D0535124

THE *varnished* TRUTH

DAVID NYBERG

THE *varnished* TRUTH

TRUTH TELLING

and

DECEIVING

in

ORDINARY LIFE

THE UNIVERSITY OF CHICAGO PRESS
Chicago and London

David Nyberg is a professor in the Graduate School of Education at the State University of New York at Buffalo, where he teaches philosophy.

THE UNIVERSITY OF CHICAGO PRESS, CHICAGO 60637
THE UNIVERSITY OF CHICAGO PRESS, LTD., LONDON
© 1993 by David Nyberg
All rights reserved. Published 1992
Printed in the United States of America
02 01 00 99 98 97 96 95 94 93   1 2 3 4 5 6

ISBN (cloth): 0-226-61051-9

Library of Congress Cataloging-in-Publication Data

Nyberg, David, 1943–
    The varnished truth : truth telling and deceiving in ordinary
life / David Nyberg.
        p.   cm.
    Includes bibliographical references and index.
    1. Truthfulness and falsehood.   2. Deception.   I. Title.
BJ1421.N83   1993
177'.3—dc20   92-20637
                                                        CIP

⊗ The paper used in this publication meets the minimum requirements of the American National Standard for Information Sciences—Permanence of Paper for Printed Library Materials, ANSI Z39.48-1984.

For Nancy

Clever beyond hope is the inventive craft he possesses. It brings him now to ill, now to good.

Sophocles, *Antigone*

CONTENTS

Part Three   *Deception and Moral Decency*

ACKNOWLEDGMENTS

This book began as a sabbatical project at Oxford University in 1986. I would like to express my deepest gratitude to the Principal and Fellows of Mansfield College, whose attentive hospitality made my year in Oxford as comfortable for me personally as it was profitable for this work. I am grateful also to the members of the university Sub-Faculty of Philosophy for allowing me to join them through election to temporary membership in the Philosophical Society. Harry Judge provided for many practical necessities in his role as Director of the Department of Educational Studies by appointing me research associate.

During the year I had invigorating discussions with Hugh Collins, J. R. Lucas, Steven Lukes, R. A. Mason, Joseph Raz, Oliver O'Donovan, David Wiggins, and John Wilson. The intellectual stimulation of these encounters and the personal relationships that developed were—and remain—enriching.

I am indebted to Sidney Bloch and the members of his study group at the Warneford Psychiatric Hospital in Oxford for their constructive comments on the paper they heard, which appears here much revised as chapter five.

Thanks also to Kathryn Morgan and Denis Phillips for their excellent and witty responses to my Presidential Address which introduced the central themes of this book at the Philosophy of Education Society meeting in Boston in 1987. And to my friends Barbara and Don Arnstine, Stephen Brown, Kieran Egan, Richard Liebmann-Smith, Jonas Soltis, and Ronnie de Sousa for their essential encouragement and sound advice during trying times.

My agent, Kathi Paton, and editors at the University of Chicago Press—John Tryneski and Christine Bartels—made the transition from manuscript to bound books as pleasantly rewarding as that ticklish process is ever likely to be.

No father could be more happy with his son than I am with Noah, whose quality of mind has drawn my attention to subtle aspects of deception and morality that I had not appreciated, and whose quality of spirit sometimes makes my heart soar like a hawk. My beloved wife Nancy has been a fierce protector of writing time, a sagacious yet forbearing reader of what I manage to scribble down, and a bottomless well of confidence in me and in us. I think she must be a gift of the gods.

INTRODUCTION

This book explores one fundamental truth of everyday life, namely, that even under ordinary circumstances, when the chance of getting caught is not great, almost all of us are willing to deceive others or deceive ourselves, with untormented conscience. The way I see it, deception appears to be normal rather than abnormal, a workaday attribute of practical intelligence. While it is certainly the case that we use deception of self and of others as a mean of coping with fear, we have learned to use deception for many other purposes as well: to tolerate stress, to gain a sense of control over the uncertain aspects of our lives and the future, to enhance our own well-being, to gain and protect privacy, to help others anonymously, and so on. As our minds have evolved, as practical intelligence has become more and more refined, as we have learned the subtleties of substituting words and symbols for weapons and violence, thereby changing the nature of power in social relations, deception has come to play a central and complex role in social life.

I don't mean to suggest that we do nothing but deceive each other all the time; however, I do mean that all of us can point to numerous occasions in our own experience when we felt the choice to deceive was morally appropriate. Nevertheless, many philosophers continue to argue that if deception were to become common it would pose a serious threat to individual and social stability. Therefore, in their view it must be considered to be a categorical moral wrong. This is the standard view in moral philosophy. Likewise, the standard view in behavioral science is that "mental health," or "normal human thought," is characterized by a well-established, clear, voluntary contact with reality, free of the need to distort, deny, repress, or otherwise misrepresent or lie about that reality. In this view, deception, and especially self-deception, is assumed to be always rooted in anxiety or fear, and is taken to be symptomatic of possible mental disorder, signaling a breakdown in one's contact with reality.

On the contrary, a healthy, livable human lifetime of relationships with others is to me inconceivable without deception; furthermore, I hold the prescription that life should be lived without aid of self-deception to be a distinctly unfriendly idea. I think deception is in our nature, and it is there for some reason: the mind does not evolve in ways harmful to itself.

To rail against this ubiquitous phenomenon—which seems to play an undeniably successful role in the evolution of nearly all species—as being either immoral or unhealthy in principle seems to me disingenuous if not desperate. Does morality forbid all deception? Does unhealthy fear or anxiety lie beneath all self-deception? I don't think so. These conclusions are just too simple to handle the moral and psychological complexity of deception. In this book I challenge both of these views by showing how some deception and self-deception are necessary both to social stability and to individual mental health. I will also go a step further and defend the idea that sometimes it is unhealthy and immoral not to deceive. The moralistic–mental health requirement of being set against all deception is as wrongminded as it is to loathe and distrust all bacteria—which would necessarily include the ones responsible for wine and cheese and the normal digestive functions. It is clearly a mistake to ignore context and consequences in evaluating bacteria, only some of which are culprits of disease. Others can contribute to the flourishing of life. The same can be said of some deceptions, including self-deceptions. We deceive, among other reasons, so that we might not perish of the truth. But we deceive carelessly, thoughtlessly, inhumanely, and selfishly at our peril. The question whether it is ever acceptable to use deception is not quite on target. We should ask instead how we may deceive whom about what and for how long.

I certainly do not intend to dispute the truism that truth telling is very important to the development of knowledge in science and scholarship (in fact I have little to say about these activities since my focus is on ethics). But, to paraphrase Harley Granville-Barker, the trouble with using truth telling as a guiding principle in moral conduct all the time is that one ends up thinking of one's attitude instead of the usefulness of what one is doing. What I intend to explore at some length, and from several angles, is the question whether truth telling has been morally overrated, and deceiving naively underrated as means for achieving desirable results in social life. I wonder about what the "unvarnished truth" could possibly mean, and what it might contribute to the richness of our lives, if it were to take over as the norm in practice. I know in my own case that I want neither to tell nor to hear all the truth that could be said about myself. I suspect I'm not alone in this desire: few are willing to hear what they don't want to hear, to say what they cannot bear to say. At the same time, we do need to be able to trust others and to be known as trustworthy ourselves. Hence my title: *The Varnished Truth*.

I have rewritten this book many times trying to make the ideas in it interesting to a broader audience—ideas that have grown while teaching moral philosophy and philosophy of education for sixteen years. This is a serious but not a scholarly work; I make no claim to a new standard of precision or thoroughness, and I write not for scholars but for readers of diverse background who have an interest in the subject. On the other hand, it is a book intended to arouse thoughtfulness by challenging the familiar, to stimulate moral concerns though no moral is neatly drawn, and to encourage those who want to act decently but find themselves unable or unwilling to act exclusively on the basis of strict and rigid moral principle. Even though not meant to be scholarly, it is a philosophical book in the sense of its being an attempt to challenge the adequacy of our current conceptions of truth telling and deceiving, to discover some hidden assumptions about the moral nature of our relationships with others, and to achieve a clearer understanding of the problems involved in being a morally decent person.

As a philosopher, and as a teacher of philosophy, I have always been more drawn to sniping at a subject than laying down a barrage against it. Half a dozen attempts to see a point, each from a different perch, satisfy me more than one grand and overwhelming push from A to B. Another way to express this methodological choice is to say I prefer to work in the pattern model of explanation rather than the deductive model. According to the pattern model, something is explained when it is so related to a set of other elements that together they constitute a unified system. We understand something by identifying it as a specific part in an organized whole. In the deductive model, on the other hand, events are explained by subsuming them under general laws, by showing that they occurred in accordance with those laws, by virtue of the realization of certain specified antecedent conditions. Much good philosophical work is done in this model, which calls for a cognitive style that is "postulational" and formal. But that is not my choice here. Instead, I try to use the pattern model and a cognitive style that is somewhat "literary" and informal. My objective is to provide readers with a recognizably realistic evocation and description of deception in relation to familiar elements of everyday life, in a manner that is both informative and entertaining.

There is a structure to the evocation, and a design to the description. The book is organized by three questions about the relationship of truth telling and deceiving:

1. What does it mean to "tell the truth"?
2. What is deception for?
3. How does deception fit in with moral decency?

The first chapter describes the terrain in which this exploration takes place, by arguing that truth telling is morally overrated and deceiving has been underrated as means for aiding decent people negotiate the intricacies of their environments to produce a livable life. Then, in part 1, the concepts of truth, lying, deception, and self-deception are examined in that order. Chapter 2 sets the stage by surveying the major theories of truth. This chapter is placed at the beginning of part 1 for the reason that both lying and deception logically require a concept of truth for their very definitions. This chapter also addresses the question why the idea of "the truth" has fascinated human minds for so long. Chapter 3 sets out some distinctions between lying and deceiving and proposes a four-part logic of lying. The nature of deception is examined in chapter 4, followed by a similar treatment of self-deception in chapter 5.

Part 2 focuses on some questions about the propriety of, and the manner in which, we use deception in the practice of civility, in friendship, in teaching and raising children, and in the adversarial system of law.

Finally, in part 3, I try to show how an appreciation of the sophisticated and complex role that deception plays in the back-and-forth of daily life can fit in with a clearly tenable and proper ethical point of view that is more concerned with moral decency than with moral perfection.

I have tried in this book to give an authentic reckoning of the role of deception in our lives, and thereby alter our map of knowledge about moral decency. Deception is not merely to be tolerated as an occasionally prudent aberration in a world of truth telling: it is rather an essential component of our ability to organize and shape the world, to resolve problems of coordination among individuals who differ, to cope with uncertainty and pain, to be civil and to achieve privacy as needed, to survive as a species, and to flourish as persons.

1 TRUTH TELLING IS MORALLY OVERRATED

Charm is a way of getting the answer yes without asking a clear question.

Albert Camus

A little inaccuracy sometimes saves tons of explanation.

H. H. Munro (Saki)

A man who tells the truth should keep his horse saddled.

Caucasus Proverb

With an ever weakening resistance, I have come to admit that the need for misrepresenting some aspects of truth and reality in my own life is nearly an everyday occurrence; in times of crisis it can be compelling.

This book is about the moral complexity of truth telling and deception. It attempts to understand the complementary roles of truth telling and deceiving in ordinary human communication. It records a struggle to see why, when deceiving is publicly condemned, it is privately practiced by almost everybody. Perhaps the reason for this seeming hypocrisy is that both the public condemnation of deception and its private practice are indispensable to the smooth running of our social lives. It is even possible that deception could be an important aspect of moral decency, since most people who are morally decent do in fact practice deception while earnestly maintaining to others, and sometimes to themselves, that they do not, or that they always feel guilty when they do. Deception is not easy to talk about frankly. Many people tend to see it as either odious and therefore an unfit topic for conversation, or completely obvious as "the lubricant" that keeps society going and therefore unworthy of discussion. I think our difficulty in talking frankly about it stems partly from our tacit understanding that to do so would often place us at a practical disadvantage; after all, in what cases would it be wise to tell the truth about the role of deception in *your* life?

SOME FOOLISH QUESTIONS

Imagine what you would answer if someone posed these questions to you:

Is there anything you have done that you would very much like to forget so there would be no danger of having to tell the truth about it if somebody asked?

After seven years of marriage and two children, Lisa is no longer sexually aroused by her husband, Larry. She blames herself for being frigid and does her best to depreciate the importance of sex in their relationship. On sudden notice, Lisa's job takes her to France for a week; two days before she returns home she has a heart-swelling, soul-stirring, sensational fling with a man she'll never see again. Her sexuality is vivacious once more. She knows confessing to the affair would deeply threaten Larry, whom she loves. How should she handle her eventful insight and renewed sensuality?

If Lisa told you about her affair, would you cover for her?

When you tell your friends and family about your experiences on a trip, do you strive for scrupulous accuracy or do you hope to arouse interest, which may require embellishment and exaggeration and possibly the deletion of facts?

The doctors have said they are certain you have but six months to live. One effect of this news is that you become completely unconcerned about what others think of you. Would you say or do anything differently—that is, more spontaneously or honestly?

Your two closest friends offer to tell you, with unchecked candor and without regard for your feelings, everything they think about you. Would you want them to do it?

you? These two friends ask you to do the same for them. Would

What else besides honesty do you value most in friendship?

Have you ever disliked and disrespected someone you worked for, and told them so—while you still needed the job?

Have you ever taken sick days from work when you were well enough to go in?

The insolent checkout clerk at the supermarket in the mall mistakenly gives you $10 extra change. Would you keep it? Would anything change if the clerk had been helpful and polite? If you had known the clerk personally?

The same thing happens two days later at the mom and pop corner store where you go several times a week. Would you make a fuss over giving the $10 back to signal and underscore your honesty?

How much taxable income would you feel justified in omitting from your tax return? Less than $100? $500? $1,000 or more?

Have you ever said that you never lie? Was that a lie?

For most people at least some of these questions have no obvious and unequivocal answers. We live in a labyrinthine world of puzzling objects, enigmatical events, and partially unintelligible (sometimes even mystical) relationships that we cannot hope ever to comprehend entirely. Things happen; we witness some aspects of an event from a particular vantage point; we interpret what we have taken in with our senses; we discover or compose an acceptable meaning from that subjectively limited rendering of "fact"; we express an edited, personalized version of the result, to a selected audience, at a chosen time, if we want to. There is a vast psychological distance between the "things that happen" and what we are later able to say about them, no matter how sincerely we try to be objective and to get it right. Lifelong uncertainty about the "truth" is an attribute of human sensibility; it is a product of the interplay of memory and imagination, history and choice.

I am interested here in the moral value of truth, such as we think we can know it. Some of the questions that need to be addressed are: What exactly are we required to *do* with the truth once we know it, have it, feel it, or whatever? Is there a moral command that implies a duty to dish it out without garnish to everyone who passes by? Or does the obligation not arise until we are asked to tell the truth? Does it matter who asks? Does it matter what exactly is asked in the way of truth telling? Does it matter how we feel about the situation? Must we will ourselves always to make our words and actions conform to our thoughts and feelings, regardless of all other considerations? If we wish to act morally, have we no choice but to be ardently consistent truth tellers?

We tend to assume that truthfulness and morality go together in a clear and simple way. What happens to this assumption when we ask a few more probing questions such as: Is truthfulness a moral value of a special kind? If so, what kind, and how does it fit in with other moral values such as compassion, charity, discretion, friendship? Does truth telling really have intrinsic moral value, or is it better understood as an instrumental value—should we serve it, or should it serve us? How does the answer to that question affect the injunction always to tell the truth? Do we have a right to the truth from others? If we did have such a right, would we actually use it all the time? Do we really have any idea what a world of truth tellers would be like? Is such a world what we want?

In an ordinary community of morally decent people there is a need for trust and community standards for truth telling, but an ordinary community, unlike the ideal scientific community, must continually face the ambiguous problem of when to tell how much of what truth to whom. Telling the whole truth about everything to everybody all the time is an impossibility, but even if it were possible, it probably wouldn't be desirable. The question is: of all the things we *could* say, what *should* we say?

Deception is a touchy subject. Before serious misunderstandings begin to form, it would be a good idea to state clearly that I repudiate all harmfully exploitative deceptions such as consumer fraud, insider trading, the misuse of public office and public trust for personal self-interest, kids hiding their dope and alcohol and pregnancies from their parents, husbands and wives cheating on each other, large-scale tax evasion, used car dealers painting over rust and turning back odometers, the false and vicious reasoning of racism and sexism, televangelists preying on vulnerable, semiliterate audiences, cigarette advertising, and so on. The list of reprehensible exploitations is enormous and grows longer daily. I do despise and reject all this corruption. However, it is a mistake to despise and reject all the other forms of deception, too, just because we have had experience with these contemptible ones. It would be the same kind of mistake as rejecting all politics just because we have been burned by some corrupt politicians; or disapproving of all scientific research involving humans and animals because some of it is carried out inhumanely on noncrucial questions; or discounting the value of all religious leaders just because some of them are fools and fanatical egomaniacs. We need to sort out what is and what is not morally justifiable deception, just as we must sort out moral from immoral behavior in politics, science, and religion.

There is a lot left unspoken about the role of deception in everything we do—at home, at work, in all sorts of social encounters. This book is an invitation to ponder that role, to think about the nature and the function of deception in loving, working, entertaining, educating and raising children, developing self-concepts, "using" other people, being married, keeping friendships, coping with the extremes of life's griefs and joys, looking at the indiscernible future, learning from the unreliable past, trying to live "authentically" in the present, and being alone in the privacy of our inner world. The book asks what it is about deception that we (so carefully?) manage to leave unspoken, why this is so, whether it should be so, and what to do next, once the subject of deception is out in the open. How will life appear when we have looked at the truth about deception?

As children we are taught to revere the principle of truth telling before we have achieved a clear understanding of what truth is. For a child, how is the truth different from a captivating story that takes us off into other vivid realities? From saying things that make people feel good? From whatever saves us when we are in danger? Truth, fantasy, goodness, happiness, excitement are not automatically separated in the thoughts of young children. They have to be taught to isolate truth and truth telling for special treatment. As our experiences widen, however, we also learn through wonderfully indirect and subtle means that truth telling, like every other moral principle, has its drawbacks in practice, and sometimes we have to pass over it in our calculations for getting on as decent and successful human beings.

Deception is found in every culture (only attitudes toward it differ), probably because it provides advantage in carrying out one's intentions, and because it offers a chance to escape confrontations without having to fight.[1] We humans are active, creative mammals who can represent what exists as if it did not, and what doesn't exist as if it did. And we do this easily and routinely. Concealment, obliqueness, silence, outright lying—all help to hold Nemesis at bay; all help us abide too large helpings of reality. T. S. Eliot was right when he reminded us that "Humankind/Cannot bear very much reality." In civilization no less than in the wilderness, survival at the water hole does not favor the fully exposed and unguarded self. Deception, it seems, is a vital part of practical intelligence.

PRACTICAL INTELLIGENCE

Much of human interaction is taken up with the giving and getting of impressions, which are composed of some plain truth and some fancy, some display and some concealment, something said and something suggested, something focused and something blurred. All this for the purpose of getting done what you want to do.

The Cagey Veterinarian

Dr. Gregory, a very thoughtful veterinarian who at first bridled at the suggestion that deception was a part of his practical intelligence, later gave me this example as a sort of humorous confession.

> Veterinary Deception: Always rub the pet's skin with alcohol before giving the injection. The owner has been taught for decades that this is proper procedure. Reality of Veterinary Deception: Rubbing the skin with alcohol before giving an injection does no good at all. It's pure show (it takes about five minutes for alcohol to kill a significant amount of bacteria on the skin, and that is too long to wait with an anxious animal on the table and many more in the waiting room). For me the habit is so deep that I really feel

strange when I fail to do it, regardless of the farce of doing it. It took me about fifteen years to realize that the only thing it does is cause me more pain when I prick myself rather than the dog (usually because of a sudden movement of the pet). Then I figured the alcohol probably increased the dog's pain as much as it did mine.

At first I handled the situation by injecting near but not actually at the spot I placed the alcohol, but I knew someday some sharp client who asks questions would pick up on the sham. Now I use the antiseptic chlorhexadine, which does no more real good than alcohol but does not cause the stinging.

In this case, Dr. Gregory's willingness to deceive serves as a welcome reassurance for the owner. He has combined his scientific knowledge with practical intelligence. His clients keep coming back (for excellent care); business is good; no harm done. The situation is much the same for physicians.

Acting Like a Doctor

Dr. Stephen Hoffmann has written about his need for a modern medical equivalent of chanting and playing drums in coping with many patients' wish to believe and to be healed. His experiences with patients in a hospital emergency ward have helped him realize that an important part of being a doctor is being a dramatist. On his way to meet a patient, he prepares himself:

> I must lead off with the right persona. Each type of patient—the adolescent with a drug overdose, the middle-aged man with chest pain or the depressed elderly woman—calls for a certain demeanor. A doctor tries to assume it from the outset, adjusting it as he goes on, as he would the fit of his white coat.[2]

Confronting a twenty-seven-year-old woman who has been on the Pill for five days and is worried about a stroke because she has developed a "weak foot," he adopts a calming manner, performs an examination, and delivers the good news that her strength and sensation are normal, and that it takes much longer for the risk of stroke to be affected by the Pill.

"It's not in my head, if that's what you mean," she snaps.

When I try to persuade her that nothing seems amiss, she balks. "Well, something is definitely wrong!"

I stall for a second, realizing that I've failed. I haven't responded to the need that brought her to the hospital late on a Sunday night. Even though I've done what was medically called for, I never like it when a patient leaves feeling angry or dissatisfied; I tend to take such reactions personally. What's more, the threat of malpractice is seldom far from my mind. While I believe I've exercised proper judgment, I know that in the charged atmosphere of the courtroom, good judgment alone doesn't always suffice. It's time, then, to improvise. Like Prospero in *The Tempest,* only through "some vanity of mine art" can I make "my project gather to a head."

Dr. Hoffmann goes on to do what he has learned many people expect of doctors: he performs the artful ritual of the medicine man, calculated to make the patient feel better. He resorts to theater:

I stage a dazzlingly detailed neurologic exam. There are props: a reflex hammer and an ophthalmoscope, each of which I move about in carefully choreographed patterns. There are dramatic asides— thoughtful "hmmm's"—and flourishes, too, like the motions I put my patient through to test for rare, abnormal reflexes. I even bring in special effects, such as a black and white striped tape which I move back and forth hypnotically before the woman's eyes, testing for subtle changes in her vision. Throughout it all, I'm careful to concentrate on my delivery, timing my words, smiles and gestures for best effect. My last act is to order an X-ray of the neck to make absolutely sure that impingement of a nerve root isn't the cause of her problems.

The doctor's final act is to talk with his patient once again. He states that the thorough workup has revealed nothing wrong but acknowledges the fact that her symptoms are surely bothering her and encourages her to come back for more tests if they persist. She is pleased and grateful. "For sheer healing power," he writes, "nothing can match the theater."

This kind of dissembling is common among doctors, but motives vary. When is it done for the sake of the patient, and when for the doctor's own self-interest, whether for the further cultivation of his image as God's chosen helper or for the prudent reason of protecting himself against potential litigation? Doctors do slant the truth sometimes to avoid making patients feel angry or unimportant. That's what medical jargon is for: you come in feeling a pain in your back and leave with knowledge that your problem is lumbosacral sprain. The pain is still there but you feel better about it because it has been professionally recognized and identified.

Dr. Hoffmann acknowledges that his kind of theater is expensive, and that health care costs rise because of it. Patients pay the bills for all the props and flourishes. Is the cost worth the show?

> What should I have done, then? Stop short of any drama and allow her to leave unhappy? Dispense the unembellished truth and let her walk away with serious questions about her health—and my competence? Before I can give the matter more thought, though, the charge nurse tells me that I have another patient. I clear my voice and straighten my white coat. Curtain time is never far away.

The High IQ Half-Wit

Now let's consider someone unwilling to deceive, and the price of his "sincerity."

Richard had just been accepted as a doctoral candidate in a psychology department which is generally acknowledged to have one of the best programs in the country. His undergraduate grades were nearly perfect, his GRE scores were in the highest percentile, he had an IQ score (whatever that means) of 160, and his application file contained recommendations chock-full of praise for his academic achievements along with predictions of great future success. The faculty members of the department were unanimous in ranking him their number one candidate.

As expected, Richard performed brilliantly in his course

work and research. He was successful in attaining a large grant to support his dissertation, which won an award for being the best in its field that year. In light of his sparkling record as a superior student with superior intelligence it is no wonder that he came to think very highly of himself. But Richard's self-esteem grew along with his achievements to such an extent that he became unselfconsciously arrogant, intolerant of others whose minds were not as quick and nimble as his own, and a boastfully self-promoting advocate of his theory of intelligence, which he argued was original and perhaps even revolutionary. He was so consumed with himself, with laying the foundations for the distinguished career he envisioned, that he earned a reputation as an arrogant SOB. When his advisor and other concerned faculty confronted him with this fact, Richard showed no inclination to alter his behavior. He believed some people had a right to be arrogant; his record and his obvious intelligence justified his attitude, he thought, and he was not about to be pressured into playing games of pretending differently.

Surprise, surprise. All of Richard's classmates were offered good positions upon their graduation, but he was turned down after every interview. He was first in the class, but he did not receive a single job offer. Why? He was too dumb to hide the fact in his interviews that he was an arrogant SOB, and nobody wanted to have him as a colleague, no matter how high his test scores, no matter how distinguished his dissertation. He failed to see the value in pretending to be less arrogant than he sincerely felt he had a right to be. He also failed to realize that his future professional success depended in some degree upon meeting the social requirements of the place where he did his work as well as upon that work itself. While he had achieved a high score on an abstract IQ test, he had a relatively undeveloped practical intelligence to go with it. His classmates' practical, or contextual, intelligence included the knowledge that sometimes *seeming* can be more important than stubborn, no-nonsense veraciousness. They clearly fared better than Richard. They knew something he didn't—they knew how to act appropriately in an interview context.[3] No doubt they had accepted the wisdom of such advice as was recently offered to college graduates:

During the Interview:
Don't act as if you're squeezing the recruiter into your
busy schedule. Even if you're the kind of student
who is in demand, you'll increase the number of offers you receive if you appear enthusiastic. Come
across as a soon-to-be-professional. Dress comfortably but appropriately, and in most cases, conserva-
tively. Practice your handshake so that your grip is
firm and friendly. Be yourself. Experienced recruiters
can spot students who say things they think the interviewer wants to hear.[4]

(There is a deep irony in all this diligent trying and practicing to
"be yourself." We'll look at it more closely in chapter 5.)

Interviewing is for impressing the interviewer (who has already read all about you), if you want the job. Sometimes that
means seeming to be more or less of something than you really
feel. Refusing to acknowledge this, and sticking instead to the ideal
of If-I-feel-it-then-I'll-say-it-because-it's-true, may have the virtue
of being purely sincere, but it is not always the practically intelligent course to take. It is a great distortion to believe you are speaking the truth simply because you say what you think. It is possible
to be sincere and wrong. It is also possible to be sincere, right, and
dumb. Could it be that to employ this form of deception discreetly
is an important part of what it means to be contextually, or practically, intelligent?

Maybe this question ought to be incorporated into Richard's
theory, and into his thinking about his next job interview. It is even
likely that consideration of the question will lead Richard to a more
realistic view of his own strengths and limitations, a view that will
have the effect of further enabling him by broadening his intelligence, and at the same time teaching him the cost of arrogant
veracity.

DECEPTION FROM THE BOTTOM UP
AND TOP DOWN

Dr. Gregory and Dr. Hoffmann learned that pretending was
part of their jobs as healers, a lesson Richard had not yet come to

grips with as an academic psychologist. It is not always clear what motivates a desire to pretend—it is sometimes self-interest and sometimes the interests of others. Nor is it always clear whether pretending will benefit or damage a particular relationship. Dr. Hoffmann's next patient may react in an altogether less appreciative way to his performance. Perhaps Richard's ineptitude at pretending worked out for the best—if not from his own, then at least from his would-be colleagues' point of view.

A basic philosophical question is raised here that bears on the course this book will take: should we evaluate the inclination to deceive in each instance and determine its moral status in the particular circumstances given? This is the view from the bottom up. Or should we think about it more abstractly, as an exception that always needs justifying against a background of truth telling, and determine its moral status in principle, once and for all? This is to look at deception from the top down, in the way such philosophers as Sissela Bok look at lying.[5]

Since I disagree with some important aspects of Bok's approach and with some of her most important general conclusions, it would be useful (at least to those readers who have not read Bok), and fair to her, if I outline here what I take her to be saying, so our differences can be clearly seen. Before doing that, however, I want to state that I am not interested in lining up all my authoritative ducks in a row to do battle with hers, nor am I interested in building a comprehensive, systematic refutation of her work. Rather, I want to use her book to illustrate the top-down approach, which is representative of some widely held beliefs about truth telling, and then, in the following chapters, I want to display as best I can the bottom-up approach, to raise doubts and questions, to encourage people to reconsider, to think again about what they take for granted on the subject of deception.

What is Bok's book about? She appears to be chiefly motivated in her writings by two concerns. The first is for what she sees as the casual attitude so many professionals take to the practice of deception in their work (business, government, law, medicine, etc.), compared with her own troubling experience in facing hard choices about truth telling. Her second concern is about the "striking recent decline in public confidence not only in the American government, but in lawyers, bankers, businessmen, and doctors."[6] Bok suspects there is a causal relationship between the casual attitude of professionals toward deception and the decline in public confidence, although we don't really know whether this perceived "decline" in public confidence is actually the result of improved methods in the polling of public opinion, or of better investigative reporting that brings more information to the public eye about what has long been going on behind the scenes, or—as Bok implies—whether it reflects a palpable increase in the practice of deception. Whatever the correct explanation may be, her concerns are sincere and serve as strong motivation to become more clear about matters of truth telling.

On the assumption that this casual attitude about truth telling is both morally wrong and destructive of public confidence, Bok formulates the central question she hopes to answer: "Is there, then, a theory of moral choice which can help in quandaries of truthtelling and lying?"[7] The way she states her question gives us a clue as to what she assumes at the outset, and determines at least partially the route she will take in answering it. First of all, she wants to develop a *theory,* which is a statement of the general laws or principles of something; in this case that something is the rational activity of deciding whether to lie. She intends to propose a theory that can tell us when a decision to lie is morally justified or at least excusable, a theory that will, if put into general practice, help to reverse the decline in public trust, thereby improving the moral character of society. Her approach is deliberately abstract in its focus on theory, principles, and rational decision making, although the tone of her arguments is often quite personal. Unlike most philosophers who take this top-down approach to the study of lying, she does not trouble herself for long with questions about the nature of truth, or of truth telling, which can easily end up frustrating the entire enterprise. Nor does she confront the immense complexity of deception broadly conceived. Instead, she chooses to look primarily at clear-cut lies. She defines a lie as "any intentionally deceptive message which is *stated.*"[8] This definition is meant to separate lying from the larger category of deception which includes, but is not limited to, such statements.

Her search for a theory of choice is initiated on a strong

presumption against any lie's being excusable or justifiable, but with an awareness that "sometimes there *may* be sufficient reason to lie."[9] She presumes further that "lying requires a reason, while truth telling does not."[10] By this she means that every lie is a suspect deviation from an orthodox norm of truth telling and as such, each decision to lie requires a rational exoneration. So the value of her theory will be to provide the principles that can be used to judge the reasons given to defend any decision to lie.

Her conception of the problem emphasizes the long-term general effects of the "practice" of lying on whole societies. In her view, the major reason why lies are morally wrong is not simply that they cause "immediate harm to others." It is rather that they harm the liars themselves and harm the "general level of trust and social cooperation. Both [harms] are cumulative; both are hard to reverse."[11] This image of generalized harm is central to Bok's position and deserves a fuller description:

> . . . even if [liars] make the effort to estimate the consequences to *individuals*—themselves and others—of their lies, they often fail to consider the many ways in which deception can spread and give rise to practices very damaging to human communities. These practices clearly do not affect only isolated individuals. The veneer of social trust is often thin. As lies spread—by imitation, or in retaliation, or to forestall suspected deception—trust is damaged. Yet trust is a social good to be protected just as much as the air we breathe or the water we drink. When it is damaged, the community as a whole suffers; and when it is destroyed, societies falter and collapse.[12]

This vision of how lies may lead to social collapse is a slightly modified version of Kant's absolutist position on why truthfulness should be considered an unconditional duty:

> Truthfulness in statements which cannot be avoided is the formal duty of an individual to everyone, however great may be the disadvantage accruing to himself or to another. Thus the definition of a lie as merely an intentional untruthful declaration to another person does not require the additional condi-

tion that it must harm another. . . . For a lie always harms another; if not some other particular man, still it harms mankind generally, for it vitiates the source of law itself.[13]

Hesitantly, Bok rejects the absolutist prohibition of all lies, even though she maintains allegiance to the justification for it:

In the absence of some vast terror associated with lying, which goes far beyond the presumption against lying stated [earlier], I have to agree that there are at least *some* circumstances which warrant a lie. And foremost among them are those where innocent lives are at stake, and where only a lie can deflect the danger.

But, in taking such a position, it would be wrong to lose the profound concern which the absolutist theologians and philosophers express—the concern for the harm to trust and to oneself from lying, quite apart from any immediate effects from any one lie.[14]

On the subject of warranted lies, Bok's language remains extremely reluctant: "Only where a lie is a *last resort* can one even begin to consider whether or not it is morally justified."[15]

Bok explains that the reasons one may offer as an excuse for having told a lie usually appeal to one or more of these four principles: "that of avoiding harm, that of producing benefits, that of fairness, and that of veracity."[16] Her analysis of these principles leads her to say that "inevitably, most of these excuses will fail to persuade."[17] Furthermore, no reason offered as an excuse need even be evaluated "if the liar knew of a truthful alternative to secure the benefit, avoid the harm, or protect fairness. Even if a lie saves a life, it is unwarranted if the liar was aware that a truthful statement could have done the same."[18] But then she softens this a little by saying that "because the reasons themselves are present to larger and smaller degrees, one cannot always say that a lie seems or does not seem excusable."[19]

Accepting reasons as *excuse* is essentially forgiving a wrong; forgiving does not mean that the wrong was not wrong, only that it is forgivable. Accepting reasons as *justification* is another matter. To justify a lie is very different than to excuse one. It is here, on the

question of justifying lies, that Bok makes her most significant contribution to the theory she has set out to develop.[20] First, she sets
down the conditions of justification:

> To justify is to defend as just, right, or proper, by
> providing adequate reasons. It means to hold up to
> some standard, such as a religious or legal or moral
> standard. Such justification requires an audience: it
> may be directed to God, or a court of law, or one's
> peers, or one's own conscience; but in ethics it is most
> appropriately aimed, not at all one individual or audi-
> ence, but rather at "reasonable persons" in general.[21]

In this statement we can see again the abstract character of her top-
down approach. In Bok's view, justification is a matter of scruti-
nizing concrete instances of individual behavior in the light of
religious, legal, or moral standards (principles) before an audience
of fictional characters (reasonable persons in general, or the ideal-
ized "moral agent") who are taken implicitly to represent more
principles (about right and wrong, rational and irrational, etc.).
While acknowledging a difficulty in assuring the "reasonableness"
of any available public, she adheres to the approach nonetheless.

After a detailed discussion of publicity—the willingness to
make a public statement and defense—which Bok believes is a crucial constraint in justifying any moral choice, she thus summarizes
her findings on the theory of choice with regard to lying:

> Such, then, are the general principles which I believe
> govern the justification of lies. As we consider differ-
> ent kinds of lies, we must ask, first, whether there are
> alternative forms of action which will resolve the dif-
> ficulty without the use of a lie [lying can be an option
> only as a last resort when no truth telling alternative
> is possible]; second, what might be the moral reasons
> brought forward to excuse the lie [the best are self-
> defense and life-saving, or extreme triviality], and
> what reasons can be raised as counter-arguments [for
> example, no one should be subject to deception with-
> out informed, voluntary consent]. Third, as a test of
> these two steps, we must ask what a public of reason-

able persons might say about such lies. Most lies will clearly fail to satisfy these questions of justification.[22]

The publicity test is the key: what would other (reasonable) people say about the decision to lie, or the particular lie itself (Bok is not entirely clear on which she means). In the remainder of her book, Bok takes up some kinds of lies that might conceivably pass the three-part test. Lying to enemies, for example, may be justified, but only when: there is *no* truth telling alternative; there is a *crisis;* and there are openly (lawfully) declared hostilities. The overall conclusion yielded by Bok's discussion of many challenging examples (placebos, letters of recommendation, private lives of public figures, the timing of crucial economic policy changes, perjury, and many more) is neatly summarized in her own words:

> Some lies—notably minor white lies and emergency lies rapidly acknowledged—may be more *excusable* than others, but only those deceptive practices which can be openly debated and consented to in advance are *justifiable* in a democracy.[23]

Bok warns that both the spread and abuse of lies can be expected if we don't have, and use,

> clear-cut standards as to what is acceptable. In the absence of such standards, instances of deception can and will increase, bringing distrust and thus more deception, loss of personal standards on the part of liars and so yet more deception, imitation by those who witness deception and the rewards it can bring, and once again more deception.[24]

She then invokes the authority of Augustine to make her point even more dramatically: ". . . little by little and bit by bit this will grow and by gradual accessions will slowly increase until it becomes such a mass of wicked lies that it will be utterly impossible to find any means of resisting such a plague grown to huge proportions through small additions."[25]

Both in her own words and in her citation of Augustine, Bok relies on what logicians and lawyers call the slippery slope argument to set up what I call the domino theory of lying. The slippery slope argument goes like this: If I'm allowed to lie once about this subject, then I will lie about it again, and then I'll lie about other things as well. Furthermore, if I'm allowed to lie, then you'll want to lie, and soon you will lie about everything, and then everybody will want to lie about everything, too. This progression will damage and eventually destroy public trust. The way to prevent this from happening is to adopt a policy that makes lying so difficult to get away with that no one will even want to try. This is the concept of deterrence. (The same concept is used to justify capital punishment for some crimes. However, there is no evidence to support the hopeful assumption that such a policy works to deter the crimes in question.)

My view, on the other hand, is that trust in others is a co-operative, life-preserving relationship that often depends upon the adroit management of deception, sometimes even lying, for its very subsistence.

We can always get a philosopher to translate personal troubles into ethics, but there is often a cost for this service. Paradoxical as it sounds at first, we may achieve simplicity at the cost of clarity. If I want to know whether I should deceive *you*, about *this, now*, the philosopher is likely to rephrase my question into something like: "When should one tell the truth, or something less?" Replacing the particularity of "I" with the generality of "one" tends to simplify the problem right from the start by abstracting from the details of personal involvement. That could be a mistake, and I think it often is a mistake in the top-down perspective on moral questions, because by achieving distance (abstraction, generality) on the subject, we lose the ability to perceive its telling details. I am interested in particular cases and the boundaries of contrast in discrete relationships more than I am interested in abstractions and universal principles. The impersonal generality of top-down moral theory comes from the expectation, or the wish, that the truth about morality will turn out to be simple. That wish for simplicity entices the philosopher to search for the fewest possible principles to cover the greatest number of cases. In contrast, the personal particularity characteristic of bottom-up moral theory reflects an appreciation for the details required for achieving clarity.

Like other domino theorists Bok is stricken by the question, "What if everybody deceived everybody else!?" The answer is, of course: everybody already does. We all value the truth and yet we are *all* ordinary human deceivers; we neither want to know all the truth nor tell it all. Deception is not so much a plague as it is part of the atmosphere that sustains life. The dread domino was toppled thousands of years ago ("I said in my haste, All men are liars."—Psalm 116:11), and deception has been part of the status quo ever since. Social life without deception to keep it going is a fantasy. Bok's top-down view does not allow her to see this, or to agree with it, because the oversimple principle of truth telling is in the way. We'll look more closely at these two perspectives on moral judgment in chapter 10. For now, it can be said that both views agree on at least one part of the problem, namely, that people should not deceive simply whenever they feel like it.

TRUTH TELLING IS MORALLY OVERRATED

As I said, this book is about the moral complexity of deception. The central problem is this: even though we have come to know that life without deception is not possible, we have not diligently trained ourselves to deceive thoughtfully and judiciously, charitably, humanely, and with discretion. As George Steiner has argued, "the human capacity to utter falsehood, to lie, to negate what is the case, stands at the heart of speech . . . and culture."[26] A sympathetic account of deception is absolutely necessary to an adequate reckoning of human conduct, and therefore to an understanding of useful moral principles and moral education.

The truth telling injunction is deceptively simple. It sounds not merely possible but positively easy: Give plain and frank expression to what is in your mind; don't misrepresent your thoughts or feelings. But should we really refrain from lying to a violent criminal simply because there may be a truthful alternative? Should we answer a child's every question about sex, divorce, death, and disease regardless of any probably disturbing, even destructive consequences of doing so? Should we give frank expression to every strong feeling of contempt, envy, lust, and self-pity? Should we tell our friends the truth when we believe it will shatter their self-confidence? The list of possible "exceptions" is endless, and many of them are justifiable even if they fail to pass Bok's three-principle test.

What in the world is so awfully good about telling the truth all the time? Why should we feel obliged to excuse or justify every exception? Haven't we got the value of truth telling just a little out of focus? Can it be that truth telling is morally overrated?

Let's now take a look at some different ways of understanding the idea of truth, as a first step in our inquiry into the moral complexity of deception.

PART *one*

WHAT IT MEANS TO "TELL THE TRUTH"

2 VARIETIES OF TRUTH

What is true is what I can't help believing.
                                    Oliver Wendell Holmes, Jr.

All truths are half truths.
                                    Alfred North Whitehead

What is truth? I don't know and I'm sorry I brought it up.
                                    Edward Abbey

In order to understand deception, we have to begin by looking at truth in some detail because deception requires a conception of truth for its very definition.

Why does the truth matter so much? What is it about the idea of truth that has so fascinated human minds for all of recorded history, and probably before that? Why does our society have such fierce prohibitions against all manner of denying, distorting, reversing, hiding, and "disrespecting" the truth? Where did we get the idea that the truth will set us free? How did the truth come to be an object of worship not only among the religious, but among the secular as well? What is the root of the moral value we place on truth? Perhaps like other enduring idols, it becomes and remains an object of worship precisely because we cannot ever know for sure what it is, what it means, but we can't quite ever manage to forget about it either. Anything that we cannot know but cannot forget is certain to be compelling. We apparently need the *idea* of truth whether it's true or not.

The truth: the everlasting search for truth, the reverence for truth, the power of truth, the goodness of truth, the *obvious* necessity of truth, not to mention the pragmatic usefulness of truth, and its beauty—all of this is compelling. There is something about being human that makes us care deeply about truth. What is that something?

Looking as far back in our recorded cultural history as we can, to the ancient Egyptian guide to immortality, *The Book of the Dead* (c. 4000–1500 B.C.), we find that "falsification" is one of exactly forty-two sins which the deceased must deny in order to gain entrance to life's pleasant extension in the Elsewhere. This is a clue that anticipating death has long been a disturbing problem and that the truth plays a role in redemption. Or, to put the point more broadly, the truth plays a role in helping us cope with our fore-knowledge of death. I wonder, if we couldn't imagine our own death, whether we would have a much different view of the value of truth. I expect that the truth represents something that we feel *ought to be certain* in a life that is uncertain, a life that leads inexorably on to an even more disturbing uncertainty, the Elsewhere. The truth is a fix on things—or maybe just a fix—that we need to make it through the turbulence of living in profound puzzlement. It is our species' absurdly exciting predicament to have the capacity for imagining more than we can know. Imagination has no limit. We can always imagine knowing more than we actually can know. The object of such imagining, in some cases, is what we call the truth. Indeed, some people believe that the only way to apprehend the deepest, profoundest truth is through intuition. I think it is fair to say that most of us want *something* in the world to be certain, and we will look anywhere for a clue to what it might be. Some go to the mysterious wells of aesthetic imagination and the shadowy illuminations of religious narration. Others turn to the precision of logic, mathematics, and science. Yet others go into themselves, into the soul, as directly as they can through introspection, without scientific, aesthetic, or religious mediation. All of these approaches have value with regard to the aim of finding certainty. The truth is what we make it out to be, what provides for us a solid wall to rest our backs against. Am I saying that the truth is the product of hu-

man imagination—that the very ideal of truth is an invention—that
we can never know what the truth is because it doesn't exist except
in our imagination? Am I saying that the truth is something we
make up in order to cope with death?

Well, yes and no. Truth is a symbol for something we take
to be certain. I do believe that we *want* there to be something certain
in this world, because belief in certainty can make us feel good. It
can make us feel *very* good. One of the most famous examples of
prudential belief, attributed to the seventeenth-century mathema-
tician Blaise Pascal, is about the existence of God. He worked out
this formula, known as "Pascal's wager": If God does not exist, it
does no harm to believe in God anyway; but if God does exist, we
disbelieve at our peril; therefore, the best bet (because there is no
way to lose) is to believe in God. Pascal himself was a sincere believer but also a skeptic whose probings revealed that, in science as
well as in religion, certainty was out of reach. He tried to show, in
the wager argument, that in a state of uncertainty it is not unreasonable to believe in God, when the choice whether to believe or
not might have profound effects on our lives. Pascal may have
thought that if people began by making a Pascalian wager, eventually they would become sincere believers, too. Even if he was motivated by this thought, his argument still seems to me more
prudential than evangelical.

Generally speaking, we have a tendency to think that if
something makes us feel very good, if something brings about a
highly desirable and satisfying feeling of harmony and well-being,
then perhaps that something, because it is so highly valued, is what
we mean by the goodness of truth. Hence, truth is love; love is
truth, whether you think it's God that loves you or only Nancy
does. The fact is that we all need to be taken care of; otherwise we
are liable to become utterly distracted by the anxiety of living a
meaningless life until our brief moment beneath the sun is termi-
nated by the chilly isolation of death. What makes us feel taken care
of, feels like the truth. When I think of the nurturing role that belief
in truth plays in our lives, I have an image of truth as being at home,
with the smell of bread baking in the oven.

On the other hand, finding oneself astride the peak of a

mountain at sunrise, or anchored in safe harbor close by an island of stillness in heavy seas, or thigh-deep in a rustling field of ripe golden grain on the eve of harvest, or even camping out at Walden Pond, one might be convinced that truth is (in) nature. The truth is to be found in the squeeze and yield of time, in a cycle of endless regeneration, in the perfectly balanced composition of air and fire and earth and water, wherein nothing is really lost through change nor can anything be truly possessed, as the forms of life continuously alter in marginal ways while staying essentially ever the same. In this view, truth is almost melodious. It is the music of the soul in harmony with the music of the spheres. This image of truth is of one complex unity, a single sound, made up of all the different tones together. All is one; nothing is to be understood separately. Ommmmmm.m..m...m....

The best scientific minds also are attracted to the unity of knowledge, or truth, and sometimes for very similar reasons. Hedwig Born, the wife of Max Born, wrote of their good friend, Einstein:

> It is probably not surprising that it was he who helped me to be an objective scientist, and to avoid feeling that the whole thing was impersonal. Modern physics left me standing. Here was only objective truth, which unhappily meant nothing to me, and perhaps the possibility that in the future everything would be expressed scientifically. So I asked Einstein one day, "Do you believe that absolutely everything can be expressed scientifically?" "Yes," he replied, "it would be possible, but it would make no sense. It would be description without meaning—as if you described a Beethoven symphony as a variation of wave pressure." This was a great solace to me.[1]

During Einstein's severe illness in 1918, Frau Born was a frequent visitor. On one visit she asked whether he was afraid of dying. "No," he answered. "I feel myself so much a part of all life that I am not in the least concerned with the beginning or the end of the concrete existence of any particular person in this unending stream." Such was the sense of unity he found in all of nature, all of life; such was the comfort of his vision of certainty. It is also true, however, that a year or so after Einstein said this his mother came to spend the last few months of her life with him, and when she died he wept like an ordinary man. Such are the limits of our visions and the comfort they afford us.

THEORIES OF TRUTH

(Those readers who may find this section a little too complicated and involved in theories of truth for their interests should go straight to chapter 3, keeping in mind the general point that there is disagreement among philosophers as to the meaning of "truth" and "truth telling.")

Philosophers have been concerned with the concept of truth from the beginning. They have for the most part tried to understand *what truth is,* and have not focused, as I have, on the psychological need for it. It is perhaps an impossibly difficult task to understand what truth is. Nevertheless, there is near universal agreement that it is important to try, no matter how difficult it seems. Einstein put his concern with truth in modest terms: "The important thing is not to stop questioning," he said. "Curiosity has its own reason for existence. One cannot help but be in awe when [one] contemplates the mysteries of eternity, of life, of the marvelous structure of reality. It is enough if one tries merely to comprehend a little of this mystery each day. Never lose a holy curiosity."[2] Whether driven by a need to cope with death in the big picture, or by a holy curiosity about the marvelous structure of reality, the search for truth goes on, and our reverence for truth endures. Philosophers have developed four major theories of truth. Looking at each of them briefly may help us sort out the difference between true and false, as well as between truth and deception.

The Coherence Theory of Truth

This is the big picture view of truth, characteristic of great rationalist systems in metaphysics (accounts of reality as a whole) or in mathematics and physics. The idea is that you can't say that a statement, or a judgment, is true unless you can say that it coheres with a system of other statements. Every true statement, then, is a member of a system of other true statements, and all of them are tied together logically.

In pure mathematics the test for the truth of a proposition is whether it can be logically deduced from other propositions (or axioms) in the system. The point here is that within the system, everything fits in with everything else. A limit on our ever knowing the truth of a statement is the degree to which we can also know all the other true statements in the system. If we can't know them all, then we have to admit that a statement might possess only a degree of truth (and an undetermined degree of falseness). The criterion of truth for a statement or judgment is other statements. If I say, "Today is February 29, 1989," you can know whether it is true only by referring to a set of calendar statements already learned and accepted—learned, not given; accepted, not determined.

It is a weakness of this theory that truth is the product of one statement sticking together with statements that are independently assumed to be true. In the big picture, which includes what is thought, what is experienced, and what simply is, there may be at least two statements assumed to be true, but different from one another, that may be used to test the statement in question. How are we to decide between them for the *real* truth?

Another weakness is the puzzling meaning of "degrees of truth." We can ask how much truth there is in a statement—and how much of what is not true has been included. Then we can ask how much truth is required for a statement to be considered true enough, more true than not true. For example, I say, "My father is bald"; but he says, "No I'm not, because I haven't lost all of my hair." My father's hair has been thinning for years to the point where there are mere wisps remaining on top, but his sides are still reasonably full around the ears and the base of his skull. Is he bald or not? When will the statement "My father is bald" become true, if it isn't true already? Would it matter if we decided exactly how many more hairs he must lose to qualify as bald? What is the *final* hair that must go to tip the balance? Coherence theory can't answer the question.

We can also ask whether a true statement tells all of the truth in question: a wholly true statement is not the same as the whole truth. I may testify truthfully in court that I have never seen this man before, while failing to mention that I have seen his image on film, heard his recorded voice, and recognize him for the person I know him to be.

In any event, what the coherence theory of truth does for us is to give the reasons for the truth or falsity of statements-in-relation-to-other-statements. It does not help us determine the truth of facts or experience. Statements about statements may be true because they stick together in a rationalist system, but statements about experience are true because of what the world is like. On that question, coherence theory is properly quiet.

The Correspondence Theory of Truth

"Correspondence" means mutual response, or the answering of things to each other; it suggests congruity, harmony, and agreement. The term has been extended to denote a relation of similarity, or analogy.

Although coherence and correspondence sound as if they mean almost the same thing, there is a difference philosophers point out. Bertrand Russell, for instance, held the view that truth is to be understood as some kind of correspondence between belief and *fact,* whereas coherence theorists argue that truth consists in the way beliefs hang together in a system of beliefs—facts of experience being for them beside the point.

Aristotle's account of what truth is may still be the simplest way of stating the gist of correspondence theory: "To say of what is so that it is not so, and to say of that which is not so that it is so, is false; while to say of what is so that it is so, and of what is not so that it is not so, is true."[3] Even so great a mind as Aristotle's, however, attracts its gleeful critics. Eubulides of Megara took great joy in criticizing Aristotle's views, and one of his best efforts was his "paradox of the liar," in which he invites us to consider the truth of such statements as: "All generalizations are false." According to Aristotle's description of correspondence theory, the statement (itself a generalization) is true only if it is itself false, and false only if it is true! The paradox remains a serious problem for philosophers to this day.

In the commonsense view of this theory, it goes without saying that the world contains facts, and that there are beliefs which

refer to these facts and by this reference are either true or false. The
possibilities are these:

	Fact	Nonfact
Belief	1 (Truth)	3 (False belief)
Nonbelief	2 (Disbelief)	4 (Unknown)

In the first case, we have belief in a fact, a correspondence of belief
and fact, or truth. In the second case, we have a failure to recognize
the fact, and therefore we don't see, or have, or believe the truth.
In the third case, we actively believe something that is not factual,
so we hold a false belief. Finally, in the fourth and most mysterious
case of not believing something that is not a fact, we have a sort of
backhanded way of expressing a truth: we disbelieve what is not a
fact, which is what we should do if we are to avoid error and see
the truth. But of course we may not know what we are doing here,
we may not be aware that the object of disbelief is not a fact. Or we
may fail to believe something because we don't even know about it
(in which case we would fail to believe it even if it were a fact).
Anyway, in this theory, the only time we can say we have got the
truth is when we believe a fact.

We should keep in mind the difference between there being
a fact and there being a statement about that fact. It is a fact that
fire consumes oxygen, and I believe it does; so on that issue I've
got the truth. But what is it that I believe here—the fact itself,
which I have not knowingly confronted and proved to my own
satisfaction, or a statement about that fact, which I have encoun-
tered enough times in the right places to believe it absolutely? I
believe the statement. The statement corresponds to a fact. Therefore, my belief corresponds to the fact, too. Whether my belief is
true depends upon how things are, not upon statements about how
they are. The statements are merely links between beliefs and facts,
and truth is not dependent upon statements at all. That's the nerve
of the correspondence theory.

One last point about statements: they can be expressions *of*
truth, which suggests that truth is a property of objects, or facts;
or they can be expressions *with* truth, which suggests that truth is
not a property of anything, but is rather an adverb (to speak truthfully is to speak in a certain way). It is possible, then, to speak
truthfully (sincerely?) about something that is not factual, so long

as the speaker believes it. Such an expression would be truthful, but not *of* the truth.

The Pragmatic Theory of Truth

The search for truth is really a search for belief. Historically, the pragmatists thought visions of truth as existing apart from human investigative activity to be absurd. They were far more interested in science and human conduct than in metaphysics.

For William James, the purpose of thought was not to get "reality" right, it was to form ideas that would satisfy the thinker's interests. So an idea that generated a concrete, particular effect in the life of an individual—this is what he meant by "practical"—became an important belief. Beliefs that provide "vital benefits" may be regarded by the individual as true. In this sense, if a formula for faith in God produces vital benefits for the believer, it is to that extent true. The same generally can be said of the formulae of science. The distinction is that in science, formulae are subject to public verification and can be proved false when they fail the tests. Not so for religious and other metaphysical beliefs, which cannot be verified or falsified. But so what, if such beliefs cannot be verified? They continue, unverified, to produce vital benefits. Truth is, as the pragmatists would have it, what works.

This is an extreme view that seems to say more about the *value* of certain beliefs than about their meaning or truth potential. After all, something that works to make you feel good is different from something that works out to be correct. Value is a practical aspect of truth, but there is more, as John Dewey, another pragmatist, argued. He thought truth "happens to an idea" when it works out in practice that there is a correspondence between the idea and facts. He used the example of a man lost in the woods who develops an idea (a plan) of how to get home. When he finds his way home, he is in a position to say his idea "agrees with reality," or, in other words, is true. Truth, then, is a variable associated with successful confirmation of an idea. In fact, truth and confirmation mean the same thing for this pragmatist.

There is a problem with this view. Say a Wall Street trader sets up an illegal deal over the weekend, based on insider information, but the FTC investigator doesn't confirm his hypothesis that the trader has committed the crime until the next Friday. Does it follow that "The trader committed the crime" wasn't true on the weekend but became true on the next Friday just because it was confirmed? No, not really. Confirmation happens at a particular time, but what is confirmed has already happened and was true before it was confirmed. It simply wasn't known to be true.

A second aspect of the problem has to do with the human role in *making* truth. Dewey suggests that an investigator's confirmation is what makes a statement (hypothesis) true. But what can we say about the statement "It will snow in East Aurora every April 15"? We can wait and see, but we cannot do anything to *make* it true unless we can make it snow.

Setting these problems aside for the moment, we can say that Dewey's lasting contribution to our understanding of "truth" is that he taught us to look at the process of free and open investigation, which includes encounters with new ideas and other people, and so to realize that we have no better criterion of truth than the confirmations which result from the process. The human urge behind this process is not so much to represent a fixed or given reality as it is to participate in the community of discourse. The outcome of participation in this community Dewey described as a kind of unpredictable growth, of both individuals and the community as a whole. In saying this he showed us the mistake of trying to free "the true self" so it could then lead us to see "the real truth," which is imagined to lie beyond the human capacity for confirmation.

The next, and final, theory on our list says a lot more about the relationship between "the true self" and "the real truth."

The Performative Theory of Truth

The idea that truth has to do with a way of speaking rather than with objects or facts themselves is an important part of the performative theory. For example, when you say, "I promise," you don't just describe something, you are performing an action. You aren't just making a statement, you're *making* a promise. Similarly, in this theory, when you say, "That's true," you are performing an act of agreeing with, endorsing, admitting, emphasizing, or granting a statement. You are saying, "Yes, I agree with that." A performance does not correspond to any fact, it *is* a fact, and as such cannot be either true or false.

I heard a lecture once, given by a philosophically minded musician, on the nature of performance. He began by saying that a performer uses the score as a starting point and tries then to get to "the work." The work itself is what the composer meant, or intended the work to be. The score is a representation of that intention, but of course it must be incomplete in some respects. For example, directions such as "fast" or "slow," "loud" or "soft" are vague and relative to the passage that comes before and the way that passage has been performed. The duration of particular notes, the tempo, the definition of parts, the overall sound (romantic, ebullient, somber, etc.)—all of these are suggested in the score but subject to further interpretation, too.

The lecturer went on to say that he thought of the work as a "type" of which performances were "tokens." (Think of the first letter of the alphabet as a type, and A, a, **A**, *a*, **A, a**, etc., as tokens of it. These tokens are in a sense performances of that letter as a type.) We have some rules governing such performances, but all of them count as performances, and it is difficult to say that any one of them is clearly wrong or a failure. Failures come of unintelligibility, not of interpretation. (Sometimes the rules can be broken without loss of intelligibility: Always use capitals for proper names and for starting sentences—but it is okay to write "e.e. cummings is a poet who never used capital letters.")

A further point to note is that performing is different from merely quoting or reciting. Performing is like asserting a proposition about the work; it's an attempt to say something about the work that is not completely obvious from looking at the marks on the page that make up the score. Quoting or reciting is just sticking to the marks and risks missing the work altogether. In rehearsing for a performance, players will say things to each other such as "Make it sound sincere," or "Do it with authority," or "Get into it; get involved in it."

All this raises the interesting question of who *is* the final judge of what the work really is. The composer? But she may be blind to a certain property, or may forget parts that others see.

Performers? But they must rely on their own interpretations, and fill in so much with parts of themselves, their own feelings and experiences and preferences. Audiences? But audiences only hear performances. Well, then, critics and philosophers? But they differ among themselves (as a matter of professional pride, it sometimes seems), so how are we to tell which one is correct, which ones wrong? How can we find the truth about a performance, or about the work itself? Perhaps the answer is that there is no such thing as the work in the first place. All we have is the score, plus in some cases what the composer says about it, and the best we can hope to do with it is perform it as we see fit, appreciate or criticize the performances, and forget about "the work."

At the close of the lecture I remember thinking that in certain respects we could conceive of the U.S. Constitution as a score that is performed by successive Supreme Courts, whose responsibility it is to do justice in ever changing social contexts to what the framers meant, what they conceived and negotiated together as the work. This way of looking at the Constitution helps reveal the deep truth of the familiar, cynical-sounding remark that the Constitution is whatever the Supreme Court says it is.

Can we use some of these ideas to help us understand what it is to tell the truth? What it is to deceive? Maybe. Let's see.

An extreme case: totalitarianism. In Stalin's Russia, Mao's China, as in Orwell's *1984,* truth is the same as what is "politically correct." When the physical records of events—statistics, names, maps, books—can be eradicated and the ordinary sense of truth is unobtainable, then truth can be proclaimed, and renounced, at any time the self-appointed proclaimers think it appropriate to their cause. Such extreme contempt for truth works away at the distinction between what is true and what is false until the difference is no longer recognizable even to the functionaries. The effect is liberating: they don't know that they are lying, and in one twisted sense of the matter, they are not lying, since to lie you must believe something to be true and say it is false, or believe it to be false and say it's true. For these sad creatures the situation is different. They actually believe the falsehoods they tell others. The triumph of totalitarianism is to annul what's true by authoritative act so that non–truth tellers cannot be accused of lying. Wickedness and treachery, yes; but not lying.

Totalitarian functionaries are not performers, really, because they merely recite and quote the score, without the added effort of interpreting the meaning to get at the work. In this example, if the work is historical truth, then the score is a fraud anyway—as if the Messiah had been transcribed into a military march—and no re-cital, quotation, or performance could possibly represent the work.

Acting in plays. Do actors become the characters they play? Do they believe what they say? Not really. In acting, you don't become somebody else, seriously, you just become somebody you might have been. So it's not so much a lie if you say things with conviction that you don't believe, as it is a performance of the truth as it might have been for that somebody you might have been.

Acting in your own life. Is a life better thought of as a work, a score, or a performance? Or as all three, somehow evolving as a whole? If you are the author, and the life is still in progress, there can hardly be a work, a whole meaning behind the score or the script. Never-theless, there could be a script with roles to play. If there are many roles (somebody's child, somebody's spouse, somebody's parent, somebody's employee, etc.) then we need many selves to play them. Indeed, a "self" may be thought of as a performance in a play for approval. This is the way Erving Goffman[4] (and William James long before him) thought about the self. There are as many selves as there are roles, and each of these is modified further in the eyes of the beholder.

This view of the self, which stands in contradistinction to the idea of a real self, the "real me," is a consternation to some who feel that there ought to be one sincere, authentic Self. Many selves mean confusion and even a sense of phoniness, self-contradiction, lack of integrity, insincerity—making one feel like an imposter. On the other hand, a more positive interpretation of this state of affairs is that one is flexible, complex, multidimensional, much more than any single label could suggest. (We'll come back to this in chapter 5.)

SELF-EVIDENT TRUTH

There is one kind of truth that is special enough to warrant a further word or two. Philosophers call it "self-evident truth," which means it "always must be true, does not conflict with other truths, and admits of no exceptions," but does not necessarily mean "obviously true at first glance." There are self-evident truths in logic and mathematics, for example, "All bachelors are male," or "Every sister has a sister or a brother," or "All brown sea otters are sea otters." The first two statements are self-evidently true to anyone who knows the English words used to make them: "bachelor" is defined as "unmarried male of marriageable age"; "sister" means a female considered in her relation to another person having the same parents. (As usual, there are semantic if not logical exceptions. It does not sound exactly right to say that the Pope is a bachelor, or that a man temporarily between his fourth and fifth wives is a bachelor, even though both meet the technical criterion of "unmarried male of marriageable age." For that matter, saying "Gerry has a bachelor's degree" tells us nothing of Gerry's gender or nuptial status. "Sister" can also mean a member of a religious order, a nonreligious sisterhood, or a body of nurses, but the sense remains figuratively the same. Every sister in this sense would have a sister in the same sense.)

The case of the sea otter is slightly different. That statement is true because it fits a valid logical form, namely, "Every A that is B is A." So we have "Every otter (A) that is brown (B) is an otter (A). We could also have "Every bachelor that is Swedish is a bachelor," or "Every sister that is a teacher is a sister." Trivial, maybe; but self-evident, surely.

It is also self-evidently true that the shortest distance between two points on a plane surface is a straight line,[5] and that 7 is a prime number. Such self-evident truths as these are not *obvious* to us all, because some of us won't see why two points on a plane have this property or know what a prime number is. Self-evident truths are not always obvious to everyone; however, they can be deduced, or proved, by a series of self-evident steps. For example, for a number to be a prime number it cannot be divided without remainder except by 1 or by itself. Seven cannot be divided without remainder except by 1 or by 7 ($7/1 = 7$; $7/2 = 3$ $r1$; $7/3 = 2$ $r1$; $7/4 = 1$ $r3$; $7/5 = 1$ $r2$; $7/6 = 1$ $r1$; $7/7 = 1$). For any readers who did not previously know what a prime number is, and who did understand this example, it has just now become obvious that the statement "7 is a prime number" is self-evidently true.

IS THERE SELF-EVIDENT TRUTH IN MORALITY?

It is self-evident that there can be self-evident truths in mathematics and logic, but can there be any such truths in morality? Is there anything self-evident (that is, anything that always must be true, does not conflict with other truths, and admits of no exceptions) about what is good or right? I don't think so. Moral rules often conflict with one another and demand exceptions. I suppose the main point is that the formal properties of a logical judgment are not the same as the formal properties of a moral judgment. Though we may dislike saying so, the truth value of "Betraying the trust of others for private gain is immoral" is contingent on context (perhaps the others are plotting a crime and you tip off the police to escape blame for yourself) in a way that the self-evident truth of "A is A" can never be.

Is truth telling always good, always the right thing to do? Certainly it would be an awful world if we could trust no one ever to tell the truth. We need to be able to trust the testimony of others, because their testimony extends our experience of the world and helps us gather new information. Trust is a belief in the connection between testimony and truth. If truth were randomly connected with testimony, if we could never have reason to rely on what others say to us, then not only would we be miserably confused and anxious, but language itself would be useless. (Of course, if everybody *always* lied we could eventually figure out the pattern and infer the truth; random truth telling is much more difficult to decipher.)

Truth telling is not always good, but it's a good thing, morally and practically, that most people have a tendency to tell the truth, as they see it, at least when there is nothing important to gain by not telling the truth. The greater good of the community needs looking after by the individuals who benefit from it. We often act for the greater good even when no law compels us, and the disposition generally to tell the truth is an instance of a kind of voluntary contribution to society that can be construed as a moral good in the sense of its being useful and agreeable. (Compare this way of conceiving the value of truth telling with the domino theorists' conception described in chapter 1.) This tendency for truth telling probably comes from the simple and direct way we learn to talk: we observe and learn the names of what we see. Getting the names right is a thrill (look at the baby laugh and thrash about excitedly with each early successful "mama," "doggie," "baby"), an accomplishment that brings us closer to the community of talkers and listeners. Non–truth telling is a deviation from this simple and direct way, and it requires a self-conscious effort. It must be remembered, however, that another universal way for learning language is through stories, and stories are anything but simple and direct with respect to the truth.

Both of these processes—observing and naming, and listening to stories—promote credulity as well as veracity. We learn to believe what we are told: what mommy and daddy say is all the evidence we need for learning the way language is used, for grasping the fit (the correspondence) between the world and the spoken word. In addition, by listening to stories, we learn to believe what we want to believe. We learn about the marvelously exciting and enlivening side of believing in events and things and ideas that cannot be discovered within the bounds of our own personal experience. Stories, like testimony, extend our experience and help us imagine what we cannot see.

The happy tendency to tell the truth most of the time is a blessed comfort, and a piece of moral luck. As we all know, however, it is not always prudent to tell the truth. Occasionally there is a lot to lose by telling the truth, and something to be gained by not telling the truth. It goes without saying that nobody tells the truth all the time. This fact serves as warning that the tendency to believe everything we are told is, therefore, a sort of brain bypass. The credulous don't doubt, don't think, don't question. They may even want to believe impossible things, as did the White Queen in Alice's Wonderland:

"I can't believe *that!*" said Alice.

"Can't you?" the Queen said in a pitying tone. "Try again: draw a long breath, and shut your eyes."

Alice laughed. "There's no use trying," she said: "one *can't* believe impossible things."

"I dare say you haven't had much practice," said the Queen. "When I was your age I always did it for half-an-hour a day. Why, sometimes I've believed as many as six impossible things before breakfast."[6]

Wanting strongly enough to believe something, even something impossible, can sometimes give us the impression that the object of belief is self-evidently true. God exists. God is good. Human nature exists. Human nature is good. Good exists. Good is good (now there's *something* we can all agree is self-evidently true!—never mind that it doesn't tell us anything). Now what about the notion that truth telling is good? Is that a self-evident moral truth? Deception is bad—is that a self-evident truth, too? Neither proposition fits the criteria outlined for self-evident truth, so I would have to say the answer is more complicated than that. I would go further and say there are no useful, meaningful self-evident moral truths because, unlike the situation in logic and mathematics, we can't even agree on what morality is, or what it means, and we certainly have not produced or discovered a body of moral knowledge that all of us would agree is *knowledge.* How can we have moral truth without moral knowledge? What we have is belief, and wanting to believe.

My main concern in this chapter has been to explore several theories of truth in order to set up the broad and general question this book is about: If we can't (and if philosophers can't) agree what the truth is, or what exactly it means to tell the truth, how then can we be so sure that "truth telling" is some sort of ultimate moral principle? I am trying to raise doubts about what is taken for granted as "the truth" and thereby open the question whether our conceptions of truth telling and deceiving are adequate when tested against what we actually do as a matter of practical intelligence.

The remaining chapters explore from many angles the relationship of truth to morality.

3 THE REVERSE OF TRUTH HAS A HUNDRED THOUSAND SHAPES

What is the use of lying, when truth, well distributed, serves the same purpose?

W. E. Forster

If we seek real rather than technical truth, it is more true to be considerately untruthful within limits than to be inconsiderately truthful without them.

Samuel Butler

The idea of deception is very broad, perhaps so broad as to be beyond grasping completely, especially when self-deception is included with the deception of others. To get some idea of how inclusive the idea is, consider dividing the world in two: first, there is telling the whole truth to everybody all the time (an ideal that we can strive to approximate, but that is actually impossible to practice because even though most people want to be truthful, they don't want to be too truthful and not quite all the time); and second, there is everything else we do. If this "everything else" is different from telling the whole truth all the time, then it represents not telling some part of the truth about something, in some way, to some degree, to someone, for some time. Of course, "not telling the truth" may simply mean sitting quietly alone, not saying anything. In this case, there is no attempt to communicate with another person, so deception is not really an issue—except possibly as self-deception (the subject of chapter 5). However, "not telling the truth" may also mean outright lying. I see lying as a relatively straightforward subcategory of deception, though it has its own complexity as an adaptive behavior which is sometimes very effi-cient in solving a whole range of problems. Like it or not, lying works, when it works, very well.

Perhaps it would be a good idea to explore the logic of the lie before turning to some of the nonlying, but still deceptive, al-ternatives to truth telling, which involve consciously adding or subtracting something from what you take to be the truth in the process of communicating with another person.

THE LOGIC OF A LIE

If we are to think of lying as intrinsically wrong, then all lies are wrong merely because they are lies, no matter what the con-ditions which produced them, no matter what conditions they produce. But does lying, or anything else we do, have a clearly unambiguous, absolute or intrinsic value? If we really believed lying was absolutely or intrinsically wrong, we would do it, or be seriously tempted to do it, only when some competing value over-whelmed our inclination not to do it. But this is surely not the case, as can be shown by pointing out the frequency of what are called "white lies," that is, lies told when supposedly nothing important is at stake, and "justifiable lies" told when something very impor-tant is at stake. There are lies for all occasions, as well we know, but we aren't consistent; we neither lie all the time nor abstain completely. We are much more consistent in *declaring* that lying is always wrong, because we think that's the right thing to say.

It would be helpful to get a clearer picture of what lying is before we make moral judgments about whether it's always wrong to lie. Here's an attempt to sort out the logic of the lie.

A lie has four parts:
1. A statement, something spoken or written;
2. A belief in the mind of the statement-maker;
3. An intention in the mind of the statement-maker;
4. The character and rights of the person addressed.

Let's take a look at each of these parts to see how they help define a lie while keeping it separate from other forms of deception.

First, the statement. For there to be a lie, something must be said. A shrug, a pointed silence, a glance, or a space on a ques-tionnaire left blank may be deceptive, but if nothing is actually stated it's hard to see what would count as a lie. However, not any old statement will qualify as a potential lie. If I say, "Please shut the window," or "Good morning," or "Ouch!" you would be hard pressed to demonstrate that what I've said is either true or false. So, only statements that could conceivably be known or believed to be true or false will count in defining a lie. (There's a problem with these, too, because some of them—"It's cold," "She's mature," "My brother follows the Republican line"—are so vague they can hardly be the subject of a definite lie.)

Second, the liar's own belief about the statement. The standard definition of lying as "saying something you know to be false" is not quite right. For example, you ask me the time. I look at my watch and see that it's three o'clock, but I say it's four o'clock. As it happens, my watch is slow and it really is four o'clock. Did I lie? Yes, most would agree. But did I say something I *knew* to be false? No. In fact, I said something that is true but which I *believed* to be false.[1] This example shows that lying is saying something you think is false, no matter what the fact. It works the other way around, too: asserting as false something you believe to be true. The key to the idea of lying is not what in fact is true (or false) but what is in the liar's mind. (Again, there are problems, this time with the *strength* of a belief. We never believe only one thing at a time, and one belief will often be mixed in or mixed up with others which dilute the strength of our certainty about it. Strong beliefs make clearer cases of lying than weak beliefs.)

Besides beliefs, the liar must also have an intention with regard to being truthful or untruthful. A liar must want to make somebody believe something that the liar does not believe, or disbelieve something that the liar does believe. Usually, getting somebody to believe something is not an end in itself, but a step along the way to some other goal. The intention, then, involves not only the desire to create a belief but to do so for some further purpose that the liar wishes to accomplish. People lie to satisfy selfish motives for manipulation, to be sure; but we also lie to attract attention, even love, or to impress others with exaggerated abilities or accomplishments; and commonly we lie like crazy to avoid harm, punishment, and blame. (Again, intentions can be strong or weak, like beliefs, and we are not always perfectly clear about them ourselves. Weak, muddled intentions confound the question of whether or not a person is lying.)

Fourth, there is the tricky question of the object of the lie—the person on the receiving end. We have been assuming that in ordinary conversation both parties have a right to an honest effort to share truthful information. Making a statement is sort of like making a general promise, or giving an assurance, that what you say is true, or at least that you think it is true. The two speakers have faith in one another and in the statements made on both sides. Immanuel Kant wrote what is perhaps the most famous formal statement of this view: "The duty of truthfulness makes no distinction between persons to whom we may owe this duty and those toward whom we may repudiate it, but is an unconditioned duty which is valid in all circumstances."[2]

This is the formal moral context, or "the rules of the game," of truth telling. Now, what happens when the person asking for information is an assassin who is looking for your friend? Does the assassin have a right to expect you to play by the rules which govern truth telling and lying, or are you both now playing another game entirely? If you think the assassin has forfeited the right to expect you to tell the truth according to the ordinary mutual trust obligations in conversation, then you are no longer operating within the context in which truth telling and lying can be sensibly defined. The very ideas of true and false are inappropriate and irrelevant, and so lying does not enter even as a possibility.

That is because a lie cannot be committed when truth is irrelevant. This is clearly the case in teasing, telling jokes, making up tall tales for amusement around the campfire, as well as some other forms of entertainment. It is also the case, though perhaps less clearly so, in situations of extreme danger. For example, it is not the point in responding to the demands of an assassin to share honest information, and not even he genuinely expects, or has the right to expect, the truth from you. The point for you in such an exchange is self-defense and defense of other potential victims. The assassin's point is to find and kill the intended victim. Perhaps an analogy will help make this clear. Just as "murder" is not exactly the right term to describe the killing of another person in fright, terror, or frantic desperation brought on by the deceased (voluntary manslaughter), or by the negligent operation of an automobile (involuntary manslaughter), or in self-defense (justifiable homicide), "lying" does not exactly describe the trickery and falsehood we use to disarm the assassin. The point I am trying to make here is that the condition of the listener's right to expect the truth is an important part of the "communication games" of truth telling and lying. Accepting this condition means that in a range of communication games (e.g., entertainment and danger) the burden of having to justify uttering falsehoods is lifted completely. However, when the logic of the lie is understood in terms of the first three parts only, without this fourth one, then, when we lie to an assassin, we must try to justify it by calling it "lying to save one's skin." (Bok might excuse such a lie, but she could not justify it if there were any truth telling alternative.)

I realize this point is controversial. Kant couldn't take it seriously because his focus was on the unconditioned duty of truthfulness, which implies that we must make no distinction among those to whom we owe the duty. As we shall see later in this chapter, Pastor Trocmé would absolutely disagree on this point, too, but for different reasons, and while Huck Finn would be puzzled, he would no doubt be grateful for finding a way to get off the hook.

To sum up, then, we can say that lying means making a statement (not too vague) you want somebody to believe, even though you don't (completely) believe it yourself, when the other person has a right to expect you mean what you say.

THE PURE AND SIMPLE LIE?

No lie is just a lie. It is a lie told to somebody about something for some reason at some time with some more or less probable results intended. Lying, like telling the truth, is complex and frought with difficulties. There is a treacherous transition from believing something, thinking it through in one's own mind, to saying it out loud to someone else. Even though we may not always experience fully the complexity of this transition, to speak a simple truth is an impressive mental accomplishment. "Speech is a misrepresentation of psychological reality, not because everyone is a malicious liar, but because that inner reality is fugitive and only poorly fits the devices of expression it finds."[3]

Describing the way(s) lying enters in this process of communicating is a complex problem. Assessing the moral status of particular lies is perhaps equally complex. Finding a pure and simple lie may be as difficult as finding a pure and simple truth.

> *Daniel:* Last night, after the most satisfying evening we've ever had together, I told Nora that I loved her. I felt the love, I even felt myself wanting to love her, and I was thinking about my future with her in it.
>
> *Allen:* That's terrific. I know you've wanted a woman in your life for a long time. You must be elated.
>
> *Daniel:* I was last night. When I told Nora that I loved her, it was true. I'm sure it was. But now, I don't know. I feel differently. I don't think it's true anymore.
>
> *Allen:* Did you lie to her?
>
> *Daniel:* No! I don't think so. I don't know. Did I?

There's no question that a statement such as "I love you" can be true at one time and false sometime later, merely because circumstances (feelings, insights) change. But does this example involve lying? Daniel made a statement (not too vague, although "I love you" is not too clear, either) he wanted Nora to believe which he thought he believed (though perhaps not completely) but which, as it turns out, he does not now think he believes. Nora certainly had a right to expect the truth from Daniel, and we can believe he tried to say it. But did he? The key question is whether he believed "I love you, Nora" at the time he spoke. The lock on the question is our feeble ability to know exactly and completely what we believe at any given time, especially at times of heightened emotion, speculation, optimism. (In the words of Heinrich Heine, "Oh, what lies there are in kisses!") Does believing "I love Nora" feel enough like believing "I want to love Nora; I hope I can" so that you might honestly confuse the two states of mind? Did Daniel lie? I don't know. Even he doesn't know for sure.

MARK TWAIN AND THE PRINCE OF WALES

Mark Twain tells this story in his essay "My First Lie, and How I Got Out of It":[4]

> I have an English friend of twenty-five years' stand-
> ing, and yesterday when we were coming downtown
> on top of the bus I happened to tell him a lie—a
> modified one, of course; a half-breed, a mulatto: I
> can't seem to tell any other kind now, the market is
> so flat. I was explaining to him how I got out of an
> embarrassment in Austria last year. I do not know
> what might have become of me if I hadn't happened
> to remember to tell the police that I belonged to the
> same family as the Prince of Wales. That made every-
> thing pleasant, and they let me go; and apologized,
> too, and were ever so kind and obliging and polite,
> and couldn't do too much for me, and explained how
> the mistake came to be made, and promised to hang
> the officer that did it, and hoped I would let bygones
> be bygones and not say anything about it; and I said
> they could depend on me. My friend said, austerely:
> "You call it a modified lie? Where is the modifi-
> cation?"
> I explained that it lay in the form of my statement
> to the police.
> "I didn't say I belonged to the royal family: I only
> said I belonged to the same family as the Prince of
> Wales—meaning the human family, of course; and if
> those people had had any penetration they would
> have known it. I can't go around furnishing brains to
> the police; it is not to be expected."
> "How did you feel after that performance?"
> "Well, of course I was distressed to find that the
> police had misunderstood me, but as long as I had
> not told any lie I knew there was no occasion to sit
> up nights and worry about it."

In this delightful essay Twain also expressed the belief that most lies
are acts and speech has almost no part in them. He had special scorn
for the crowd we call today the Silent Majority who, in their or-

chestrated acts of silence, support "the tyrannies and shams and inequalities and unfairnesses that afflict the peoples. . . ." In his mocking conclusion he pokes away at such hypocrisy:

> To sum up, on the whole I am satisfied with things the way they are. There is a prejudice against the spoken lie, but none against any other, and by examination and mathematical computation I find that the proportion of the spoken lie to the other varieties is as 1 to 22,894. Therefore the spoken lie is of no consequence, and it is not worth while to go around fussing about it and trying to make believe that it is an important matter.

I agree with Twain that the spoken lie is of relatively little interest when compared to these "other varieties of lying," which together make up what I call the field of deception. That's the next subject.

THE REVERSE OF TRUTH

It's the artfulness we have evolved for avoiding both truth telling and lying at the same time that interests me most—the varnishing, the adding and subtracting, the partial display and concealment of what one person takes to be the truth while communicating with another. As a communicative strategy, deception is so often rewarded that it would seem to have become unavoidable and indispensable. It may actually serve to promote and preserve emotional equilibrium on a personal level, and a civilized climate for communicating with each other and living our lives together on a social level.

It is important to stress, given the strong pitch in these early pages for a revaluation of deception, that truth telling has had, and always will have, a very important place in moral conduct and, indeed, in all of social life. The point is that we need not assume it to be a moral good in every instance, nor need we assume it to be present as the background in every situation. People don't tell the truth merely to tell the truth. They tell the truth for some reason. Truth telling is a means for accomplishing purposes. So is deception. My approach to an understanding of deception is not the usual one (top down) of focusing on the virtue of truth as a given, then finding ways to make benevolent compromises. It is rather to focus on human communication (bottom up), then to see what roles both truth telling and deceiving play in furthering that process toward the achievement of worthwhile goals. The patterns and designs we create for telling the truth and deceiving express who we are, both as individuals and socially, in relation to others. Both honesty and deceit are rooted in us, in our capacities and desires, and both should be used with discretion at least, if not with stronger moral expectations such as "Avoid doing harmful things and try to do good whenever you can."

I would like to offer some brief examples to illustrate some of the moral complexity of truth telling, lying, and deceiving, and through them try to show that the grounds of our common presuppositions about deception may be faulty, that conventions of truth telling are inadequate to the problems we know and share. The presuppositions and conventions I refer to are those associated with the top-down perspective on moral philosophy that is derived from formal, universal principles. Such principles can inspire us, to be sure, but they can also play tricks on our understanding, and they can sometimes demand of us more than we can possibly do. The principle that one should never lie, except as a last resort when no truth telling alternative is possible, is an example. It is far from clear what this principle means for us in the light of Michel de Montaigne's insight: "If falsehood, like truth, had only one face, we would be in better shape. For we would take as certain the opposite of what the liar said. But the reverse of truth has a hundred thousand shapes and a limitless field."[5]

It is fascinating to imagine "the reverse of truth" in Montaigne's sense and apply that sense to the dilemmas posed by the principle of truth telling in the lives of ordinary people who try hard to do the right thing but who find they cannot make moral judgments solely on the basis of formal, universal principles. For the moment let's assume that aiming for moral decency is enough of a challenge, and that moral perfection is out of reach. People can be so much worse than merely decent. For that reason, being merely decent must be regarded with favor—and not damned with faint praise. Mere moral decency is never homicidal, which is more than we can say of many "purer" moralities. The goal of moral decency is to do the best we can in the circumstances, all things considered.

Lying to Save Your Friend

Take, for example, the situation Mark Twain posed in *Adventures of Huckleberry Finn* as Huck and his friend Jim, a slave, drifted on their raft toward the place where Jim would become legally free.[6]

> Jim said it made him all over trembly and feverish to be so close to freedom. Well, I can tell you it made me all over trembly and feverish, too, to hear him, because I begun to get it through my head that he *was* most free—and who was to blame for it? Why, *me* . . . I couldn't get that out of my conscience, no how nor no way. . . . I tried to make out to myself that *I* warn't to blame, because *I* didn't run Jim off from his rightful owner; but it warn't no use, conscience up and says, every time, "But you knowed he was running for his freedom, and you could a paddled ashore and told somebody."

Huck has a crisis of conscience. The morality he has learned in rural Missouri tells him it is wrong to help slaves escape. It is stealing from the slave's owner, in this case, Miss Watson, who has done Huck no harm. But his morality clashes with his feelings, with his sympathy for his friend.

> My conscience got to stirring me up hotter than ever, until at last I says to it, "Let up on me—it ain't too late, yet—I'll paddle ashore at the first light, and tell." I felt easy, and happy, and light as a feather, right off. All my troubles was gone. . . . When I was fifty yards off, Jim says:
> "Dah you goes, de ole true Huck; de on'y white genlman dat ever kep' his promise to ole Jim."
> Well, I just felt sick. But I says, I *got* to do it—I can't get *out* of it. Right then, along comes a skiff with two men in it, with guns, and they stopped and I stopped. One of them says:

"What's that yonder?"

"A piece of raft," I says.

"Do you belong on it?"

"Yes, sir."

"Any men on it?"

"Only one, sir."

"Well, there's five niggers run off to-night, up yonder above the head of the bend. Is your man white or black?"

I didn't answer up prompt. I tried to, but the words wouldn't come. I tried, for a second or two, to brace up and out with it, but I warn't man enough—hadn't the spunk of a rabbit. I see I was weakening; so I just give up trying, and up and says—

"He's white."

We all learn morality in some kind of community, somewhere, and most often what we understand as "the morally right thing to do" is what that community has taught us to understand. In this episode, Huck suffers a conflict between his own natural sympathy and a morality which tells him it is wrong to help slaves escape.

Huck *knows* what his conscience says is the right thing to do but he *feels* sick about it. In the end, sympathy—his fellow-feeling for Jim—wins out over conscience, and Huck lies to the two men hunting for runaway slaves. Huck believes that in lying he has acted weakly and wickedly. He cares for honesty and gratitude, and this requires him to give Jim up. But his love and compassion struggle against his conscience. He chooses for Jim and the hell that he believes awaits him, on the basis of irrational feeling and against the many reasons he has for giving him up. All the reasons are on the side of conscience. He has no principles or arguments on the side of feeling—he simply sees himself as failing through weakness to do what he believes to be right. Twain's masterful touch of irony shows how weakness sometimes leads to right action. Or to put it another way, how morality sometimes requires what it normally forbids.

When sympathies are broad and kind like Huck's, and the morality in question is bad, or at least contains aspects and concepts we deeply disapprove of, then things will work out well. But moral principles can also help us, when sympathies are questionable or confused. In this sense, principles that embody our best sympathies can help us when our feelings are not at their best.

So, sympathies and principles should be thought of as checking and balancing each other: sometimes principles become untenable because of the strength of our feelings; sometimes feelings must be overridden. Experiences will evoke responses that can change the way we think and the way we choose to apply the principles we hold. Feelings are vital to moral conduct, but they are not everything. Sometimes they must be subordinated. The same may be said of moral principles. Sometimes we must rise above principle to do the right thing.

Not every reader will be convinced, however, that Huck did the right thing by lying. Even Montaigne, whose wise words were quoted above, had a very strong aversion to lying: "Truly, I am not sure that I could bring myself to ward off even an evident and extreme danger by a shameless and solemn lie."[7] He wasn't the first to feel this way. St. Augustine argued that lying is wrong even to save chastity.[8] And before that, in the *Iliad,* Homer has Achilles say: "Hateful to me even as the gates of Hades is he that hideth one thing in his heart and uttereth another."[9]

Lying to the Nazis

This passionate hatred of lying is a central theme in Philip Hallie's miraculous—but real—tale of goodness in his book *Lest Innocent Blood Be Shed.* During World War II, in a small Protestant town in southern France called Le Chambon, villagers and their clergy saved thousands of Jewish children and adults using only one weapon—secrecy—against the Vichy government and the Nazi SS. Pastor André Trocmé, known as "the soul of Le Chambon," inspired the entire village through his deep, invincible morality and caused goodness to break out in the midst of that episode of horrible, lunatic inhumanity. His morality included the principle "Never lie," and he steadfastly refused to tell a lie, even to the Nazi SS, when his own and his young son's lives were in evident and extreme danger. Here is an excerpt from this remarkable story (Trocmé was on the Gestapo death list and he had been arrested):[10]

Soon the German police would interrogate him and demand to see his papers. His identity card gave his name as Beguet, and they would ask him if this was indeed true. Then he would have to lie in order to hide his identity. But he was not able to lie; lying, especially to save his own skin, was "sliding toward those compromises that God had not called upon me to make," he wrote in his autobiographical notes on this incident. Saving the lives of others—and even saving his own life—with false identity cards was one thing, but standing before another human being and speaking lies to him only for the sake of self-preservation was something different. Telling the policeman a lie face-to-face would mean crossing a line that stands between the false identity card that saves a human life and the betrayal of one's fellowman and of one's God.

He decided that when the German police questioned him, he would say, "I am not Monsieur Beguet. I am Pastor André Trocmé." Having made this decision, he became calm; his conscience was quiet.

But a thought shattered his calm: Jacot was waiting for his father in front of the station, and he did not know his way back to their friends in Lyons or to Le Chambon. He was a sensitive, very emotional boy, deeply attached to his father. How his horror would grow as the hours passed and his father did not return!

If anyone had asked for his papers, Trocmé, and quite possibly [Jacot] as well, would have been deported and destroyed, because Trocmé would have told the truth.

Trocmé—the pastor, the father—was able to deceive with falsehoods on paper and with silence, but he was not able to speak a lie to another person, no matter to whom, not even to prevent the Nazi SS from destroying his son and putting an end to his own successful work that had saved, and would continue to save, thousands of lives. Like Huck, Pastor Trocmé became calm and his conscience was quieted when he decided to tell the truth. There can be great power and solace in deciding to face the truth and tell it. But unlike Huck, Trocmé would actually have gone ahead and told the truth to someone who most people would think did not deserve to hear it. He was a man of enormously strong conviction and dedication to moral principles. He was, because of this, a hero. He was also, because of his principles, ready to sacrifice himself and his son to the Nazis. (In this case, he was lucky. He escaped by slipping out of one line into another; and he found his son.) What was it that he saw as the crucial difference, the life and death difference, between deception and lying? Hallie's book doesn't tell.

For the hero who would risk loved ones, even life itself, for the sake of truth, for belief in an ideal—for such a hero, what is the golden rule?[11]

Whereas Huck was puzzled about what he was supposed to do when the situation seemed to call for a lie, Pastor Trocmé was certain. Huck felt he lacked the spunk of a rabbit, but clearly he showed great strength of caring for his friend, and he was able to resolve his conflict on the strength of this feeling for a particular individual in special circumstances which demanded that an exception be made to an otherwise firm obligation to tell the truth. Trocmé showed great strength in overcoming his feelings by relying on a moral principle which for him was absolute, a truth for which he was unwilling to make any exceptions.

Lying to the Children

These opposing views are played off against each other in Virginia Woolf's portrayal of Mr. and Mrs. Ramsay in *To the Lighthouse*. In one scene, they have a problem deciding whether to take the children on a promised boat trip the next day. He knows the barometer is falling and the wind is due west, so he snaps out irascibly that there will be no possible chance of going. She, on the other hand, still hopes the wind might change and doesn't want to disappoint the children prematurely, so she is unwilling to tell them the trip is canceled. She tells the children simply that it might be fine tomorrow, and for their sake, she hopes it will be. He curses her for "flying in the face of facts," is enraged by the "extraordinary irrationality of her remark," and accuses her of telling lies. Woolf describes Mrs. Ramsay's reaction to her husband's cursing in these words:

> To pursue with such astonishing lack of considera-
> tion for other people's feelings, to rend the veils of
> civilization so wantonly, so brutally, was to her so
> horrible an outrage of human decency that, without
> replying, dazed and blinded, she bent her head as if
> to let the pelt of jagged hail, the drench of dirty wa-
> ter, bespatter her unrebuked. There was nothing to
> be said. [12]

Mr. Ramsay's prideful pursuit of truth was for Mrs. Ramsay rashly uncharitable. Her passion was for clarity, relationships, and a caring morality. His was for simplicity, rules, and a principled morality. His mind was arranged more like a piano keyboard, hers like a painter's palette. Both, of course, are appropriate to their respective arts, but they are also in some ways fundamentally incompatible.

GOOD AND EVIL, LIGHT AND DARKNESS, TRUTH AND . . . ?

The great battle between principled truth telling and lying represents a deep, strong current in our moral and religious traditions. It's another way of describing the timeless mythic opposition of Good and Evil, Light and Darkness—categories that have no fixed or fixable extent but serve the essential role of guiding our talk and conduct along general, if ill-defined, pathways. We declare that truth telling is in principle good; lying is in principle evil. Indeed, we act as if we believe society holds together only by threads (the thin twisted yarns?) of truthful speech and that lying is somehow a direct assault on the foundations of civilization itself. We have to set up the problem of truth telling in these extreme terms and represent lying as some kind of malignant devilry; otherwise, who would give a hoot?

Deception, however, is another matter. We are more reluctant to tackle this aspect of communicating and behaving because deception is much more difficult than lying to isolate and define. Deception is seldom as explicit or direct as lying and we are uncertain how, in the long run, it affects the well-being and practical operation of society. Some say deception is worse than lying because it contributes to an insidious and progressive adulteration of clear thinking, honest feeling, and therefore human communication and trust. They believe in the ancient adage that the truth will set you free, and they honor the ideal of truth telling for its supposed purity, as peoples everywhere have been attracted to the purity of gold. Where would we be without the golden ideal, the glorious luster of the pure and simple truth?

Others say we create a rich mixture of truth and falsity so that we might live better lives; they say we have developed the arts of deception so that we might not perish of pitiless reality, and we deceive for the very practical and forceful reason that we have a future to look after. They say a mixture of truth and falsehood makes an alloy that is very durable and useful, though impure, like brass and pewter. They ask where we would be without such familiar "truth alloys" as good manners, excuses, irony, compromise, discretion, jokes, stories, privacy, and hope. They quote Oscar Wilde who said, "The pure and simple truth is rarely pure and never simple."

At the risk of mixing my metaphors beyond recognition, I would like to close this section with a reference to something I said in the Introduction—the suggestion that the moral perfectionist requirement of being set against all deception is like telling us to loathe and distrust all bacteria, including the ones responsible for wine, cheese, and normal digestive functions.[13] It is clearly a mistake to neglect context in evaluating bacteria, only some of which are culprits of disease; others contribute to the flourishing of life. The same may be true for deception, which is not only, or always, a moral problem. Its moral status is defined in terms of other notions such as hurting, dignity, fairness, and friendship. It is, therefore, a morally complex idea. The tough proposition we have to consider is how and why to deceive whom about what and for how long. Can we learn to use deception in our communications with each other more thoughtfully and judiciously, charitably, humanely, and with discretion? Can we learn to sort out the harmful from the beneficial uses of deception, to avoid the moral disease caused by excessive self-interest—and instead put our minds to making the wine and cheese, to seeking aid in the digestion of reality, to making life flourish?

The truth has great literal and allegorical power. That is sometimes a good reason to approach it from the side. I think this is what Emily Dickinson was trying to tell us when she wrote:

> Tell all the Truth but tell it slant—
> Success in Circuit lies
> Too bright for our infirm Delight
> The Truth's superb surprise
> As Lightning to the Children eased
> With explanation kind
> The Truth must dazzle gradually
> Or every man be blind—[14]

4 SHOWING AND HIDING: THE LOGIC OF DECEPTION

A liar is a man who does not know how to deceive, a flatterer one who only deceives fools: he alone can pride himself on his cleverness who knows how to make skillful use of the truth.

Vauvenargues

A man's most open actions have a secret side to them.

Joseph Conrad

Half the people in America are faking it.

Robert Mitchum

There are some professionals who are remarkably adept at managing their expressions—salespeople, flight attendants, lawyers, therapists, spies, politicians, magicians, actors, champion poker players, writers, and thieves, to name a few.

John Hamrak, one of the most inventive con men of the first years of this century in Hungary, and an accomplice dressed as a technician walked into the office of an alderman in City Hall. Hamrak announced that they had come for the clock which was to be repaired. The alderman, probably because of the great value of the clock, was reluctant to hand it over. Instead of further substantiating his role, Hamrak responded by calling the alderman's attention to the extraordinary value of the clock, declaring that it was for this reason that he had come for it in person.[1]

Hamrak's strategy was to point to one salient truth in order to re-direct the alderman's attention from another. So, even though the con man spoke only the truth, he was not entirely sincere. He did mean what he said about the value of the clock, but he was decep-tive about his intention in coming to get it. He knew that the alder-man would be likely to consider him an honest man because he had emphasized the great value of the clock, thereby insinuating that he shared the alderman's responsibility for it.

Deception requires strategic skills in speaking, writing, and other forms of expressive behavior—including facial and bodily ex-pressions. Through these we make impressions, or encourage oth-ers to form their impressions of us in a certain way. We all have strategic skills; some are just better than others.

Hamrak was encouraging the alderman to commit a com-mon fallacy in thinking about other people: The Good Person Fal-lacy. The mistake is to think that if a person clearly does something morally good—return a misplaced wallet, give to charity, risk in-jury to help another, or in this case tell the truth—then that person must be good, must be a Good Person. A Good Person does not steal, therefore, . . . whoops!

We can turn it around, into the Fallacy of the Bad Person, which is the same kind of mistake. If we think deception is morally bad, and this person deceives, then we think this person is a Bad Person. These fallacies prevent us from seeing the distinction be-tween actions and persons. When my son misbehaves, I don't tell him he's a bad boy, a bad person; I tell him he's a good boy who just did a bad thing. Robin Hood robbed and stole like crazy—but he gave away what he stole from the rich to help the poor. Was he a Bad Person? A Good Person? Or was he a person who did bad things for good reasons?

Deception is not something that only bad people do. We are all ordinary deceivers. And deception is not always morally bad: the police very likely had to use deception to catch Hamrak and retrieve the clock. There can be no doubt, though, that deception is a moral concept. Even deception used for entertainment is subject to moral reaction. Socrates wanted all the poets and storytellers banned from Athens because they did not tell the truth; they created fictions and myths that the children who listened to them would later have to unlearn if they were ever to see the truth clearly. Likewise, Orson Welles's masterful radio program, "The War of the Worlds," was so realistic in depicting an invasion from space that people flooded telephone lines with panic calls for information on how to protect themselves. Welles was criticized for misusing his genius for deceptive entertainment in an irresponsible way.

In our society, there is a tension between the moral principles about deception and the moral practices of everyday life. Usually, the morals in practice are less exacting, less demanding, and perhaps more subtle than the moral "law." Philosophers such as Kant tell us that truth telling is categorically good and deception is always bad. Our civil codes and moral testaments spell out just when, by law, truth telling is required (giving evidence in court, writing contracts, etc.) and when, by custom, exceptions may be made (as in the Talmudic general principle that lies are forbidden, except when uttered to make peace). There is an exception recognized in formal law as "puffing" or "chaffering." The legal scholar Charles Wolfram summarizes the law's attitude to the practice this way:

> Some deals are too good to be true, and some representations are too preposterous, jocular, suspicious, or trite to induce reasonable reliance. A measure of salt is required particularly if the person making the representation is one of adverse interest, as will ordinarily be the case in negotiating. "The habit of vendors to exaggerate and of purchasers to depreciate the value of the article which they are selling or buying is well known." Both contract and tort law recognize loose but not terribly broad categories of these conventionalized lies upon which no one may reasonably rely in determining to enter into a contract. The categories relate to some, but by no means all, statements of future facts, opinions—particularly opinions about matters of quality, value, and authenticity—and intentions.
>
> Such misstatements excepted from creation of liability are known as *puffing* or *chaffering*. The exceptions are based on assumptions about human behavior in business dealings and on "reasonable

standards of fair dealing." For both purposes judges draw meaning in part from what they believe to be prevailing market practices. Those practices do not always insist on the truth. It may be permissible under them, for example, to lie about one's intended use of a piece of property in order to prevent the intending seller from asking a higher price.

The puffing exception is not based on belief in legal magic that turns some lies into truth. It is based on the reasonability of the reaction of specific listeners to specific misstatements. Importantly, that means that contract negotiators must accept gullible persons for the naifs they are: a gullible person's greater readiness to rely may be held reasonable under some circumstances. Generally, the puffery privilege to lie one's head off has not been favored, and in many instances its legality comes down to a jury question of the materiality of the statement and the justifiability of the auditor in relying on it.[2]

Wolfram uses the term "lie" loosely to indicate any number of deceptive ways of expressing oneself, but otherwise his meaning is clear. His summary is very useful in pointing out the interplay between formal law and assumptions about informal human behavior and "prevailing market practices." Deceptions of various kinds are accepted as integral to our way of life, and the function of formal law is to keep them from getting out of hand. I would say the same about morality in general: it is unrealistic and unacceptably invasive of personal privacy to insist on a world without deceit, but it is necessary for everybody's welfare—especially for us gullible naifs—to maintain a balance between deceiving and truth telling, to prohibit people from lying their heads off, to prevent injury and suffering caused by betrayal, cheating, and other kinds of treachery.

THE LOGIC OF DECEPTION

The notion of deception is much more elusive than the notion of lying. Telling a lie is one way of deceiving people, but what can we say about the difference between a straightforward lie and the less direct ways we all use to "manage information"? Let's try to set up some conceptual fences that might contain this elusive notion of deception.

A first stab at a definition: Deception is the shrewd and sober art of "showing and hiding" which is meant to control what is and is not perceived, assumed, or understood. The point is to present a situation in a way that will encourage some person(s) to develop a confident but mistaken hypothesis, which in some way serves our purpose. Or, we could say that deceiving is the business of persuasion aided by the art of selective display.

Now let's look at the various ways we can hide and show.[3]

Hiding

Hiding has at least three major subcategories:

1. Disappear: to fade, vanish, or become invisible either under cover or by blending in with the background.

Polonius tries to deceive Hamlet by taking cover behind a curtain so he can eavesdrop on a conversation between Hamlet and his son, Laertes. His ploy does not work out well, however, as Hamlet hears a noise and plunges his dagger into the old man, not knowing who he is.

You see me coming up the aisle in a department store and remember that you owe me $10, so you step into the crowd at the bargain table, hoping I won't see you; if I do catch sight of you, you're in the perfect location to plead for more time to repay the debt.

One method common to many animals in the ocean is cryptic coloration that allows the animal to resemble some part of the environment enough to disappear. Certain shrimp and kelp crabs blend in with the plants they rest on during the day. Flatfish have pigment cells that adapt to the ocean's bottom where they live. Squid have an extraordinary ability to change color to match sunlight in deep water, or moonlight near the surface.

2. Disguise: to become unrecognizable by adding to or modifying your characteristics. "It is a paradox that secretiveness plays the same role as boasting: both are engaged in the creation of a disguise."[4]

The mayor wants to find out more about life on the streets

of his city, so he buys some used clothes from Goodwill, lets his beard grow for a week, doesn't bathe or comb his hair, and walks around as if he were homeless for a few days and nights.

You cover your feelings of embarrassment, anger, and revulsion with a gracious smile when someone who has just met your charming sister tells you how much alike you are, when you know she is also pathologically manipulative and greedy.

Spider crabs have learned to decorate themselves with bits of algae, sponges, wood chips—all manner of materials—until they are well protected from spiny lobsters, sea otters, and other predators, who would make a meal of them if they could only find them.

Deception of this kind has an aesthetic side, too, in connection to a need to recount what we want others to see or hear, much embellished beyond fact. Tolstoy's description of the boastful young officer Rostov is an example:

> Boris saw that Rostov was preparing to make fun of Berg, so he skillfully changed the subject, begging Rostov to tell them how and where he got his wound. This pleased Rostov, and he began a circumstantial account . . . exactly as men who have taken part in battles always do describe them—that is, as they would like them to have been . . . but not in the least as they really had been. Rostov was a truthful young man and would never have told a deliberate lie. He began his story with the intention of telling everything exactly as it happened, but imperceptibly, unconsciously and inevitably he passed into falsehood. He could not tell them simply that they had all set out at a trot, that he had fallen off his horse, sprained his arm and then run from the Frenchmen into the woods as fast as his legs would carry him. Besides, to tell everything exactly as it had been would have meant the exercise of considerable self-control to confine himself to the facts. It is very difficult to tell the truth and young people are rarely capable of it. His listeners expected to hear how, forgetful of himself and all on fire with excitement, he had rushed down like a hurricane on the enemy's square, hacked his way in, slashing the French right

and left; how his sabre had tasted flesh, and he had
fallen exhausted, and so on. And that was what he
told them.[5]

It is a cheerless fact of life that, with very few exceptions, our experiences fall quite a bit short of the fabulous. What's the harm in
bringing on smiles and admiring laughter by telling our lives as if
they were less tame and more impressive than they really are? Rostov, like most of us, seeks to satisfy his audience and himself by
shaping and structuring, embellishing, dramatizing, condensing,
fancying up the content of an experience to give it a pizazz which
it lacks on its own.

3. Distract: to escape notice by creating uncertainty in the
perceiver. The magician entertains by focusing our attention on his
right hand while his left slips a card up his sleeve.

Your husband goes to his first pornographic movie *and* has
an affair while out of town. He returns to tell you shamefacedly of
that one night he went to the movie with a friend, which is the
truth. He wants to talk about the episode because he feels guilty
about it. You never think to ask about an affair, because a man who
is ashamed of going to a blue movie surely would not be unfaithful.
(Remember the Fallacy of the Good Person?)

Showing

As Balthasar Gracian advised his readers in the seventeenth
century, "There is no need to show your ability before everyone."[6]
Showing, like hiding, has at least three subcategories:

1. Mimic: to present yourself as another real, well-known,
recognizable individual.

We all impersonate honest people.

Mama's boy has gone off to college where he begins to wear
different clothes, adopts a manner far removed from his parents'
ways, accumulates a treasure of small possessions charged with sentiment, and creates a new self-image; without deliberately trying
to, he becomes a different sort of person, an independent, sophisticated, astute—and now critical—observer of his former family
life. Nevertheless, when he goes home for Thanksgiving dinner, he
reverts to his accustomed role and acts like the boy his mother

knew. He now has two views of himself—one of his own, and one for sharing with his mother.

Poets, symbolically for the rest of us, may feel the need to make appearance conform to private self-image. Here are a few of the more famous ones:

> It is the young Ezra Pound at a London dinner party wearing an earring and drinking from a finger bowl. It is the Californian Robert Frost assuming the role of a New England farmer, without ever really farming. Yeats invented for himself the genealogy he thought a poet ought to have, though in that poem of his last years, "The Circus Animals' Desertion," he strips away his contrived images, his masks, his props, to
>
> > Lie down where all the ladders start
> > In the foul rag-and-bone shop of the heart.
>
> T. S. Eliot did not achieve his fixed persona all that readily. He had to try a number of masks before he found the one that fitted. In his very early European days he thought of settling down in Paris and gradually writing in French. He then adopted Latin Quarter clothes. In his first London period he painstakingly combed the Americanisms from his speech. At one point he wore a monocle, and when he had taken rooms in Burleigh Mansions he called himself Captain Eliot. Osbert Sitwell noticed that he wore pale green face powder to accentuate his sense of suffering. In 1923 he shocked Richard Aldington as they walked past Marlborough House by tipping his hat to the sentry. It was, as his most recent biographer observed, "the wrong gesture to the wrong person, suggesting that he did not yet understand the society which he wished to join." Edmund Wilson called him a "self-invented character."[7]

There is a good deal of mimicry in nature, too, as evolution favors the trickster. Why do animals employ such trickery? For many of the same reasons we humans do: to save their skins, to make themselves more attractive to the opposite sex, and to find food. Putting one over on your competitor, predator, or prey gives you an edge on survival.

Angler fish actually mimic fishing by dangling bait in front of their own mouths from a spine that serves as a "rod." When the duped victim goes for the bait, he's devoured by the angler. There is a "cleaner fish" that gets its food by grooming parasites from the skins and mouths of bigger fish, and there are "cleaner fish mimics" that have learned to masquerade as their harmless cousins in order to get close enough to take their victims by surprise.

2. Counterfeit: to invent a fake reality. Counterfeiters and forgers raise an interesting question: what is the difference between fake and genuine?

If an imitation is totally successful, how is it different from what it imitates? If Elmyr de Hory, the late art forger, can paint a fake Matisse or Modigliani that gives you the same pleasure you get from looking at the real thing, is your experience any less genuine, any less good?

If I invent a friendship with you because we need a friendship to get along with each other in our work, and the fake friendship actually produces contentment, is it ultimately any different or less good than a "genuine" friendship?

Emma pretends to love a seventy-five-year-old widow whom she has known for many years, because she knows the old woman needs to be loved by someone. The experience works for both of them to bring contentment and satisfaction, but at least on Emma's side, the love is invented. Her motive is compassion; her technique for expressing that compassion is counterfeit friendship. No one knows what the widow really thinks.

In many cases, this kind of showing is also hiding, as when we pretend well-mannered respect to hide feelings of indifference or contempt, or when we make a limited offer in negotiations to hide the extent to which we'd go to make a deal.[8]

There is a kind of "innocent faking" that afflicts public discussions and all forms of public documentation, as in the following story,

> told by a man who for some years held a post in the Military Secretariat of the British War Cabinet. The

years of his office were some of the most important in the whole history of British Government; they brought him in contact with persons, Churchill and others, whose actual words would be invaluable to any biographer, in the years during and just after the last war. The Cabinet minutes, when released, would seem to get as near the truth about the personalities involved, statesmen, generals, administrators, as anything could do. Alas, that truth will never be known, owing to the method of recording these minutes, which this assistant secretary has explained as his almost daily job. First his function was to take down by shorthand or notes what the ministers, or those summoned to advise them, actually said. Like all human discussion, perhaps especially in time of stress, this was virtually without form, incoherent, illogical, illiterate, and frequently inconclusive. It was therefore the function of this official, a trained academic scholar as well as a civil servant, to rewrite the whole affair, and give it the form it ought to have taken, to substitute in order, logic, and expression what he judged the participants had meant to say, not what they actually did say: for example, to make sense of a well-known explosive British general, who was so impatient of mere words that he often said China when he meant Russia, or Italy when he meant Germany: and so on. Yet the process of this innocent faking did not stop there. If the assistant secretary, at the next Cabinet meeting, had read back as minutes those beautifully composed and logically ordered conversations, the speakers would have recognized so little of the speeches now assigned to them that they would refuse to accept them as a true record. He therefore had to introduce a sufficient amount of illogicality, human failing, and, above all, conventional diction, to persuade the members of a British Cabinet that this was what they might each one conceivably have said. The finished result, the final article of the future biographer's so-called evidence, is therefore at least two removes away from anything that was actually said and that actually happened.

This must apply now to the proceedings of so many institutions anywhere, all over the world.[9]

3. Misdirect: to emphasize an alternative to your real interest.

The halfback runs hard for the sideline in an obvious end-run, then suddenly cuts straight up field before the defenders can change their direction. Such a runner is said to have "good moves."

Dean Acheson puts a "good move" on Congress by speaking in terms "rather clearer than the truth" about the perils of Communism spreading throughout the hemisphere and gets the funding policy the administration wants.

Maya Angelou provides another example of good moves in her book *I Know Why the Caged Bird Sings:*

> Knowing Momma, I knew that I never knew Momma. Her African-bush secretiveness and suspiciousness had been compounded by slavery and confirmed by centuries of promises made and promises broken. We have a saying among Black Americans which describes Momma's caution: "If you ask a Negro where he's been, he'll tell you where he's going." To understand this important information, it is necessary to know who uses this tactic and on whom it works. If an unaware person is told a part of the truth (it is imperative that the answer embody truth), he is satisfied that his query has been answered. If an aware person (one who himself uses the strategem) is given an answer which is truthful but bears only slightly if at all on the question, he knows that the information he seeks is of a private nature and will not be handed to him willingly. Thus direct denial, lying and the revelation of personal affairs are avoided.[10]

All of these kinds of hiding and showing suggest that deception is more like "editing the truth" than denying it altogether.

Eight Ways to Deceive

The examples of hiding and showing illustrate deception in action, but they don't really expose the framework of this kind of communication. It might be helpful at this point to sort out the elements of deception and arrange them in a simple pattern, so we can see the logical possibilities at a glance.[11]

In cases of deception there must be a person who either contributes to causing, or chooses to allow, somebody else to acquire a belief, continue believing, stop believing, or be unable to believe something that is thought to be true or false. Let's try to organize this mess of possibilities:

A. Four ways of doing something to deceive:

1. Contribute to causing S to acquire a false belief; straightforward lying is always like this: "I am not a thief."

2. Contribute to causing S to continue in a false belief: "Nurse, don't tell 14c that he's dying; he thinks he can will himself to recover and I want to keep his hope alive for the time being."

3. Contribute to causing S to stop believing something true: "Surely you don't for a moment believe that *I* could have done *that*!?" "Members of the jury, no matter how convincing you may think the prosecutor has been, I put it to you that my client has not been *proved* guilty, and is *therefore not* guilty."

4. Contribute to causing S to be unable to believe something that is true: this is simply hiding the truth. "Where did you find Tigger, dear?" "At Danny's house." (Yes, I promised Mom I would not climb the tree at Danny's, but the cat was caught up there and it was *so easy* to get her down. What she doesn't know won't hurt her.)

B. Four ways of "letting it happen":

5. Choose to allow S to acquire a false belief: "Today is bonus day: did the boss talk to you?" "Yes." (She did, she said hello.) "How much did she give you?" "You don't want to know." (Zero, again.) "That much, eh?"

6. Choose to allow S to continue in a false belief: "Does she give you that much every year?" I wink.

7. Choose to allow S to stop believing something true: "And I thought all along that you didn't really understand my tastes—now you've shown me wrong with this vase:

only someone who knows me well could have chosen it."
I look down to half-conceal a coy smile. (X gave the vase to
me last year; actually, I didn't like it, so I passed it on.)

8. Choose to allow S to go on without a true belief: "My
sister would be wild with envy if she knew how much we
travel; let's avoid the subject when she's here, ok? Let's talk
about all the things we do at home."

In assessing a potential deception, we have to know what's
in the deceiver's mind with regard to the belief itself and with regard to S's beliefs. Self-awareness, intention, deliberateness, and responsibility are inherent in both modes of deception—by either
"contributing to" or "allowing" the distortion of reality as you take
it to be in S's mind. These features serve to help us distinguish
deception from mistakes, accidents, and other unintended errors.

The second four cases raise the interesting question of distance, or involvement. How far does the influence of "allowing"
actually go? Do I "allow" strangers to think whatever they will
merely because I don't step in to straighten them out on some issue?
How far do others' rights to expect the truth from you actually
extend? If a neighbor asks how much I make in a year, am I in
any way obliged to provide an answer, because by not answering
I am "allowing" him to think it's more (or less) than he makes?
How responsible are we for what others may assume, compared
with what we offer as assertions of what we really believe? Does a
lawyer have a responsibility for her adversary's independently mistaken assumptions about the evidence, or his carelessness in failing
to ask the right questions, which result in a stronger case for her
client?

The key to answering these questions can be found by determining the presence of an intention to deceive. Without such an
intent, there can be no deception.

THE FIELD OF DECEPTION

Now that we've got a sketch of the logic of deception, let's
look at the field in which it is used. Whenever we want to evaluate
the moral status of a concrete instance of deception, we should take
into account at least these six categories of concern.

The situation, or context: the time, place, and particular event. This includes consideration of relationships that are continuing, that have a past and future. *Sometimes* deceiving violates a relationship and is therefore odious. But it is just as true that *sometimes* full exposure of a truth violates a relationship, betrays trust, and divulges information that was not, for good reason, freely offered. A good friend is someone who knows that not everything that could be said ought to be said.

Public and private places are each controlled and protected by different sets of rules and customs: you regularly hear singing in a church; you never hear singing in a bank. There are some places where truth telling is expected and even required, but there are other places where it is not. Your host's dining room is not the courtroom; the theater is not the stable; the bazaar is not your doctor's office.

Defining a discrete event is not always easy. We think all events have a beginning and an end point, but when do these occur? Did the car theft begin when the sixteen-year-old broke the window of the car, or when he smoked the pot at his friend's house the hour before, or when his abusive father threw him out of the house as a fifteen-year-old, or when as a hungry ten-year-old boy he discovered the meaning of hopelessness in a ghetto of poverty? An event is an experience that starts to form at some time and ends up somehow, but in a life full of experiences it's hard to tell how one event can be separated from the others.

The actors: Who is doing what to whom? Who is directly involved? Does everybody have an equal right to the same (amount of) truth? Is deceiving a Nazi any different from lying to a bounty hunter looking for runaway slaves, or deceiving children about the likelihood a picnic will be canceled because of bad weather, or exaggerating your personal qualities and achievements during a job interview, or asking a higher price for a used outboard motor than you really want to get, or deceiving the IRS by underreporting your income by $500, $1,000, $5,000?

Who is indirectly involved? How far and in what direction do the effect ripples ripple? Is everybody involved? Is all deceiving always morally wrong, because society is based in trust that we will speak the truth and so any violation of truth telling must be seen as a crime against humanity—even though some particular individual temporarily may not have the right to your truth? On the other hand, should we measure the moral goodness or wrongness of deception by estimating (and calculating when we can) the amount of pain it helps us avoid for ourselves, and prevent for others? Or does the morality of deception come down to an intuitive judgment of the best we can do in each case, in the face-to-face circumstances, all things considered?

The purpose: Why is this happening? Does the deceiver have a clear and fully conscious purpose? What is it? Can the purpose be separated from the choice of deception as a means to accomplish it? Is deception the only, or best, way?

What knowledge or belief does the deceiver have that is being misrepresented? Is there good reason not to offer the knowledge, or the belief, freely?

The manner: How is the thing being done? Is the deceiver free and able to shape communications with the other person in any of several possible ways to achieve the purpose? Is the deceiver making good use of the insight that anything that can be said, can be said another way?

Is the deceiver lucidly aware of what's going on? Sometimes people are also mistaken or confused in addition to being deceptive in presenting false information, or in presenting correct information in a misleading way.

What is the "cost" to the relationship(s) involved of doing things *this* way? Is there a less costly alternative that is morally acceptable?

The consequences: How interested should I be? Is the situation so trivial that it doesn't matter whether truth prevails or not? Are we joking? How serious is this? Is this merely entertainment? Is truth even relevant?

Is the outcome of the situation crucial in some way that makes truth telling either required or clearly subordinate to some other considerations—such as preserving someone's psychological equilibrium, or economic welfare, or even saving a life?

Are there unintended but anticipated consequences that matter? For example, if a teacher pretends to be a very strict disciplinarian at the start of the school year as a means of maintaining order and shaping expectations for future conduct in the classroom, she can anticipate, although she does not intend, that some students will dislike her for being strict.

Seven beliefs that limit the obligation to tell the truth. People have rights to certain information, but not to *all* information.

Not all people share these rights equally; they can be forfeited by renouncing other moral values.

Truth telling naturally goes along with most voluntary agreements, but when you involuntarily get into a situation with another person, you have to choose whether truth telling is reasonable.

People should avoid harming others.

People should help others when they can.

When there's a choice, put people before things.

We should bear in mind that there is a great pressure on all individuals to acquire accurate information and at times to transmit inaccurate, or less than accurate, information as a means of survival: "Deception is an expected feature of all relations between imperfectly related organisms."[12]

GARY COOPER'S POLKA-DOT DRESS

Patricia Neal tells this story about her relationship with Gary Cooper, who was her great love:

> One evening he appeared with his usual armload of groceries. There was a special bag for me that delighted him enormously. It contained a summer dress of red material with white polka dots, yards of skirt and a big red belt. It was just a cheap off-the-rack dress, but Gary could not wait for me to wear it. I went to my bedroom and slipped the dress on. It bunched up like a great sack and the bodice sagged. It looked like hell on me. So I made up a story that I could not present myself in it just yet. The next day

I took it to a dressmaker, who fitted it and lined the bodice with elastic to hold it tight. The dress was saved. I loved it and proudly wore it for Gary, who was none the wiser. Sometimes a woman must be clever enough to make a gift look as grand as it was meant to look.[13]

Indeed, this clever alteration of reality produced a result that only caused greater happiness between two people. Did she deceive him? Yes. Was it morally okay for her to do what she did to Gary Cooper, for the reason she had, in the way she did it, in those circumstances? She helped him do what he wanted to do, but couldn't do on his own. They both were aiming to make the other happy by giving each other their respective gifts. How much should we care that deception was used in bringing about the resolution to a potentially painful and embarrassing episode between these two people?

Right. But now consider the fact that this episode took place during their long-term affair, which they tried to conceal from Mrs. Cooper. Patricia Neal's little deception was nested in a much larger one that involved a third party. Does that change anything? Well, yes and no. It does change the context and the people involved indirectly, but it doesn't really alter the episode itself. What it does change is our view of the two lovers' relationship, which rests on the unstable and unappealing bed of betrayal. We begin to feel sympathy for Mrs. Cooper and correspondingly less sympathy for her husband's feelings about his lover's new dress. So we have a situation which involves a morally acceptable deception within a morally unacceptable deception. Or is that too simple a conclusion?

Right. But what about Mrs. Cooper's own affairs, some of which her husband knew about before he took up with Ms. Neal? Is this some kind of "Tit for Tat at the Coopers"? Does that change anything? What if they wanted to remain married for several reasons—she was Catholic and they had a child—but not for sexual companionship? And what if they invented a loving relationship with each other that included this right to seek others for what they could not give each other, a relationship that provided contentment and genuine comfort at home, as well as genuine passionate love away from home?[14]

IN THE BEST OF ALL POSSIBLE WORLDS

I have heard some people say—they must have been philosophers—that in the best of all possible worlds there would be no deception. This doesn't sound right to me. In the best of all possible worlds people would have to like each other quite a lot, but people still would be very different from each other in many ways, some of them inevitably less agreeable than others. I can't quite imagine how we all could manage to express every one of these disagreeable differences in perfect, enthusiastic candor without inhibition, without recourse to the arts of display and concealment, to people whom we liked very much and by whom we wanted to be liked in return. Rather, it seems to me that communication absolutely free of deception of all kinds is suitable only for people who like each other very little, or don't plan to be together very long. Conversation is only partly based in truthful exchange of accurate information; the other basis is the support that each side knows is available when needed.

To live decently with one another we do not need moral purity, we need discretion—which means tact in regard to truth. I know a lot of people who say they never deceive others and never want to be deceived themselves. I don't know anyone, however, who has actually, honestly given up all capacity for deception, or who would never again, under any circumstances, privately wish to be deceived—if only in order to preserve a sense of dignity, a feeling of self-respect.

5 SELF-DECEPTION: WEAKNESS OR WISDOM?

Once he finds out who he is, what can
Console him?
         . . . for on earth
Everyone who lives, lives in a dream.

Calderon

I don't want to know. I don't want to know anything. I refuse to know. And I refuse to say anything. And I will not, and there is an end of it.

Ivy Compton-Burnett

If there is such a thing as a basic human quality, self-deception is it.

Colin M. Turnbull

We may say at the onset that the whole of life is too much to take. True, we have a strong need to see, to feel, to sense, to know—this urge to experience and understand is something humans boast of in talking about themselves as a species and as individuals. But it is just as true that we also have a strong need *not* to see, to feel, sense, or know a lot of things. Perhaps more than we are prepared to realize; certainly more than we will talk about. This human trait for self-deception, for voluntary blindness, numbness, dull-mindedness, and ignorance is definitely not something we boast about. After all, if we let this cat out of the bag, we would threaten a finely tuned and expertly regulated social system of selective perception, exposure, and understanding. Human self-deception is one of the most impressive software programs ever devised.

MUST I WANT TO KNOW ALL THAT I COULD KNOW?

Which of us would like to know the day of our death? Few, I would guess. Why?

Imagine for a moment there is some bit of knowledge in the world about you, something you don't yourself know directly, but nevertheless something that you *could* know if you wanted to. *Must* you want to know it? Is it ever right to ignore it, sometimes going so far as to put completely out of mind the possibility of knowing it? Let's say further that you even suspect what the knowledge is, but since you don't actually have it, there is still room for doubt, even for denial, and you want to strengthen the doubt, fortify the denial, because you believe the knowledge will be bad news. Preserving uncertainty may be a strain—remaining ignorant on purpose requires effort—but at least in uncertainty there is room for hope. So you decide to balance the cost in strain against the benefit in hope, and gradually the strain diminishes as its cause slides out of conscious focus.

Would it make any difference if the knowledge in question were the time and cause of your own death? Take for example the 125,000 Americans who are at risk of developing Huntington's disease, which is caused by a dominant gene inherited from a parent. If you have the gene, you will have the disease (a late-onset degenerative disease of the nervous system) and there is a good chance you will pass on the gene to your children. Symptoms normally won't show up until the victim is thirty-five to forty-five years old, or even much older, when many may already be parents. There is no cure for the disease, but now there is a test that can predict for some people at risk whether in fact they have the gene. If they don't have the gene, all's well. If they do have it, no one can help them. They will know how and when they will die. They will also know that their children have a 50 percent chance of inheriting the gene, which will kill them, too.

For some people at risk the test can provide knowledge to replace the mixture of fear and hope they live with. Doctors estimated that three out of four adults at risk would want the test when it became available. It turns out, now that the test is being offered, that far fewer have signed up. The majority of this group seem not to want the knowledge doctors could provide. Or, rather, they may want the knowledge that they do *not* have the gene, but they are unwilling to take the risk of finding out that they do have it. They apparently prefer the anxious uncertainty of "What if?" to the depressing reality of "How soon?"

It is possible that adults at risk know themselves well enough to anticipate suffering a debilitating depression that would surely follow confirmation of the disease. They may envision a life of monstrous dread and dysfunction, leading eventually to suicide as the symptoms first begin to appear. Self-knowledge then may counsel against the pain of coping with the truth. Some of us may know very well that we need hope to survive, that there are some things we must strive not to know, even if that attitude looks to others like denial and self-deception. Sometimes the truth does not set you free; it destroys the sense of freedom that hope provides.

WHY AREN'T WE ALL PSYCHIATRISTS?

I'll tell you, sometimes knowing the truth is a curse. There must be a reason why we are not all psychiatrists and detectives. Unwise attention to some truths can botch one of life's essential activities—avoiding anxiety. Only from an extremely abstract and unfriendly view of life can this imperative be interpreted in every case as a malady requiring the cure of insight. Insight is supposed to lead to truth, which in turn is supposed to make life whole. Well, maybe so. But I can't help wondering why, if truth is all that curative of our anxieties, we spend so much time and effort *helping* it to elude our grasp. If we really wanted to know the truth, and wanted others to know it too, wouldn't it be rather simple and straightforward to vow always to speak it and always to ask that it be spoken to us? Couldn't we behave as scientists do (at least those who don't fudge the data) in their self-corrective method of seeking truth, and work cooperatively, sharing and double-checking everything, in our common search?

We don't do that, obviously. We do everything in our power to avoid, distort, conceal, reverse, deny, and fancy up the truth whenever we think we can gain something by doing so, and when we stand a better than fair chance of getting away with it. Freud knew this. He also knew that sometimes we go too far and make ourselves sick with self-deception. That was his whole practice, after all: teaching people how to recognize destructive self-deception and replace it with a more constructive kind called self-knowledge. In psychoanalysis, this is achieved by uncovering the "narrative truth." However, there are problems in getting the narrative straight, as every patient and analyst knows.

> Throughout the analysis, the patient is confronted with the conflict between what is true but hard to describe—the pure memory—and what is describable but somewhat untrue—the screen memory or, more generally, any kind of compromise formation.
>
> The form of these creative efforts is guided by the narrative tradition; as the vague outlines take on form and substance, they also acquire a coherence and representational appeal, which give them a certain kind of reality. Narrative truth can be defined as the criterion we use to decide when a certain experience has been captured to our satisfaction; it depends on continuity and closure and the extent to which the fit of the pieces takes on an aesthetic finality. Once a given construction has acquired narrative truth, it becomes just as real as any other kind of truth; this new reality becomes a significant part of the psychoanalytic cure.[1]

Patients tell doctors less than they know; doctors tell patients more than they know; and both seem to want it this way. However, we—both the patients and the doctors—are inclined to deny this, as well as the further accusation that we lie to ourselves on purpose to get what we want, in order to save face. The source of such denial runs deep.

> It was Freud's contention, after all, that neurotic resistances were such as to force the subject personality to contrive intricate devices whose goal was to keep from that personality even valuable insights which could prove useful to him.[2]

Reports of mental states, or dispositions—thoughts, memories, feelings—are made in structured contexts, and they are made through selected expressions (there are many expressions for any given event, experience, or thing) that do not always preserve the truth value of the phenomenon being reported. A well-chosen expression allows us to capture a thought and protect it at the same time. We can present the truth so wadded up in verbal cotton batting that there is no danger of it ever being felt, even though it is there.[3]

Why does this "malady" of clouded awareness persist despite all the moral protestations of the doctors, whether they be physicians, philosophers, or religionists? It persists because we know in our bones that self-knowledge isn't all it's cracked up to be, and because self-deception is a strategy we cannot hope to live without. We simply must avoid too much anxiety, and learn somehow to cope with life's surprises. Discovering the pure and simple truth about ourselves (which is rarely pure and never simple, if Oscar Wilde was right) is not necessarily an adequate means to that end.

It is hardly possible to expose self-deception without simultaneously encouraging it. That's because we normally don't seek the truth about ourselves merely for the sake of knowing the truth. Instead, we seek information and self-images which are agreeable and useful, whether absolutely true or not. We need a balance between the agreeable and useful and the truth, a balance which makes it easier for us to live with ourselves, with each other, and to accommodate all those odd bits of unexpected experience that are slung our way by luck.

It is not very nice to challenge every little bit of deception, or to expose all suspected self-deception in the course of civilized interaction. Well-mannered living depends upon innuendo and ambiguity and the decency not to point out hidden messages when they are not so well hidden as the messenger thinks they are. It can be downright hazardous to know how others really feel, or to know how we ourselves feel about certain subjects or individuals. It is a very good idea, most of the time, to focus on messages deliberately offered rather than on what leaks out around the seams.[4]

THE CRAVING TO BE APPRECIATED

Any adequate explanation of deception must embody the one law of human nature we can infer from the last century of psychological theory, namely, that people need to think well of themselves, and to do so they need to be thought well of by somebody else. Our common ground is a need to appear to be better than we think we really are. (Be yourself at all times. If that isn't good enough, be somebody else.) This need acts to restrict candidness in offering truthful information to certain others on certain subjects at certain times. It even interferes with conscious self-knowledge. It is the craving to be appreciated that motivates much deception of others and deception of self.

This aspect of human nature has been the subject of much psychological research generated during the last thirty-five years by Leon Festinger's theory of cognitive dissonance.[5] The theory focuses on predicting behavior resulting from the tension that exists when two or more of one's ideas, beliefs, attitudes, or opinions are psychologically inconsistent. Recognizing such inconsistency tends to make us feel foolish; to avoid, or overcome, feeling foolish is one of the strongest motivations at work in everyday life. Thus, we may say there is a very strong need to resolve the tensions of cognitive dissonance. Research has shown that "individuals will distort the objective world in order to reduce dissonance. The manner in which they will distort and the intensity of their distortion are highly predictable."[6] One of these ways is to begin to believe our own lies, or other deceptions, when there is insufficient external justification for them. A classic study of this change of belief was carried out by Festinger and J. M. Carlsmith.[7] The investigators asked college students to perform a very boring series of tasks (packing spools, turning screws, etc.); afterward they asked the students to lie about how boring it was to the next subjects who were scheduled to perform the same series. Some of the students were paid twenty dollars to say the tasks were interesting and enjoyable, others were offered only one dollar to tell the same lie. After the experiment was over, the "lie-tellers" were asked to rate the series of tasks as dull or enjoyable. The results were clear. Those who were paid twenty dollars rated the tasks as being dull, which they were. But the students who were paid only one dollar actually rated the tasks as enjoyable. Festinger and Carlsmith concluded that when there is a large enough amount of external justification ($20), people are willing to lie without believing the lie themselves, but when this amount is meager ($1), people will move in the direction of believing the lie themselves, as a way of reducing their feeling of foolishness for accepting one measly dollar to tell a lie. This is sometimes referred to as the "saying-is-believing" phenomenon.

Elliott Aronson reformulated Festinger's theory to focus attention on the individual's self-esteem.

> Basically, this reformulation suggests that dissonance is most powerful in situations where the self-concept is threatened. Thus, for me, the important aspect of dissonance in the situation described above is not that the cognition "I said 'X'" is dissonant with the cognition "I believe 'not X'." Rather, the crucial fact is that I have misled people: the cognition "I have said something I don't believe and it could have bad consequences for people" is dissonant with my self-concept; that is, it is dissonant with my cognition that "I am a decent, reasonable, truthful person."[8]

This reformulation is based on the insight that we, all of us, crave to think well of ourselves to such extent that we are willing to change reality when it doesn't fit our self-image.

If we take what people talk about most of the time as a good indicator of what's important to them, then affirming self-worth must be at the core of human life. There is no more interesting topic of conversation than oneself, as Oscar Wilde somewhere so impertinently put it. We cannot just live; we must live worthily if we can, and *seem* to do so if we can't always. Whenever we want to present ourselves as a certain sort of person—honest, reliable, intelligent, or whatever—we create an appearance. That is, we mediate, or redesign, what comes naturally. (If being honest, reliable, and intelligent came naturally, we wouldn't have to try to *appear* so. We would *be* so.) We try to cultivate a personality, develop a character that suits our purposes; we try to make ourselves into a person who we can imagine would be a better person (more successful? more lovable?) than the one we would naturally be. We want our actions to be justified, to spring from reasons and motives that are worthy of the person we wish to be.

Naturally, given the distance between what we are and what we wish we were, some amount of other-deception and self-deception is an essential requisite for carrying on. For ordinary people, being ordinary is not enough; we need to be more than ordinary and for that we sometimes need the salutary assistance of illusion, which in a curious way becomes a basis for self-esteem. We might say that illusion is compassion's remedy for the disappointment of reality.

THE "PARADOX" OF SELF-DECEPTION

Who can seriously doubt that we do deceive ourselves? On the other hand, who can explain why and how we manage to do it so well? The very idea of self-deception is fundamental and elusive at the same time—perhaps that's why trying to come to grips with it can be so annoying.

What is it about self-deception that makes it such an irritating concept? Although it is familiar to us as an experience, when we think about it as a concept it appears paradoxical. We know we do it, and others do it, but still it would seem to be logically absurd and impossible that we can. How can "I" make "myself" not believe something that "I" already believe? Self-deception confronts us with a real experience that appears to be logically impossible. But then human beings have never confined themselves to do or believe only what logic allows.

We can get a sense of how self-deception is possible when we compare "deceiving yourself" with other similarly reflexive English expressions. "Amusing yourself" is not the same thing as amusing others, but you can do it, even by retelling yourself jokes and laughing at them as if you didn't know the punch line. "Reminding yourself" about something that you already know, but apparently don't know *now*, is a common enough experience. "Teaching yourself" is not like teaching others because "you need to know what you teach in order to teach it to others; but you teach yourself something precisely when you don't know it."[9]

There is a weak sense of paradox involved in the act of self-deception from which no special logical problems arise. That is, the paradox may be only an apparent contradiction, one that might be resolved at a deeper level of scrutiny. For example, I pride myself on the fact that I am a person who loves the symphony. You point out that I haven't actually gone to the symphony for more than two years. It appears that I am deceiving myself by speaking one value and acting on another. When I think about it, I discover that what I really love is recorded symphonic and chamber music, played at home. I don't like going out to hear music. However, I do support my local symphony with an annual donation because I like the idea of having a symphony in the city, even though I don't like to go myself. So the truth is that I do like recorded symphonic music, and I do like supporting the institution, but I still don't like the bother of getting dressed up and driving to the music hall.

There is, however, a stronger sense of paradox with which we must reckon. Is it possible for one willfully and intentionally to deceive oneself? Some have argued that such self-deception is logically paradoxical and therefore absurd, an impossibility, at best a metaphor for some other state of mind such as wishful thinking.[10] But what is the salient difference between self-deception and wishful thinking? Is it not the way one deals with new evidence against the belief held?[11] The self-deceiver resists stubbornly and ingeniously the implications of the evidence, while the wishful thinker will usually acknowledge, however reluctantly, the new evidence as counting against the belief. For example, I believe the professor is genuinely impressed with my work because of her generous and enthusiastic praise. Then you tell me she does the same for nearly everyone, possibly because she's kindhearted or wishes to avoid long conversations. I now have two ways to interpret the new evidence you have presented. If I'm a wishful thinker, I will reluctantly accept what you say, or perhaps I'll ask some other students about their experiences with the professor; in the end, I'll revise my estimate of my professor's attitude toward my work. On the other hand, if I'm a self-deceiver, I'll discount what you say as sour grapes, and I'll point out that while she may be insincere with all of her other students, her attitude toward me is genuine.

The difference between these two ways of using evidence hinges on the existence of a clear distinction between rationality and pseudorationality, or rationalization, a distinction that is notoriously hard to maintain in thinking generally and particularly in self-reflection. Thinking about oneself, about one's way of seeing things and interpreting what one sees, is such a muddled business that it might sometimes be impossible *not* to deceive oneself. At any rate, being honest about self-deception means giving up the purely logical analysis of the concept, the strictly literal reading of it that produces a formal paradox. *It* is not simple because *we* are not simple. Human beings are messy, digressive, intensely heartfeeling, and mysterious. Self-deception merely confirms this fact.

Is there no way to maintain that self-deception is an act of an integrated personality managing somehow to believe and not believe the same thing at the same time? It is easy enough to understand how in deceiving another person I could believe A and try to pretend I don't, or pretend I believe B and want the other person to believe B, too. But how can one person do this sort of thing internally without giving away the game?

NO PERSON IS ONLY ONE PERSON

Most fundamentally, the idea of deceiving oneself is a threat to our sense of wholeness and our integrity. It seems to imply that we must think of ourselves somehow as double selves rather than as a psychological unity. Otherwise, how could we explain one person playing both deceiver and deceived at the same time? It would seem that we either pose some kind of split personality or deny that self-deception is taking place at all. Neither of these alternatives feels right to me. Let's explore another possibility.

People hold all sorts of beliefs at any given time, so many in fact that it is difficult to keep them all sorted out and consistent with one another. Some of these are bound to be incompatible, even contradictory, especially for those of us who are lazy, harried, muddled, distracted, careless, insensitive, forgetful, and who are constantly changing our minds as life goes on. But self-contradiction, or inconsistency, is not the same as self-deception. Not all mistakes and distortions, incomplete pictures and flat-out illusions are self-deceiving—but some are. Which ones? What is special about self-deception?

In a word: purposefulness.[12] In Herbert Fingarette's terms, when we believe, or at least strongly suspect, something to be true and yet turn away from it, disbelieve it on purpose, in order to evade the consequences of facing it—then we are deceiving ourselves. When we declare one belief for the purpose of denying another that we take to be true—that is self-deception. Notice that this is not merely a case of being indecisive, or changing one's mind when new evidence comes along; it is a case of holding two beliefs at the same time and using one to repress the other. Self-deception is skillful maneuvering to achieve ignorance when clear, conscious understanding threatens to break through.

> Beliefs exist to "correct" reality, and to the extent that reality is—or represents—the truth, or is at least the source of the truth, beliefs are necessarily a variant of lies. Our need to believe becomes dominant precisely where our knowledge of reality is either insufficient or unpleasant or both. It should come as no surprise to us that [people] use their systems of belief as congenial forms of denying crucial truths.[13]

Past reality is what happened. Present reality is what one experiences as having happened. Such experience is shaped as much by wishes and fears as it is by fact. Thank goodness that reality can be revised in so many ways, and that we have vagueness, ambiguity, and faulty memories to save us from at least some of reality's sharper edges. But it should be noted that we cannot escape criminal liability through what lawyers call conscious avoidance—by taking deliberate steps to prevent our discovering facts that would unequivocally demonstrate to ourselves the criminality of our conduct.

There is much to be said for this description of self-deception as conscious, purposeful manipulation, but I think I've put the case too strongly if it is taken to encompass all self-deception. I don't think it is right to assume that we are always, or in general, explicitly conscious of what Fingarette calls our "engagements in the world," by which he means what we do, and what we understand of the world and ourselves, our projects, activities, motives, feelings, memories, and so on. We may certainly experience all of these engagements, but we "spell out" in explicitly conscious terms only some of them. We are selective in choosing what to attend to and what to leave unattended. "Rather than taking explicit consciousness for granted, we must come to take its absence for granted; we must see explicit consciousness as the further exercise of a specific skill for special reasons."[14]

There is no need to spell out everything. It probably is not possible anyway. First, it just takes an enormous amount of skill to bring engagements into sharply accurate, explicitly conscious focus. Imagine trying to spell out your improvisations in a tennis match or a musical jam session as you are playing. Only some of our experience is in focus, the rest is background—some of it very far back, indeed. It takes skill to focus, refocus, and bring into focus the right things in the right ways at the right time.[15]

Second, our engagements are so numerous and complex that we wouldn't have time to spell out all of them even if we wanted to and had the necessary skills. Imagine yourself, as just one trivial example, at dinner with your mate, trying to spell out the vicissitudes of the day's work and various of the day's encounters with friends and temptations, striving to say something intelligent and gratifying about the meal, showing yourself to be sincerely interested in what your mate may be trying to spell out to you, having to deal with troublesome memories of a lost friendship evoked by that unwonted aroma emanating from the soup, and striving to consummate the romantic mood that this particular engagement is supposed to induce. Lordy lord, that is a mindful. (And all that's without children at the table!)

Spelling out engagements so they become explicitly conscious is not only complex and time consuming, it can be a disruptive nuisance, too. There may be good reason not to spell out some particular engagement, to avoid becoming explicitly aware of it. When there is such reason, there probably is reason also to avoid explicit consciousness of what you are trying to avoid and why. Self-deception is the purposeful avoidance of spelling out certain engagements—just leaving them unfocused in consciousness, in the background, so to speak.

For example, I could say to myself that I am angry and frustrated at having just missed the last train to London that would have made it possible for me to keep my date for dinner with you. I know I'm frustrated and angry because I'm flushed, edgy, indignant, and am stamping my way to a phone booth so I can call you with an apology, blaming a string of students, taxi drivers, and "the crowd" for my—for *our*—misfortune. After the call, however, I find myself in a state of pleasant anticipation. Before me lies a suddenly free evening, the prospect of an unhurried drink, perhaps a movie, and a late supper on my own. I mark this striking shift in my state of mind as evidence that I am a person who can cope, who can make the most of a bad situation. I do not care to think further about why I risked missing the train by taking that last appointment.

Our judgments whether or not to spell out various engagements with the world depend on something more than evidential reasons; they depend on something like a sense of personal identity. I want to be (known as) *this* kind of person; therefore, I cannot afford to spell out *that* engagement because to do so would damage my sense of myself and spoil my appearance to others. (I am not the sort of person to miss a train deliberately in order to have a valid excuse for breaking a date with you, all because I couldn't face telling you that I just don't feel like making the effort to be with you, and because I couldn't face telling a lie. That is definitely not the sort of person I am.) Because of this I must say the person thus engaged was not I.

This account sounds common enough, accurate enough. People do deny some of their experience as properly belonging to their "real" self. Augustine thus dispensed with his whole childhood. But why, after all, is it important that we do this? Why are we not willing to avow openly all of our engagements (actions, emotions, memories, etc.) and then choose whether to spell them out? In other words, why don't we settle for deceiving others and not ourselves?

The answer may lie in the difference between being an individual which is a given, and being a person, which is an achievement open to all who are willing to put in the effort. An individual is merely a discrete being with potential to become someone whom we would describe in terms of character, or personality. Persons are individuals who have made something of themselves over time, as conscious moral beings: making and thinking, adding this, discarding that, accepting this, rejecting that, until a synthesis, or confederation of selves, takes shape. Everyone knows how important learning is to this process, but have we forgotten how important *forgetting* is in achieving the sense of person we envision? One reason we manage on the whole to remain sane is that we are so good at forgetting what is disagreeable (fears, failures, pain, disabling confusion, and so on). We are not, nor should we become, *all* that we experience, plan, do, feel, and perceive. We are necessarily selective about what goes into making up our character.

The actual choices of what to spell out and what to forget, what engagements to pursue, avoid, or enter "as another person," may well turn on the strength of one's interest in personal integrity. Integrity is made up of chosen and discarded engagements regulated by some sense of pattern or by pride. There is no end to it, really, as old choices resurface and new ones are confronted. Integrity depends on what is forgotten as surely as on what's remembered. Integrity is the insistence that experiences, desires, and emotions be consistent, as life goes on in all its inherent inconsistency. In a way, then, it would seem that integrity might require some kind of self-deception. Fingarette sums up the point this way:

> The less integrity, the less is there motive to enter into self-deception. The greater the integrity of the person, and the more powerful the contrary inclinations, the greater is the temptation to self-deception." [16]

Nietzsche, in *Beyond Good and Evil,* puts the point even more succinctly: "'I have done that,' says my memory. 'I cannot have done that,' says my pride, and remains adamant. At last—memory yields." [17]

We can find a sensible way to avoid logical paradox creeping into this account by asking what happens to the idea of self-deception when we give up thinking of self as a unity. [18] One consequence is that instead of facing a paradox we come to think in terms of mindlessness—how one self-in-context can routinely be mindless to certain details of that context itself, and to other selves in other contexts. For example, being father to a six-year-old, professor to twenty- and thirty-year-olds, spouse and lover to a forty-year-old, and son to a seventy-year-old not only encourages but *requires* mindlessness to certain details. When one of these selves is in control, the others are "submissive," diminished, even gone entirely from awareness. These selves are in a constant process of confederation, but they do not collapse into one. The confederation needs coherence, continuity, but not unity.

In developing this self-as-confederation concept, the psychologists Benzion Chanowitz and Ellen Langer argue that

> the problem of life becomes how to incorporate and/ or keep at a distance the disparate sets of standards that each have value in their distinct settings. Life's tale is told in terms of the distinct selves that a person cultivates and the growing closeness or remoteness of these selves over time.[19]

We can choose to protect each from the others, or to combine and thereby dissolve differences. However, only if we view Self as a unity, a magnificent singular with a capital S, must we think that inconsistency (among selves-in-context) is a weakness, a flaw in character, a sign of irrationality, and finally a malady in need of a cure.

We may wisely avoid perfect coherence in acknowledging who we are and what we are doing. However, something like compatibility among the aspects of our selves surely is essential. We do need to draw the line, but where it is to be drawn and what shape it takes is blessedly unprescribed. The line and its location will determine the extent to which we are willing to confront life as presented to us by other characters and events. Candor, clarity, courage, discretion, self-regulation will be defined and ordered in this process of acknowledgment.

Still, there is good reason to be unsure about all this. Some will decide to adhere to Matthew Arnold's view of us as each being born a unique isolated consciousness, our task being to find voice for our buried life. Arnold put it this way:

> But often, in the world's most crowded streets,
> But often, in the din and strife,
> There rises an unspeakable desire
> After the knowledge of our buried life;
> A thirst to spend our fire and restless force
> In tracking out our true, original course;
> And we have been on many thousand lines,

And we have shown, on each, spirit and power;
But hardly have we, for one little hour,
Been on our own line, have we been ourselves—
Hardly had skill to utter one of all
The nameless feelings that course through our
    breast,
But they course on for ever unexpress'd.
And long we try in vain to speak and act
Our hidden self, and what we say and do
Is eloquent, is well—but 'tis not true![20]

The longing for a true self, a unique isolated consciousness, a personal unity, is real enough; for some it's poignant and strong. But is it any more than a longing? Is unity of self any more than a subjective convenience? I suppose it's our choice to believe what we will about that. Jorge Luis Borges draws this image of Shakespeare for us:

> There was no one in him; behind his face . . . and his words, which were copious, imaginative, and emotional, there was nothing but a little chill, a dream not dreamed by anyone. . . . His passages on the fundamental identity of existing, dreaming, and acting are famous. . . . The story goes that, before or after he died, he found himself before God and he said: "I, who have been so many men in vain, want to be one man; myself." The voice of God replied from a whirlwind: "Neither am I one self; I dreamed the world as you dreamed your work, my Shakespeare, and among the shapes of my dream are you, who like me, are many persons—and none."[21]

If we choose to view the self as a confederation of selves-in-context, then self-deception looks more like a conflict that is predictably generated when different selves act mindlessly toward each other with respect to certain details of their respective contexts. An observer might infer self-deception in a person acting under the sway of one social context, then another, truthfully saying something in the first, then continuing to "know" but not saying the same thing in the next. It may be, of course, that the person is acting mindlessly with respect to the first context while occupying the second.

Indeed, it is a mistake to think of self-deception in terms that over-intellectualize it and divert us from seeing it as a means for muddling through experiences that try our resources for coping with changing contexts and getting on without intolerable losses. With this aim generally in mind, there is no fixed end to mindlessness, to what we are inclined to ignore.

PIOUS SELF-DECEPTION

Even (especially?) for very pious persons, self-deception comes in handy sometimes.

> Every Iranian knows the story of the mullah who, on his way to the mosque for morning prayers, was splashed by a dog shaking itself in a drainage ditch. The mullah, who knew he did not have time to change his clothes before prayers, refused to look squarely at the animal that had sprayed water on him and rushed on, muttering, "God willing, it's a goat." (Water from dogs is polluting while water from goats is not.) "God willing, it's a goat" is shorthand in Persian conversation for "Let's let things pass and not look too closely."[22]

Talabehs, or student mullahs, have to struggle with sexual desires in the course of becoming wise and holy. One practical stratagem developed over the years (it began as a pre-Islamic tradition of Arabia) for satisfying their sexual needs without interrupting education and professional development is the *mut'a,* or temporary marriage. Roy Mottahdeh describes *mut'a* like this:

> The temporary marriage is contracted for a specific period on the condition of the payment of a specific sum to the temporary wife. The temporary wife must have had her period three times since any previous marriage (to avoid disputes about paternity) and should not be a woman "addicted to fornication." Sunnis (who forbid such temporary marriages) as well as anticlericalists claim that Shiah shrine towns are full of de facto prostitutes. These are women who give false testimony about their past sexual relations in order to contract marriages of a day or a week with

pilgrims and sometimes with talabehs, who, in the spirit of "God willing, it's a goat," don't inquire too scrupulously about the background of their temporary wives. Mullahs, on the contrary, defend the temporary marriage as an institution sanctioned by the Prophet and used conscientiously by scrupulous Shiah Moslems, including, of course, the mullahs.[23]

Mut'a contracts are very simple. Once the duration of the arrangement and amount of payment (either to the woman or the man) have been negotiated, the marriage becomes effective upon exchange of these words: "I, [name], marry [or mut'a] thee, for the amount of [money] and for such and such period"; followed by "I accept."[24] These ceremonies do not require witnesses (and in fact are usually private), nor must they be registered formally, although they do conform to requirements that vary by locality. Temporary marriage can be as short as an hour or as long as ninety-nine years. At the end of the contract term, no divorce is necessary. Shiah doctrine permits men to have as many temporary marriages at a time as they want, one reason being that the purpose of mut'a is sexual enjoyment while the purpose of permanent marriage (nikah) is procreation. A Shiah Muslim woman, on the other hand, is permitted but one mut'a at a time, each followed by a period of sexual abstinence. "This is to identify a child's legitimate father in the case she is pregnant. The children born as a result of temporary unions are considered legitimate and theoretically have equal status with their siblings born of permanent marriages. Here lies the legal uniqueness of mut'a, that which distinguishes it ideologically from prostitution, despite their striking resemblance."[25]

Attitudes toward mut'a are mixed among Shiah Muslims and other Islamic men and women. Some see it as a religious law sanctioned by the Qur'an and the Prophet Muhammad himself, justified as a means of limiting the spread of venereal disease, sinful homosexuality, masturbation, and fornication. Others see it in secular terms as a helpful means for crossing the barriers of sexual segregation; still others see it scornfully as a hypocritical gimmick that serves special interests through self-deceptive misrepresentation—the way to get around the prohibition against "fornication" is simply to rename it "temporary marriage" [*mut'a*]. In any case, *mut'a* is a complex institution, sanctioned by religion but subject to cultural disapproval, devised for dealing with rules of law, personal and cultural values, and the profound importance of sexuality in a pious life. While there is no requirement, there certainly is plenty of room for self-deception among those who participate in *mut'a* marriage.

DISTORTION IN THE MIRROR

It is true that "no creature's mind could contain a mechanism which eliminated too many of its well-founded factual beliefs. But such a mechanism has a certain survival value for social creatures when its operation is confined to beliefs about themselves and about each other."[26]

It may be that survival in psychological terms is more closely linked with narrative coherence than with truth understood as correspondence with fact, and that when the truth we know is either insufficient or unpleasant or both, distortion is sometimes needed to maintain coherence and stability.

But distortion can be suspect and frustrating, too. The mirror is a symbol of two human interests which taken together suggest a profound contradiction: vanity and truth telling. One example of this double connotation is found in Shakespeare's *King Richard II*. Toward the end of the scene where Richard abdicates, handing his crown over to Bolingbroke, the deposed king sends for a looking glass. He wants to see who, or what, he is now that he has given everything away. The mirror shows a face that looks all right, a flattering image that gives a false notion of Richard's inward condition, which is one of wretched suffering. To Richard's eyes the mirror lies, so he smashes it in angry frustration perhaps directed at his flattering followers as well as his own foolishness in encouraging them. Like Richard, we alternate our interpretations of the image in the looking glass—vanity drives away truth, truth vanity, and the choice which shall win the day does not appear to be wholly within our control. We are not one, we are several:

> Thus play I in one person many people,
> And none contented.[27]

There are benefits to seeing things as they are not, so long as you don't stray too far from what we speak of as "agreed-upon reality." At some crucial points in our experience, maintaining the sharp distinction between what is true and what is false gives way to a need for things to stick together and be easily understood. When the object of inquiry is oneself, it sometimes makes sense to keep in check one's truth-seeking faculties.

In the end it may turn out that holding to the ideal of self-actualization, or of discovering the "real me," is the biggest self-deception of all.

DECEIVING YOURSELF TAKES TIME

The extreme literal interpretation of self-deception assumes that the original belief continues to persist beyond the point when the opposite belief is accepted, and that a person not only believes both contradictory propositions but also *sees* them *as* contradictory. If these assumptions are correct, then self-deception is impossible. Since it is not impossible (experience tells us that), we should suspect that the assumptions are not correct. We can see that the assumptions are not needed if we look at "believing A" merging into "believing not-A" as a gradual process, and if we think of awareness as having infinite gradations, like time or color. Such gradual change, like one image fading into another in a film, may actually be a rational strategy because it helps the self-deceiver avoid facing the contradiction. Deceiving oneself is a complicated activity, a performance of sorts, that takes time.

Take for example the belief "I shall succeed if I *believe* I shall succeed, and I'm not interested in seeking evidence to the contrary." This is a belief that can *make* itself come true but is not true now. If the belief is formed in the teeth of known evidence, it is irrational. But if the belief is formed by a person who does not consider such known evidence paramount and who is willing to set it aside for the "truth that comes true because of my belief in it," then the belief takes on the character of a rational plan. This is a kind of rational self-deception: by exaggerating chances of success one can actually improve them. The same is true if you substitute "failure" for "success" in that last sentence.

This process has been known in sociology and educational

theory as the self-fulfilling prophecy.[28] Tell a kid he's a delinquent, and he'll become a delinquent. Show teachers false data indicating that half the students in a given class are "late academic bloomers" and see how the teachers' attitudes and behavior, based in false belief, induce similar false beliefs in the students, who in turn actually improve their achievement test scores—including IQ test scores.[29]

IS SELF-DECEPTION EVER RATIONAL?

Can we decide to believe something? Can I have a conscious project to make myself believe what I want to believe?[30]

The answer is no when "wanting to believe" means "wanting it to be really the case." My son is dead; I want to believe he is alive, that is, I want him to *be* alive. This project is impossible and incoherent.

However, the answer is yes when "wanting to believe" means "wanting to be comfortable or in accordance with social conformity." This may be irrational, but it is not obviously impossible or incoherent. Football players often "psych themselves up" before an important game, in a deliberate attempt to instill beliefs (which may be false) about their own prowess and their opponents' weaknesses meant to improve their performance.

We do commonly believe what we want to believe just as surely as we forget disagreeable things that we want to forget. If I want to be loved by you, I want to believe I'm loved by you. I therefore act as if this desired belief were really true. In my own mind, my belief that you love me justifies my actions. This is who I am; I'm yours. And who knows, you might, because of all this, come to realize that you do love me.

Now, I can control what enters my mind on the subject, and I can process what actually does get in guided by my belief. But this guidance is not altogether direct and positive. We don't actually plan to distort evidence, but we do manage to distort it. How does this desire to believe something intervene between evidence that enters the mind and the resulting belief? We know *that* it works, but we don't know how.

How is wanting to believe something agreeable different from wanting to forget something disagreeable? What is the moral or psychological difference between forgetting something true and believing something not true? Am I obliged to believe *only* what is true, whether I can stand it or not? May I be excused from believing *every* truth I was once aware of? To what degree am I allowed, morally speaking, to pick and choose among all my memories and all possible images of my future self in order to help make life more livable?

We certainly need to forget certain things in order to get on with others and with our own project of construing a personality for ourselves. Imagine the mental chaos if forgetting were impossible! I happen to know a hopelessly jealous person when it comes to sex. She can't stand the idea of her husband being, or ever having been, sexually intimate with another woman. Early in their marriage he made the mistake of telling her the truth, which she asked for, about his sex life before they married. The story involved people she knew. She was devastated. She became obsessed; she could think of nothing else; she dreamed about it. She loathed what he had done to their relationship, which she thought had been permanently scarred. This torment lasted more than a year before she was able to "put it out of mind." She has since been able to live as if she had never heard the anguishing truth (until now, that is, when I asked her about self-deception in her life and she dredged up the damn thing so I could write about it). Isn't that enough to show that selective forgetting is morally and psychologically desirable? Does she deceive herself? Then she deceives herself. Thank God for her sake it's possible.

What we choose to forget is an important matter, of course, and I would argue that learning to choose what to release from memory, and how, is an important life-giving skill. I have no idea how to teach it, but I believe we all need to learn it somehow.

ARE WE DESIGNED TO DECEIVE?

Is there something about the design of our very nature that accounts for our natural inclination to practice deception of self and others? What we take to be faults of rationality, for example, clinging to an initial hypothesis or exaggerating salient evidence, may be strategies of a reasonable sort seen from a more distant perspective. What is it, after all, to be rational? It is to conduct oneself in accord with certain public rules that determine the meaning of rationality. Whatever the substance of those rules and that meaning, one thing is sure: we do not like the idea of being—or being thought of as—irrational. The wish not to be thought irrational is a common (dare I say universal?) cause of self-deception and deception of others. This is, of course, because we *are* irrational creatures who must struggle all our lives to become, or at least to seem, rational. We are now on the verge of the argument that it is in some sense irrational *not* to be self-deceptive, at least about our own rationality, which is linked to our craving to be appreciated. There may be a connection between self-deceiving beliefs and long-term evolutionary benefit.

Charles Sanders Peirce said something useful to an understanding of self-deception as an adaptive mechanism in his classic essay on the fixation of belief, in which he described four methods people use to "settle their opinions."[31] One of these is the method of tenacity. He saw the importance of "the feeling of believing" in determining our actions, and he thought this feeling to be deeply set in human nature. "We cling tenaciously, not merely to believing, but to believing just what we do believe."[32] When doubts are raised about a belief, we struggle to deal with them somehow. This struggle is called inquiry. The sole object of inquiry, Peirce argues, is the "settlement of opinion"; however, "we may fancy that this is not enough for us, and that we seek not merely an opinion, but a true opinion. But put this fancy to the test, and it proves groundless; for as soon as a firm belief is reached we are entirely satisfied, whether the belief be false or true."[33] Peirce notes that "in many cases, it may very well be that the pleasure [one] derives from [one's] calm faith overbalances any inconveniences resulting from its deceptive character."[34] In judging this method of fixing (false) belief, Peirce is open to its value:

> A man may go through life, systematically keeping out of view all that might cause a change in his opinions, and if he only succeeds—I do not see what can be said against his doing so. It would be an egotistical impertinence to object that his procedure is irrational, for that only amounts to saying that his method of settling belief is not ours. He does not propose himself to be rational, and indeed, will often

talk with scorn of man's weak and illusive reason. So let him think as he pleases.[35]

Peirce sees the method of tenacity as admirable for being strong, simple, and direct, even though it does not lead to truth, at least not in the way that the scientific method is likely to. When the truth in question is about external "reality," the method of tenacity is nonproductive. On the other hand, when the truth in question is about internal "reality," the calmness or wretchedness of one's mind and soul, the method may well be evolutionarily optimal.

We are made of many incompatible attributes or components that, just because they coexist, are called a person. To notice this, and believe it, is not necessarily to point to a problem that needs solving, either. There is no law that says desires or intentions must be consistent with one another. Rather than trying to change our natures by reducing human good and moral right to only that which is rational, we could accept our mottled lot more gracefully and do what we can to make this life of incompatible things a little easier, a bit less harmful.

We have to wonder about the source of the high moral premium set upon self-knowledge. Where does it come from? Why is it so loudly touted as a personal and social virtue? It would seem that we struggle with all our might and wit against gaining the hard crucial truth about ourselves; the enterprise certainly does not come naturally and easily. Freud, throughout his writings about the unconscious, contends that widely shared neurotic resistances work to contrive the most intricate devices whose purpose is to interfere tenaciously with self-knowledge. If it's so desirable, why don't we desire self-knowledge more sincerely? We talk about it one way, but actually feel about it quite differently.

Even when we do focus on truthful self-examination—say, by keeping a diary—we exaggerate and force everything. We want the truth about ourselves to be more than it is because we are looking for better selves than we are. This was Sartre's ironic insight about self-knowledge presented in his novel La Nausée. We lie, even to ourselves about ourselves, to give life meaning.

Here's a game: Invent a "Personality Diagnosis and Display Machine" that is guaranteed to be absolutely accurate, exhaustive, and ruthlessly objective. Make it interactive, so you can talk back and explain yourself. Have your friends strap you to the machine, to make sure you can't get away before it's through with you, then let them take their seats so they can learn the whole truth about who you really are. Turn it on.

Does that sound like fun? Why not? Why don't we live in a society where this is a commonplace activity, where we are the machines? There must be a reason. Perhaps it is that self-examination is really always a matter of degree, or ought to be. There is a point, and we can tell when we get there, beyond which we may not comfortably and safely go. It is not for nothing that we all have worked out uniquely personal formulas for exposure. Perfect clarity in the dangerous game of self-knowledge contains the power to destroy. Ask what happens *after* the truth is told. Is there a way to recovery if the pain is great?

We all remember what Socrates taught us: the unexamined life is not worth living. Alongside that brave bit of advice, we should also recall with appropriate sympathy the message brought home by Oedipus: the well-examined life may prove unlivable. Or, as I have heard John Barth say: "self-knowledge is always bad news."

The point is to get on with living a life as a person, not merely as a creature. For that we need to move past difficult realities such as overwhelming demands and responsibilities, losing faith or friendship, fear that we're going stupid, losing memory, falling ill, or are being found out for the disappointing person who we feel deep down we really are. We need hope and energy to cope with these difficulties and sometimes—not always—illusion helps.

OPTIMISM

We can put an awful lot of self-deception down to optimism. Lionel Tiger says that "making optimistic symbols and anticipating optimistic outcomes of undecided situations is as much a part of human nature, of the human biology, as are the shape of the body, the growth of children, and the zest of sexual pleasure."[36] William James wrote of this, too, in *The Varieties of Religious Experience*: "For practical life at any rate, the *chance* of salvation is enough. No fact in human nature is more characteristic than its willingness to live on a chance."[37] Tiger defines optimism as "a mood or attitude associated with an expectation about the social or material future—one which the evaluator regards as socially desirable, to his advantage, or for his pleasure. The attitude is both variable and complex: how optimism is defined in a particular situation depends on what the particular optimist regards as desirable."[38]

We don't know exactly why it is, but "happy ideas about their destiny appear to make people feel better in their bodies."[39] Ideas about progress in morality, politics, and economics can make physically unfit social reformers feel positively robust in their urgent enthusiasm. Physically ill patients can contribute significantly to their own recovery by maintaining a possibly unrealistic optimism about, or a sense of personal control over, their own wellness and the future.

Shelly Taylor has studied the relationship between physical health and such salient psychological factors as optimism, beliefs, and illusions. She found that a sense of personal control can have a direct effect on health:

> Belief in a sense of personal control, then, appears to have a direct and positive impact on health, just as the experience of lack or loss of control has an adverse effect on health. What is clearly implicated in these studies is the importance of *beliefs* concerning control, not simply whether control is in fact present or absent in these stressful situations. Studies in which people have been led to believe that they have control over stressful events (even when they, in fact, have no control) demonstrate that the belief in control produces dramatic effects on neuroendocrine functioning. However, among people undergoing stressful events that they perceive as uncontrollable, neuroendocrine functioning is dramatically altered in ways that can have a direct impact on immune functioning. It is no wonder, then, that controllable and uncontrollable stressful events have such different effects on health. Moreover, it is the belief or illusion of control, and not simply the existence of control, that is implicated in these relationships.[40]

Taylor goes on to discuss the importance of the placebo effect, as an illustration of the power of optimism in healing. She suggests that "perhaps the clearest evidence for the beneficial impact of unrealistic optimism on health is the powerful and widely documented placebo effect."[41] Medicine has come a long way in deciding what shall serve as a placebo. In the early days, patients were treated with bizarre concoctions of the blood and dung, teeth and hooves, and rotted flesh of many animals, among many other emetic medications. Today starch tablets and injections of pure water are more common, but it is widely recognized that "in fact any medical procedure, ranging from drugs or surgery to psychotherapy, can have a placebo effect, and the effects of these placebos are substantial for reducing pain and discomfort,"[42] as well as other symptoms. The medical historian Arthur Shapiro concludes that "placebos can have profound effects on organic illnesses, including incurable malignancies. . . . Placebos can mimic the effect usually thought to be the exclusive property of active drugs.[43]

It is not altogether clear how placebos work. We know there is a connection between certain emotion-laden beliefs (for example, anxiety) and the release or suppression of chemicals (epinephrine) in the body. If we assume that a neurochemical imbalance can cause or contribute to health problems, and if we assume further that such imbalance can be traced to the presence and strength of certain beliefs, then it would seem plausible that a change of belief could affect a restorative neurochemical change. A placebo might then be just the thing for inducing a sense of optimism and control, which would reduce depression, anxiety, hopelessness, and helplessness. Taylor summarizes her understanding of the placebo effect in these words:

> The effectiveness of placebos should not be thought of either as a medical trick or as a purely psychological response on the part of the patient. Placebo effects merit respect. The placebo achieves success in the absence of truly effective therapy. It increases the effectiveness of therapies that have only modest effects of their own. It reduces substantial pain and discomfort. It was the foundation of most of early medicine's ef-

fectiveness, and it continues to account for many of medicine's cures today. As such, it is powerful testimony to the adaptive impact of unrealistic optimism on health.[44]

In *Optimism,* Tiger acknowledges the work of Claude Lévi-Strauss, who raised a question about the evolutionary implications of what is "good to think": "Just as sexual intercourse, for example, is presumably pleasurable as an inducement toward reproductive success, so then what is pleasurable to think may well be similarly linked to human evolution."[45] One of the most beneficial pleasures of the mind may turn out to be what Taylor calls positive illusions, or creative self-deceptions.

Placebo is Latin for "I shall please." The power of unrealistic optimistic belief is real. Sometimes thinking so *does* make it so.

PART *two*

WHAT DECEPTION IS FOR

6 CIVILITY: REVEALING AND CONCEALING OUR THOUGHTS

Truth is beautiful, without doubt; but so are lies.
                                        Ralph Waldo Emerson

God made man because he loves stories.
                                        Elie Wiesel

"Why should human beings speak thousands of different, mutually incomprehensible tongues? We live in this pluralist framework, have done so since the inception of recorded history, and take the ensuing farrago for granted."[1] Logically speaking there is no reason to suppose that human beings would—or should—easily understand one another, but still it seems strange, even unnatural, that forms of speech actually inhibit understanding so widely and persistently, and that translation is so highly valued an art.

Human diversity certainly does exist in all areas of life, and it goes without saying that no two individuals are exactly alike. But consider the *scale* of differences that show up in the major parameters of human species characteristics: we can be sorted into four to seven "races" depending on how that shorthand term is used; there are three or four major types of bone structure and size; six or so blood types; but the world over, we all have the same number of teeth, essentially one kind of digestive tract, biochemial composition, and cortex. How then shall we explain the four to five *thousand* languages and dialects that are now in use? George Steiner thinks this a conservative figure and estimates that the world has known as many as ten thousand distinct tongues.[2] The human language catalog conveys an image of us "as a language animal of implausible variety and waste. By comparison, the classification of different types of stars, planets, and asteroids runs to a mere handful."[3]

What can explain such ostentatious variation, such fantastic elaboration and refinement of differences among languages that have been, throughout human history, exasperating barriers to understanding and even dangerous sources of contempt? Surely local factors and the many ways of organizing sound can't tell the whole story.

It has been estimated that an average person utters about thirty thousand words per day. Much of this is repetition, but not all. We create sentences continually. It would take ten million million years to say all the twenty-word sentences we could make in English. And all this from just forty-five little animal sounds! We combine words to make sense and achieve our purposes, but we also speak sometimes without clear purpose, perhaps as a way of keeping company with ourselves or with others. Language is a way of just being together. We use language so much because we seem to have a compulsion for self-expression and for what zoologists call "grooming behavior."

But language is also the great isolator. We could achieve a universal language, but we don't even really try. That, I think, is because we want sometimes to be alone; we need a means for separation, for controllable privacy, in addition to social grooming and intimacy with others.

What would it be like to end the punishment of Babel and get relief from unintelligible speech, do away with gibberish and ambiguity? Would Esperanto actually manifest the hope which its name implies of allowing all of us mutual access to our respective inner realities? Would that be a good thing even if it were possible? Or, to put the question another way, can the fact that we are so guardedly selective about straightforward, clear communication for the sake of complete understanding be explained by something in the nature of language? Are we stuck with an ineluctable need for translation? Does this need hint at something profound about the purpose of language itself?

What has been said of difficulties in achieving understanding between speakers of different languages can also be said of individual speakers of a common language. In fact, it is the omnipresent need for intralanguage translation that is more relevant to our understanding of deception. The majority of English speakers, for example, are enormously inventive at misleading others through concealment, conventions of emphasis, foreshortening, timing, calculated mumbling, shrewd misunderstanding, precise miswording, nonchalant nodding, meaningfully expressionless expressions, and so on, all for the purpose of controlling access to truthful understanding.

The magnitude of this effort to mislead others cannot be understood or explained if we assume that the primary purpose of language is to discover and share the truth. Our actual use of language with regard to truth telling is a signal that language has some other vital purpose of equal if not greater importance. The separateness of persons is the basic fact of language and a key to its purpose. While it is clear that language serves a universal desire to achieve and protect intimacy with a small number, and close affiliation with a few—but not all—others, it is less obvious that in order to achieve closeness with a few "insiders," a wary distance must be kept from the majority. Language can be understood as one of the arts of privacy.

Much miscommunication can be put down to carelessness and ineptitude. But if human beings were simply inept at language, good translations could be provided that would improve communication by reducing or eliminating erroneous and misleading usage, ambiguity, inconsistency, prattle, and palaver. Over time the need for translation would disappear because the translators would have created a unified, universally authorized version of Language. Such an achievement is unlikely to come about, not because we lack the intelligence but because we lack the desire. We don't want to give up the protection language affords when there is the clear danger of being deeply understood, when we would rather remain unfathomed. We are exceedingly clever at using language for concealing as well as revealing. History has shown that we can manage to cooperate quite nicely in the hard work of discovering and sharing the truth, by observing, inferring, and expressing the sense of a thing. We can do all this—when we want to. But we can do more, a lot more.

A sense of the range of what else we can do is captured in Montaigne's observation that "the reverse of truth has a hundred thousand shapes and a limitless field."[4] Montaigne may have over-estimated the simplicity of truth (the idea of truth means one thing in calculus and another in courtship), but he is dead on target not-ing the expansive nature of the "reverse of truth." We can get some notion of the vast complexity we face by looking at a few common words that convey a sense of something, a kind of com-munication, that is not, strictly speaking, the truth: negotiating, bluffing, kidding, imagining, modeling, imitating, role-playing, seeming, cleverness, artifice, cunning, guile, manner, masquerade, camouflage, dissemble, simulate, dissimulate, hypocrisy, counter-feit, irony, duplicity.

One could go on, but that is enough to suggest that our language (which includes gestures and facial expressions, as well as words) is bountiful in alternatives to straightforward, clear, truthful communication. This fact can be taken as a clue to a fundamental purpose of language, which is to regulate relationships among in-dividuals and groups of people by maintaining surveillance over information revealed and concealed. Language is a highly cultivated means for representing what exists and, more interestingly, what does not exist. Every language has words for pseudo-entities, fu-sions of language, reality, and imagination: goblin, satyr, unicorn, Zeus, utopia, Trinity, purgatory, Satan. It is just as easy to think about abstruse things as about real ones.

The proposition I am suggesting here is that deception is a prime purpose, even an essential property of language and not merely some kind of perversion of it. I think Augustine overstated the case for truth telling when he said in *The Enchiridion,* "Speech was given to man, not that men might therewith deceive one another, but that one man might make known his thoughts to an-other." We do share our thoughts, but we do so very, very circum-spectly. Talleyrand, on the other hand, was generally on the right track when he overstated the case for deception in saying, "La parole a été donnée à l'homme pour déguiser sa pensée" (Language was given to man so he could disguise his thoughts).

LIE DETECTING

Lewis Thomas, who, like the rest of us, sometimes gets discouraged about the morality of the human prospect, has reported at least one reason for thinking it is not so bad in a brief and clever essay on "The Lie Detector."[5] He informs us that lie detectors have shown that "a human being cannot tell a lie, even a small one, without setting off a kind of smoke alarm somewhere deep in a dark lobule of the brain, resulting in the sudden discharge of nerve impulses, or the sudden outpouring of neurohormones of some sort, or both." This automatic alarm, he says, must be a sign that something has gone wrong in a biological system designed to be truthful; therefore, he reasons, in a purely physiological sense, lying must be "an unnatural act," which means that we apparently are wired up as a moral species, at least with regard to truthfulness.

On the surface, it is clear to Thomas why this should be so. His explanation hints at a genetic basis for the domino theory of deception: We are a social species of interdependent individuals; interdependence requires trust; lying damages trust; therefore, evolution favors trustworthy truth tellers, and has built in this warning system to scare our brains when we are tempted to lie. This sounds like a blessing from nature for the long term. The truth may not set us absolutely free, but it may ensure some enduring role for us in future gene pools.

Lie detectors—gadgets that can record changes in heart rate, breathing, and the electrical conductivity of the skin—are still pretty primitive though. This fact sets Thomas speculating on other conceivable ways of tracking lies:

> Supposing it were found that there is indeed a special pentapeptide released into the blood on the telling of a lie, or some queer glycolipid in the sweat of one's palms, or, worst of all, something chemically detectable in balloons of exhaled breath. The next thing to happen would surely be new industries in Texas and

Japan for the manufacture of electronic sensing devices to be carried in one's pocket, or perhaps worn conspicuously on one's sleeve depending on the consumer's particular need. Governments would become involved, sooner or later, and the lawyers and ethicists would have one field day after another. Before long we would stop speaking to each other, television would be abolished as a habitual felon, politicians would be confined by house arrest, and civilization would come to a standstill.

Thomas's insight leads to the question why lying is so common and plentiful in human social behavior that, were we able to detect its every instance, civilization would come to a standstill. In the story "Tobermory" by Saki (H. H. Munro) this insight is played out in burlesque form when a cat who is a privileged observer of unmasked domestic truth and has been taught to speak English with perfect correctness proceeds to spill all the family secrets and mortify the guests at Lady Blemley's houseparty. Though very fond of Tobermory, the Blemleys realize that since he is in possession of the unvarnished truth about them, "now, of course, the only thing is to have him destroyed as soon as possible."[6] If civilization depends to this extent upon our not telling the truth, then maybe it is truth telling rather than lying that is "unnatural." Thomas wonders, as a doctor: "If you wired up the average good internist in the act of writing a prescription [for a placebo], would the needles go flying?" He also wonders about the irony that such an "unnatural act" would be practiced so widely throughout nature—not just in every human society, but among plants and animals, too.

> What is it that enables certain flowers to resemble nubile insects, or oppossums to play dead, or female fireflies to change the code of their flashes in order to attract, and then eat, males of a different species? What about those animals that make their livings by deception—the biological mimics, the pretenders, the fish dangling bits of their flesh as bait in front of their jaws, the malingering birds limping along to lie about the location of their nests, the peacock, who is surely not conceivably all that he claims to be?

Lying and other forms of deception clearly are not only a human phenomenon. If lying were an unnatural act, it would be unnatural throughout the animal and plant world. But anything that is so widely manifested in nature and so prevalent a characteristic in so many species, it would seem, is—in the ordinary sense of the word—natural. To call such a phenomenon "unnatural" surely is a bit of unjustified moralizing, or at least wishful thinking.

Lying and deceiving are with us to stay; they are in our bones. We still haven't got it clear what to think about this fact, or what to do about it, but to deny it by filing it away as "unnatural" is surely the wrong—and self-deceiving—response. Thomas and the rest of us do have reason, founded in our "moral wiring" within, for not giving up hope about the human prospect. But the good news is not that we are incapable of lying without setting off a built-in alarm; rather, it is that we have learned to deceive and to detect deception at least as well as some of the other animals and plants that have survived.

That we deceive (in order to keep civilization going?) is well established. How we manage to detect attempts at deception by others is a complementary and puzzling phenomenon, as demonstrated by certain victims of brain damage.

Brain-Damaged Lie Detectors

In patients suffering from aphasia the neurological ability to use or understand words has been destroyed. However, some people who have severe receptive aphasia (are unable to understands words as such) but are otherwise intelligent still manage to grasp the meaning of most ordinary conversation. This is because when people talk they do much more than utter words. They make gestures, they color their words with expressiveness, they vary cadence, inflection, and pitch, and of course their eyes and faces enhance the meaning of what is said. Oliver Sacks has treated many such people as hospital patients, and from this experience he has come to believe that "one cannot lie to an aphasiac. He cannot grasp your words, and so cannot be deceived by them; but what he grasps he grasps with infallible precision, namely the expression that goes with the words, that total, spontaneous, involuntary expressiveness which can never be simulated or faked, as words alone can, all too easily."[7]

Sacks compares the aphasiac's uncanny sensitivity to "tone" and feeling in spoken language with a similar ability in dogs. We recognize this preternatural skill with dogs, "and often use them for this purpose—to pick up falsehood, or malice, or equivocal intentions, to tell us who can be trusted, who is integral, who makes sense—when we, so susceptible to words, cannot trust our own instincts. And what dogs can do here, aphasiacs do too, and at a human and immeasurably superior level."

There is a complementary disorder sometimes called "tonal agnosia," which refers to a person's inability to recognize *any* expressive quality in spoken language. Words and grammar can be understood, but everything else, everything that the aphasiac responds to, is lost to the tonal agnosiac. For such a person visual cues (faces, postures, gestures, and so on) are needed to help ascribe meaning, emotion, intensity to words in sentences. Such a person is protected against being swept away by rhetorically evocative speech that makes no good literal sense.

Imagine Dr. Sacks' surprise when he walked in on a group of aphasic and agnosic patients who were roaring with laughter at the start of a televised speech by President Reagan:

> There he was, the old charmer, the actor with his practiced rhetoric, his histrionics, his emotional appeal—and all the patients were convulsed with laughter. Well, not all: some looked bewildered, some looked outraged, one or two looked apprehensive, but most looked amused.

The aphasiacs responded to the incongruities of the actor's acting, "undeceived and undeceivable by words." One patient with tonal agnosia "listened stony-faced to the President's speech, bringing to it a strange mixture of enhanced and defective perceptions— precisely the opposite mixture from those of our aphasiacs." She said, "'He is not cogent. He does not speak good prose. His word use is improper. Either he is brain-damaged, or he has something to conceal.'"

In concluding his essay, Sacks raises the paradoxical possibility that

> a good many normal people, aided, doubtless, by their wish to be fooled, were indeed well and truly fooled ("Populus vult decipi, ergo decipiature"). And so cunningly was deceptive word use combined with deceptive tone, that it was the brain-damaged who remained undeceived.

To some readers who believe the President was far less *consciously* deceptive than most politicians, that his evident sincerity was one of his greatest strengths, this story may seem far-fetched and sound like typical Reagan-bashing. To that charge Sacks might reply that Reagan was using his actor's skills to project an impression of sincerity, skills that worked to fool a good many people, but not these patients. But, the argument goes on, a good actor *lives* his role so that when he is speaking it, he *is* sincere. The question remains: was Reagan a good enough actor to be sincere even in this sense? Anyhow, the point of this section is not about Reagan, it's about some clinically interesting aspects of revealing and concealing thoughts.

It May Be Smart to Be a Bad Lie Detector

Most of us are not terribly good at detecting all the deceptions that come our way. We catch some (especially when our kids try to fly one by), and we overlook some that we suspect might be there (when we really, *really* want the car or the antique that seems overpriced), but who knows how many we miss completely? However, there is a definite possibility for improvement of our lie-detecting abilities, a possibility that raises the intriguing question: If you were capable of becoming an infallible lie detector, would you consider it an advantage or a liability for your social life to do so?

It is right and good that we catch the mendaciously maverick salesperson, garage mechanic, bunko artist, military contractor, and all their dishonorable cousins at their greedy schemes to defraud us with lies about worth and costs. We all hate it when somebody tricks us into paying too much for something we don't need or never receive. It's wrong to do that, and the guilty ones ought to be outsmarted, caught, and punished. But how clever is it to search diligently for clues to any attempt to spare the truth on a first date with someone who is trying to make a good impression in uncertain circumstances? Would you want your date to see directly into your heart at every instant? Is it right to scrutinize the dinner guests for signs of insincerity on every subject of conversation? Is your spouse entitled to get away with misleading you sometimes for the sake of personal privacy or saving face, or for the long-term purpose of preserving an enriching relationship?

There is no doubt we can develop some of the skills required for detecting such clues, but there is some question about the wisdom of becoming very proficient at it. Lie-detecting skill development starts early but takes on an explicitly public character when children begin to learn winning strategies at games such as checkers. Seeing the impending opportunity for a double or triple jump is enough to excite an eight-year-old checkers player right out of the chair—a dead giveaway to the opponent who is made wary by the commotion and subsequently blocks the jump. Sincere expression of thoughts, beliefs, and emotions is not helpful for winning at checkers; successful players learn to hide their thoughts, misrepresent their beliefs, and feign emotions they don't feel. They learn to control their bodies (don't jump up and down!), voices (groan to sound disappointed), and faces (look uninterested, or worried) so as to hide all clues to the truth. The other part of the story, of course, is learning to remember that other people are skilled at pretending, too, and to look for signs that will give them away.

The same holds true for many physically active sports as well. For example, it's hard to imagine successful play without recourse to deception in football, baseball, basketball, soccer, tennis, judo, or fencing, to name a few. Jim Brown, one of the best running-backs ever to play football, got up as slowly as possible after every tackle and always walked back to the huddle as if he were in pain. He wanted his opponents to get used to seeing him like that so that when he was in fact hurt, they wouldn't notice anything unusual. Miroslav Macir, the wonderful Czech tennis player known to his bewildered opponents as the Cat, is more successful than anyone else at masking his intentions and making un-expected shots: his shots are not technically better, but they are harder to "read" and therefore frustratingly difficult to deal with. Faking, feinting, hiding what you intend to do, and displaying what's false are all part of the game. The whole idea is to mislead your opponent into thinking something false so you can do what you want more easily, efficiently, effectively. I don't think this is exactly what the Duke of Wellington had in mind when he said, "The Battle of Waterloo was won on the playing fields of Eton," because the British don't think it very sporting to use guile, but games definitely do provide the training ground for deceptive skills.[8]

Yes, we learn to use these skills, and to detect their use by others. But there are times when we should think twice before we do. Two considerations come to mind. First, it is tiresome and discouraging, not to mention mean-spirited, to be mistrustful of everybody all the time. I would rather assume that people are trustworthy and take the risk of getting burned on occasion than live in a condition of continuous suspicion and apprehensiveness about others' motives. Second, I think of diligent lie detection as a kind of eavesdropping (prying into something private), which in some circumstances can be dumb rudeness. Part of what it means to have good manners is to let some lies go by undetected, or at least unnoticed. After all, we expect as much from others, don't we? If for some reason we find it necessary to conceal the truth of our thoughts or feelings on a certain subject, say Aunt Helen's obesity or Uncle Jack's ostentatious ascot, we don't expect some expert lie detector in the room to bang his bell and announce his discovery to all concerned. Very young children may be forgiven for this kind of insensitive behavior, but the older they get the less right they have to such forgiveness. Learning not only how but when to detect lies, as well as how and when to tell the truth about what lies you have detected, is part of a well-developed social intelligence.

How important is lie detection in ordinary social life? If we all stopped doing each other the favor of ignoring a lot of what we see and hear, could social life work at all? If we all held each other to an exact standard of saying only what we mean, and meaning everything we say, on pain of public exposure for even minor deviations, wouldn't we, as Lewis Thomas suggested, stop talking to each other? I think it's vastly better to keep on talking, keep on trusting, and keep on ignoring much that comes our way posing as the truth. And every once in a while we can huddle round the television with Oliver Sacks's patients, whose deficiencies are exacerbated in part because they cannot allow themselves to be deceived, and laugh at whoever happens to be president.

LANGUAGE AND MEANING

Language is communal; it expresses both more and less than the exact truth. The genius of language is to be found in the generation of meanings and the achievement of compromise among the meanings we share to some degree. The meaning of language itself cannot be reduced to an attempt at discovering and telling the truth.

To think of human communication strictly in terms of informational exchange governed by rules of truth telling is too narrow. Language is a response to a coordination problem in social/moral life. Language is more a reflection of what we together can accomplish than what each of us does separately. Truth telling is one good answer to the coordination problem, but I think we would do well to remember that deception is another. For example, in conversation, making someone happy is often more to the point than veracity or informativeness; so if the truth must sometimes be ignored or distorted for the sake of happiness—ignore, distort. Narrowly defining human communication as purely or primarily informational means overlooking the value of "grooming time" and much else.

Mario Pei has pointed out that language has long been thought of as "the outer manifestation of a people's soul, and the creator of their pattern of thought." In this century, Ferdinand de Saussure took the theory further and argued that language "is basically a sociological phenomenon, and must be viewed in relation to its speakers and their psychological processes." Both Pei and Saussure stress a careful distinction between "language, which is a system in which many individuals participate, and speech, the basic production of sounds peculiar to the individual speaker."[9]

Language is what people make of it, not what somebody thinks they ought to make of it. Of course there are rules, like signposts, that point the way, and people can be taught to use them. But the rules themselves can be changed.

> For what concerns the nature of language as it has operated within the memory of man, there is no denying its conventional [rather than god-given, or natural], symbolical, arbitrary [because there is no real link between the word and the object] and constant features, its link with the minds of the speakers, its fundamental purpose, which is the transfer of meaning from one human mind to another.[10]

Language Rules

In order to make forms of communication (languages) actually work, participants must adopt certain rules about true and false statements, and they must assume truthfulness as the norm. Adopting such rules means agreeing to their necessity; it does not mean that people must always conform to them. In fact, failure to conform to them is persistent and frequent. The logical point is that the effectiveness of a failure to conform, by lying or some other form of deception, is necessarily contingent upon the adoption of these rules. How well deception works depends upon how truthful the speaker is assumed to be.

The fact that language is a matter of agreement among users affords a great deal of freedom in recreating and distorting ordinary usage to the advantage of some who wish their deeds to go undiscovered. This is as true for the altruist who wishes to remain anonymous as it is for the criminal who wishes to avoid the law. Language, and language rules, can do the work of evil as easily as the work of goodness.

Hannah Arendt provides an example of the malevolent misuse of language rules in her book on the trial of Adolf Eichmann in Jerusalem in 1961. Eichmann played a central role in planning the necessary steps to carry out Hitler's orders first for the expulsion, then concentration, and finally the killing of the Jews within reach of the Reich.

> All correspondence referring to the matter was subject to rigid "language rules," and, except in the reports from the *Einsatzgruppen,* it is rare to find documents in which such bald words as "extermination," "liquidation," or "killing" occur. The prescribed code names for killing were "final solution," "evacuation" (*Aussiedlung*), and "special treatment" (*Sonderbehandlung*); deportation—unless it involved Jews directed to Theresienstadt, the "old people's ghetto" for privileged Jews, in which case it was called "change of residence"—received the names of "resettlement" (*Umsiedlung*) and "labor in the East" (*Arbeitseinsatz im Osten*), the point of these latter names being the Jews were indeed often temporarily resettled in ghettos and that a certain percentage of them were temporarily used for labor. Under special circumstances, slight changes in the language rules became necessary. Thus, for instance, a high official in the Foreign Office once proposed that in all correspondence with the Vatican the killing of Jews be called the "radical solution"; this was ingenious, because the Catholic puppet government of Slovakia, with which the Vatican had intervened, had not been, in the view of the Nazis, "radical enough" in its anti-Jewish legislation, having committed the "basic error" of excluding baptized Jews. Only among themselves could the "bearers of secrets" talk in uncoded language, and it is very unlikely that they did so in the ordinary pursuit of their murderous duties—certainly not in the presence of their stenographers and other office personnel. For whatever other reasons the language rules may have been devised, they proved of enormous help in the maintenance of order and sanity in the various widely diversified services whose cooperation was essential in this matter. Moreover, the very term "language rule" (*Sprachregelung*) was itself a code name; it meant what in ordinary lan-

guage would be called a lie. The net effect of this language system was not to keep these people ignorant of what they were doing, but to prevent them from equating it with their old, "normal" knowledge of murder and lies. Eichmann's great susceptibility to catch words and stock phrases, combined with his incapacity for ordinary speech, made him, of course, an ideal subject for "language rules."[11]

The Many Logics of Language

While members of a group can invent their own rules to standardize the group's expressions, there is little to suggest that any one set of language rules could ever apply universally. As for the universalization of languages, there is "no such thing as standardizing the human mind in the matter of linguistic expression. Each language is a law unto itself in the matter of what it considers logical, desirable or necessary."[12] Logic, desire, and necessity are all reflections of the ways people choose to categorize and organize their experiences. There is not only one logic, there are many, just as there are many ways to employ, for example, grammatical gender. An English speaker may think Hungarian illogical because it uses the same word for "he," "she," and "it." French and Spanish speakers, on the other hand, may think English illogical because it does not formally distinguish masculine, feminine, or neuter forms of gender anywhere at all *except* in the personal pronoun. Semitic has no neuter gender, so inanimate objects are distributed among masculine and feminine in sometimes peculiar ways.[13] For example, in Hebrew, for all parts of the body that come in pairs (feet, legs, eyes, ears, and even testicles) the noun is feminine—the only exception is "breast," which is masculine.

Grammatical number reflects more disagreement about systems in language. "The good girl" is grammatically the same as "the good boy," and the only "necessary" indication of number or gender is in the noun. But in Spanish, "la buena muchacha" shows number and gender in each word.

Even in the context of these competing systems of grammar, "the *purpose* of language is absolute. It is the transfer of *meaning* [my emphasis] from one human mind to another. If the form of communication used fails in this one respect, no true language can be said to exist. . . . Meaning is a community of *understanding* [my emphasis], so that for the time being you and I think in the same terms."[14]

This sounds straightforward enough, but "understanding" is a peculiar and illusory thing, and "meaning" should not be confused with "truth." We have words for experiences and ideas such as "love," "justice," "freedom," even "truth," but these words do not necessarily mean the same thing to different people. Nor should they. If all of our most important words carry exactly the same meaning for everybody, then we will have lost something of our individuality. If each of these words refers to only one experience, one idea, one understanding—then they don't refer to my experience, my idea, my understanding, nor to yours, hers, his. Then we have lost nuance.

Understanding is approximate. Meaning is approximate. At its heart, language, as the carrier of meaning and producer of understanding, is particular, not universal. Therefore, truth telling as well as deceiving are best understood as personal or communal performances, rather than as theoretical absolutes. I believe it is not quite right to argue that the existence of language is predicated on the truth, and that if we don't tell the truth all the time, then language—indeed all society—will fall apart. The purpose of language is to convey a world of richly diverse and often imprecise meaning; there is more to language than the "truth," which is a very small and somewhat rare (and therefore valuable) domain of the world of meaningful communication.

A Note on Ambiguity

To achieve understanding of poorly structured subjects it may not be the best choice to look for strictly unambiguous terms.[15] Poetry, for example, is fruitful because it generates meaning far beyond the literal. Perhaps it would be fruitful to moral understanding if we were to avoid oversimplifying the ambiguities of experience, and resisted the urge to put our moral positions, principles, and theories into words that have only one valid meaning, used to represent observations that have precisely one valid interpretation.

We rightly admire precision in the languages of science and computer programming, but in some other areas vividness, nuance, and powers of evocation are more appropriate and more valuable. A story does not need mathematical exactitude to be good; it needs to be told in an authentic voice, complete with eccentric ambiguities and charm, unconfined by the sober ideal of perfect honesty without distortion of any kind (understatement, overstatement, misstatement).

Stories, to be useful in our understanding of complex domains, should help us become more active in constructing ideas, expanding meaning, breaking down compartmentalized concepts and cases. They should help us become more comfortable and more handy with metaphor.

"That exam was murder." What this disgruntled student meant to say, literally, was something like, "That exam was too difficult for me and I expect a low grade, if I pass at all." By using the metaphor of murder, however, the student opened up a dramatic world, a scene "with him as the hapless victim innocently destroyed by a ruthless examiner who, with clear malice aforethought, carefully prepared to do him in from the very beginning of the semester. Indeed, it had all been premeditated, down to the least details of time and place."

His interpretation of this act of academic evaluation as an act of homicide reveals a world of feeling that the literal statement doesn't touch. While the metaphor itself is literally false, it is nonetheless true to the speaker's sensitivities. "It also implies a great deal more than it actually says, and for this reason, masters of metaphor are also masters of insinuation."[16]

Max Black has identified three distinct views of metaphor.[17] The first is that a metaphorical expression is used as a decorative substitute for some equivalent literal expression; it is a deviation from the plain, clear-cut style. The second is similar; it states that a metaphor is the presentation of a comparison in condensed form, and might be replaced with an equivalent literal presentation. The third is Black's own contribution to the theory of metaphor, a view he calls "interactive." In this view the two subjects of a metaphor (literal and figurative referent) are active together, and the interaction produces a meaning that has more power to inform and enlighten than the literal meanings of the two subjects themselves. This kind of metaphor is not mere substitution, nor mere comparison; it generates meaning that could not be expressed literally. Thus, when Churchill called Mussolini "that *utensil*," we have an instant insight into Churchill's opinion that we would not have with a substitution or translation such as "Mussolini's role in Hitler's plan is instrumental."

A language of words each with only one meaning permitted is a horrifying prospect, for it would deprive us of the ambiguity necessary to facilitate negotiations, adapt to change, establish communal beliefs, and even apply the laws judiciously. Edward Levi, a distinguished professor of law emeritus at the University of Chicago, believes that it is "only folklore which holds that a statute if clearly written can be completely unambiguous and applied as intended to a specific case."[18]

THE PRIMACY OF PRIVACY

Perhaps the easiest route to seeing the necessary place of deception in social life is by way of privacy, or the idea of a private life.[19] That is at once a most cherished and most ambiguous idea. In general terms, privacy means "withholding or concealment of information, particularly personal information."[20] Privacy is a means of controlling what others see and know about ourselves; it limits others' ability to pry into matters we may wish to keep secret (amount of income, sexual preferences, medical history, nail biting). Privacy also has the meaning of physical removal from social interactions as well as from the intrusions of noise. This desire for seclusion need not be the same as a desire for solitude. For solitude, you disconnect the telephone; for seclusion, you hook it up to an answering machine to screen out unwanted or untimely interactions.

How could we possibly live a life without access to privacy, without assurance that when we need it there is an opportunity for secrecy and a place for seclusion? In weighing the relative demands for either secrecy or seclusion, I agree with Richard Posner that

> when people today decry lack of privacy, what they want, I think, is mainly something quite different

from seclusion: they want more power to conceal information about themselves that others might use to their disadvantage. This is the meaning of privacy underlying the federal Privacy Act, which limits the retention and dissemination of discrediting personal information contained in government files.[21]

A life without privacy is unthinkable. How could we make love? Reflect or meditate? Write a poem, keep a diary, daydream? How could we attend to those sometimes highly self-conscious requirements of skin and bowels? How could we expect to keep our intimate doings out of the newspaper? How could we pay adequate attention to our personal inner worlds, or find peace from the demands of daily living? We need a certain amount of privacy to maintain a sense of dignity and decency, to stay sane and happy.[22] Civility itself requires privacy.

The motive for privacy is often to mislead, either by concealing information sought by others, or by redirecting attention to an alternate display which we hope will distract the hunters from the hunt. The basic strategy for avoiding an invasion of privacy is simple: one can either increase ambiguity about the real subject, or increase clarity about a false one. These are precisely the rudiments of deception: to mislead by showing and hiding. While privacy is perhaps most frequently motivated in this way, it is also sometimes motivated by a simple and straightforward need for self-protection that does not require misleading when resolute denial will suffice.

Privacy conveys advantage in achieving and maintaining a reputation, the difficulty of which for public figures is symbolized both by the highly prosperous gossip industry and by an increasing number of scandalously demeaning congressional hearings. The advantage of privacy extends beyond private life, to the world of employment, where competition for jobs, promotions, and other business associations is keen and mean. Another benefit can easily be recognized in the norm of privileged communications between client and lawyer, doctor, counselor. These communications carry the privilege of secrecy for the same reason we don't open other people's mail or read their diaries without permission. If the privacy privilege were violated at will, or without sanction, the consequence would be inhibition of communication of all sorts, an intolerably high cost to autonomy and personal dignity.

Privacy within the Family

There is a scene in Ivy Compton-Burnett's novel *A Father and His Fate*[23] that illuminates the strength of our need for privacy compared with the strength of our obligation to tell the truth within the family. Believing their mother to be dead, daughters and nephews talk together:

> "I wonder if Mother can see us now," said Constance. . . . "Perhaps she can see into our minds. Then she would understand."
>
> "We will hope she cannot," said Rudolf. "That is not a thing to be done. Anyhow by anyone who understands."
>
> "Why should we mind, if we have nothing to be ashamed of?"
>
> "Well, then there would be no reason."
>
> "You talk as if you had something to hide."
>
> "As if I had many things to hide, as we all should talk."
>
> "I do not think I have more than is inevitable."
>
> "I daresay I have not either."
>
> "He is sure he has not," said Nigel. "He has been trained in self-esteem."
>
> "I think I have," said Ursula.
>
> "I am sure I have," said Audrey.
>
> "I only hope I hide them," said Rudolf.
>
> "I trust I am not a transparent person," said Nigel.
>
> "I can say that I should not mind, if Mother looked into my heart at this moment," said Constance.
>
> "Think again," said Malcolm. "And imagine her really doing so."
>
> There was a pause.
>
> "Well, perhaps I am not quite prepared for it," said Constance, more lightly.

Like Constance, most of us have two views of ourselves. One is private and one is for sharing. The fact that honesty about ourselves always takes a conscious (even self-conscious) effort, and that dishonesty often can seem effortless and even unconscious, makes me wonder whether such honesty is a bit "unnatural" and the kind of dishonesty that protects privacy is somehow built right into human nature. Again, from *A Father and His Fate:*

> "Audrey, this way of talking is not natural to you."
>
> "I do not feel natural. If you do, and it seems you do, you are fortunate. Though I don't know that the rest of us are."
>
> "Well, we will hope you will soon return to your real self."
>
> "This is my real self. What is not natural is to show it."
>
> "I should have thought most of us showed ourselves."
>
> "We show the selves we are accustomed to show, and other people to expect."
>
> "I think I show my real self."
>
> "You show the one you have come to think is yours."
>
> Constance paused.
>
> "Of course there are things we have to conquer in ourselves."
>
> "Yes, you try to improve it and make it better worth showing."

Compton-Burnett is relentless in her attacks on ordinary pretensions of truthfulness, openness, sincerity. In her fictional families, language and personality are the only weapons used in the constant battle between domestic dictators and their powerless subjects. For the latter, privacy is sanctuary.

The Family and Outsiders

The individuals within a family need some privacy from each other, it is true, but the family as a whole needs to have privacy from other families, from outsiders, too. Part of what it is to be a "family" (whether biologically determined, socially institutionalized, or voluntarily chosen) is to be separate from others, in a special, mutual bond. To be in a family requires that there be outsiders whose access to the family is closely monitored and regulated by the family members according to their sense of, and need for, privacy. Outsiders may be invited to come into the family, to be sure, and extended families of this kind are not unusual, but they are extended by invitation only.

J. B. Priestly's play *Dangerous Corner*[24] is about a closely related theme, the questionable wisdom of disturbing the sleeping dog, truth. After dinner, the six main characters, who are related as siblings, marital partners, business partners, or some combination of these, set out to discuss the apparent suicide of a man known to them individually as brother, lover, colleague, or friend. The scene is set by the following dialogue:

> *Stanton.* I think telling the truth is about as healthy as skidding round a corner at sixty.
> *Freda.* And life's got a lot of dangerous corners—hasn't it, Charles?
> *Stanton.* It can have—if you don't choose your route well. To lie or not to lie—what do you think, Olwen? You're looking terribly wise.
> *Olwen.* I agree with you. I think telling everything is dangerous. The point is, I think—there's truth and truth.
> *Gordon.* I always agree to that. Something and something.
> *Stanton.* Shut up, Gordon. Go on, Olwen.
> *Olwen.* Well—the real truth—that is, every single little thing, with nothing missing at all, wouldn't be dangerous. I suppose that's God's truth. But what most people mean by truth, what that man meant in the wireless play, is only half the real truth. It doesn't tell you all that went on inside everybody. It simply gives you a lot of facts that happen to have been hidden away and were perhaps a lot better hidden away. It's rather treacherous stuff.

As the evening discussion unfolds, everyone is forced in one way or another to reveal some private detail, emotion, or action that involves others in the group—there has been a great deal of hidden unhappiness within couples and between friends, and real happiness but with the wrong partners, dishonesty about money, and even an accidental death left to look like suicide. Near the end, one couple, who have been exposed for pretending that their marriage was better than either of them really thought it was, are about to call it a failure:

> *Betty.* Yes, we put up a good show, didn't we?
> *Gordon.* Yes, we did. What would have happened if we'd gone on pretending like hell to be happy together?
> *Betty.* Nothing.
> *Gordon.* No. If we'd gone on pretending long enough, I believe we might have been happy together, sometimes. It often works out like that.
> *Betty.* Never.
> *Olwen.* Yes it does. That's why all this is so wrong really. The real truth is something so deep you can't get at it this way, and all this half-truth does is to blow everything up. It isn't civilized.

Later there is some hint that the real truth is to be found in illusion. This perhaps is the ironic truth about truth: sought directly for itself it will mislead you, or blow everything up; sought indirectly through illusion it may give you the deepest insight human beings can handle.[25]

Too Much Privacy

However, there is such a thing as too much privacy, too deep a solitude, too isolated a group. Complete withdrawal from society, from the reality of the public world, to turn inward as some monks as well as some psychotics do, can be a failure because it deprives the individual of so much opportunity, stimulation, and interest that comes from human community. A totally private person, to use a fine old Greek term, is an idiot—that is, a person who can communicate with no one. A not quite so totally private person, on the other hand, may turn out to be a genius, or at least a contented talent who simply wishes to minimize the obligation of "being sociable," in favor of more time to think in private. Moses, Jesus, and Muhammad all went to the desert to be alone, and out of those experiences sprang great religions. Augustine and Petrarch searched deep within their inner worlds and believed they had revealed the universe.

In any case, privacy is an unsocial, if not a downright selfish value. It is the right to freedom from contact with others when we feel like it; it is the right not to be known, or to be known only in limited ways, by controlling the flow of information about what matters to us. It would be a gross and unacceptable violation of privacy to ask that we be completely open to or with others when we don't feel like it. The intensity of our feelings about privacy is revealed in how watchfully, tenaciously, suspiciously we guard our right against an invasion of our privacy—from bureau drawers to bank accounts, from personal letters to the garden in the back of the house. We have come to regard the right to privacy as a right that everyone is entitled to. We are far, far from remembering that privacy was once a rich man's luxury, as in the days of Pompeii, when few could afford to build a wall around their garden.

At the same time, though, and somewhat contradictorily, our society espouses a morality of openness—between marriage partners, in the workplace, in politics and government. In fact, striking a balance between privacy and other public values has been, and probably always will be, a built-in, universal human problem. One of the most successful means for coping with this problem is, of course, deception. We might call deception one of the arts of privacy—along with love, poetry, and meditation. The more privacy, the less communality; the more communality, the less privacy. We can go wrong through excess or deficiency in either direction, but as long as we have the arts of deception to help us find the balance in our lives, we should be able to manage.

Every important right needs a social system to protect it. The right to privacy is no exception. It is protected for all citizens by a formal system of laws against certain kinds of invasion by certain individuals and agencies; for clients of doctors and lawyers and a limited number of other professionals it is protected by an ethical code. Perhaps more importantly, it is also protected for everyone by an extremely sophisticated though informal system of display and concealment in ordinary social discourse. Human beings have proven themselves enormously talented at maintaining privacy in the midst of interactions of all kinds. While seeming to speak the whole truth, we don't. This informal system works with such phenomenal success and regularity that I am tempted to call it a law of nature. In any case, I believe there is an absolutely crucial conjunction of communal civility, privacy, and deception that we must reckon with if we are ever to get a clear view of our actual practical morality. We need privacy to survive just as surely as we need communal civility. Neither would be possible, and more importantly, a satisfactory balance of the two would be beyond reach, without deception. That's the point. Simple as that.

THE NATURAL LAWS OF CIVILITY

In an attempt to summarize the thoughts and arguments of this chapter on a somewhat lighter note, I offer the following tentative list of "natural laws" that (should) govern civility:

Truth is a choice.

Truth has meaning only when it has several.

Logic is a way of thinking that lets you go wrong with confidence.

Deceiving is a way of talking that lets others go wrong with confidence.

One good reason for not always telling the truth is that life is already complicated enough.

Humiliation is universal. That's why everybody is a liar.

Given enough time and the inventive craft of narration, you can connect any A with any B.

Every conceivable action has at least one plausible explanation.

People will say almost anything to gain a reputation for honesty.

Assert anything with confidence and somebody is sure to believe you.

Anything that can be said, can be said another way.

We attach our honor to the art of selecting and weighing exactly what we say to whom. If you tell everything, you will be known as a bore.

The reason we are not used to telling the truth is that we are not used to facing it.

In truth telling, as in everything else, moderation is a virtue.

If I lose my ability to "handle the truth," I may as well jump in the river.

In this world, sincerity can be a drawback.

The wise are not troubled by inconsistency.

A society that made deception explicitly acceptable could not endure; neither could one that did not implicitly require it.

Be ingenious, seem innocent.

Show the deed, not the design.

Moral decency ensures for us the right to be deceived as surely as the right to truth: to extol the latter and deny the former is to misunderstand being human.

Good manners can't succeed without the lie, to be both used and let pass by.

7 FRIENDSHIP AND ALTRUISM: BE UNTRUTHFUL TO OTHERS AS YOU WOULD HAVE OTHERS BE UNTRUTHFUL TO YOU

As scarce as truth is, the supply has always been in excess of the demand.

Josh Billings

It's a rare person who wants to hear what he doesn't want to hear.

Dick Cavett

Here's a story about two friends, both wonderful writers. One of them is Bernard Malamud, a frail and very sick old man. The other is Philip Roth. After lunch together with their wives, Malamud asks if he might read aloud from the opening chapters of a work in progress, to get Roth's opinion. Here is Roth's description of what happened:

> After coffee Bern went to his study for the manuscript, a thin sheaf of pages perfectly typed and neatly clipped together. I noticed when he sat down that all around his chair, on the porch floor, were scattered crumbs from his lunch. A tremor had made eating a little bit of an adventure, too, and yet he had driven himself to undertake once again this ordeal.
>
> It turned out that not too many words were typed on each page and that the first-draft chapters were extremely brief. I didn't dislike what I heard because there was nothing yet to like or dislike—he hadn't got started, really, however much he wanted to think otherwise. It was like having been led into a dark hole

to see by torchlight the first Malamud story ever scratched upon a cave wall. What was awesome wasn't what was on the wall but, rather, contemplating the power of the art that had been generated by such simple markings. I didn't want to lie to him but, looking at the thin sheaf of pages in the hands of that very frail man, I couldn't tell the truth, even if he was expecting it of me. I said simply, and only a little evasively, that it seemed to me a beginning like all beginnings. That was quite truthful enough for a man of 71 who had published 12 of the most original works of fiction written by an American in the past 35 years. Trying to be constructive, I suggested that perhaps the narrative opened too slowly and that he might begin better further on, with one of the later chapters. Then I asked where it was all going. "What comes next?" I said, hoping we could pass on to what it was he had in mind if not yet down on the page.

But he wouldn't let go of what he'd written—at such cost—as easily as that. Nothing was ever as easy as that, least of all the end of things. In a soft voice suffused with fury, he said, "What's next isn't the point."

In the silence that followed, before Claire eased him gently into a discussion of the kind of character he was imagining as his hero, he was perhaps as angry at failing to master the need for assurance so nakedly displayed as he was with me for having nothing good to say. He wanted to be told that what he had painfully composed while enduring all his burdens was something more than he himself must have known it to be in his heart. He was suffering so, I wished I could have said that it *was* something more, and that if I'd said it, he could have believed me.

Before I left for England in the fall I wrote him a note telling him that I was off, and inviting him and Ann to come down to Connecticut the next summer—it was our turn to entertain them. The response that reached me in London some weeks later was pure, laconic Malamudese. They'd be delighted to visit, but he reminded me, "next summer is next summer."

He died on March 18, three days before spring.[1]

What is the desirable balance of truth telling and deceiving in this story? Roth avoided lying. That's good. We should do that when we can. But he also avoided telling the truth. More accurately, he avoided telling exactly that part of the truth that was uppermost in his mind, the part that best represented the reality of the situation as he saw it. He judged that part of the truth to be unsuitable in the circumstances. Instead, he tried to be constructive by redirecting his friend's attention from the central point, by consciously misrepresenting his honest answer to the question of how good the writing was. Is that good, too? Should Roth have told the dying man, whose memory and vision were seriously clouded, that his writing now came to nothing? Is that what Malamud deserved to hear? Was Malamud really asking for Roth's candid critical opinion of his draft or was he asking for some kind of assurance to help him endure a crumbly end to his life? We can never know for sure what is in other people's minds, and it is presumptuous to assume to know what other people "really" need. Nevertheless, it's a fair guess that Roth did do the right thing when he varnished the truth he had to tell, and that what passed between the two friends was an understanding more valuable and constructive than the unequivocal truth would have been.

FRANKNESS IN THE STABLE

In his journal entry for Thursday, March 8, 1849, the painter Eugène Delacroix made a similar observation about the character of frank opinions.

> In the evening, Chopin. At his house, met an original who has come from Quimper to admire him and cure him for he is or has been a doctor and has a great contempt for the homeopaths of all colors. He is a rabid music lover: but his admiration is limited, particularly to Beethoven and Chopin. Mozart does not seem to him on their height; Cimarosa is old hat, etc. You've got to come from Quimper to have ideas like that and express them with such nerve: that passes for

the frankness of a Breton. I detest that kind of character. That so-called frankness, which permits people to utter cutting or wounding opinions, is the thing for which I have the greatest antipathy. Relationships among men are no longer possible if frankness like that is a sufficient answer to everything. To speak frankly, one should, with a disposition like that, live in a stable, where relationships are established by thrusts of a pitchfork or by horns; that's the kind of frankness I prefer.

In the morning, at the studio of Couder, to talk about the picture at Lyons. He is witty, and his wife is very good-looking. If we had been frank with each other, along the lines of my Breton, we should have had a fight before the end of the meeting; on the contrary, we parted in perfect agreement.[2]

What is frankness that makes it such a highly placed but controversial virtue? It is defined by candor, honesty, sincerity, truthfulness—and is taken often to be a mark of integrity. However, it can just as often be offensive and wounding, as Delacroix found his Breton to be. If causing offense and injury is sometimes the price of frankness, then perhaps, in cases when there is no greater benefit to outweigh the loss, it would be better to forego frankness—candor, honesty, sincerity, and truthfulness—in favor of some less direct means of expression. All for the sake of preserving and enhancing relationships with other people.

Friends have the right to expect the truth from one another, but they have the right to expect more than that when the truth gets them headed down a path with no affirmative sense of destination.

TRUST, TRUTH, AND FRIENDSHIP

What does it mean when I say, "I trust you," or "Trust me"? First of all, "it is not possible to demand the trust of others; trust can only be offered and accepted."[3] If the offer is accepted, there must be some reason other than the offer itself that accounts for the acceptance. Perhaps we already know something about a person's background, through experience or reputation, which disposes us to trust, and so the present offer acts as reassurance; or perhaps we ask why we should trust and reasons are given that satisfy the question.[4] Acceptance of personal trust is risky, but the risk can be reduced a good deal through the "verbal magic" of promises:

> Part of what makes promises the special thing they are, and the philosophically intriguing thing they are, is that we *can* at will accept *this* sort of invitation to trust, whereas in general we cannot trust at will. Promises are puzzling because they seem to have the power, by verbal magic, to initiate real voluntary short-term trusting.[5]

What have we done when we have decided to trust someone? I like Annette Baier's definition of trust as "reliance on others' competence and willingness to look after, rather than harm, things one cares about which are entrusted to their care."[6] I trust you if I rely upon you to look after what I have entrusted to your care. In friendship, what I entrust is myself (and at least some of that which I value): I rely upon you to look after me. Whatever happens in friendship, then, happens in an atmosphere of reciprocal trust.

I think that trust is part of what friendship means; it is not easy to imagine having a friend whom one cannot generally trust (though there may be specific areas in which the trust is weak, or has even been abused in the past). There is no friendship without a strong sense of trust: trust is necessary to friendship. But it is easy to imagine trusting someone who is not a friend—a surgeon, for example, who is about to operate on you. So, while trust is necessary to friendship, it is by no means exclusive to friends.

Now I want to make a suggestion that may at first sound ironic: Given the nature of trust in friendship there is an important and serious role for deception to play in keeping a friendship going. How could I seriously suggest that deception has anything to do with trust and is necessary for success in friendship? As Kathryn Morgan, one of my friends, wrote after she had heard my arguments for this point of view:

> Friendship is a paradigm of a personal relation constructed in a context of intimacy, trust, mutual vulnerability, and caring. The condition for such a relationship over time is deep, detailed knowledge of

another's life, character, desires, ends, and interests in a mutually understood context of trusting openness which is incompatible with the principled intent to deceive. Such conditions are built in because friendship, ideally, is the paradigm of a simultaneously disinterested and caring relationship where the relationship itself is the *raison d'être* for the pact of truth telling.[7]

She went on to ask, "Why does the king *need* a jester? To tell him crucial truths about himself, to prick the balloons of self-deception *through* the sharpness of his jests." The point she wanted to make was that a friend is someone who is willing to hurt you with the truth when it is in your interest to know it. "Ideally," she argued, "we rely on our friends for sincerity, for insight because of the knowledge and caring that previous compassionate acts of truth telling have both constructed and protected." The point is well taken, but the two qualifications she adds make all the difference: a friend will tell you the truth *when it is in your interest* to hear it, and he will tell it *compassionately*. That's what I think, and under her formal objections, I suspect that's what my friend thinks, too. Friendship is not defined by disinterested truth telling alone, but by compassionate acts performed in the friend's interests. Friendship is based upon trust that your friend will look after you and what you value. There is plenty of room in compassion for handling the truth, for being less than frank, for not telling all of the right story, for playing with some of the balloons of self-deception to keep them aloft instead of pricking them all.

This discussion has been limited by the unspoken assumption that friendship is a two-party relationship, rather than a network of several people who are involved to differing degrees with each other. In some cases, friendship may involve just two people at a time, but mostly our friends know each other. Thus, what I say to one affects the others. There may well be conflicts among friends that become exacerbated by truth telling; in telling *this* truth about you to *that* friend, I fail in my obligation to look after your friendship with him. While honoring his trust in my veracity, I may dishonor your trust in my good judgment and discretion.

My friend has read approvingly Sissela Bok's book on lying and agrees with her that "*whatever* matters to human beings, trust is the atmosphere in which it thrives."[8] It would be hard to argue with that, and I'm not sure I want to; but still, I wonder what we are getting at with the metaphoric "atmosphere of trust"? Bok actually suggests that "trust is a social good to be protected just as much as the air we breathe or the water we drink. When it is damaged, the community as a whole suffers; and when it is destroyed, societies falter and collapse."[9]

The irony that goes unappreciated in this thinking is that an "atmosphere" of trust is itself a delicately balanced mixture of the essential gases of communication, namely, truth telling and deceiving. An atmosphere of pure truth telling is no more fit to support friendship than an atmosphere of pure oxygen is fit to support life.

Compassionate Truth, Compassionate Lie

Recently on the television program "L.A. Law," I saw an illustration of a compassionate admixture of truth telling and deception that strengthened a friendship. Abby, a young attorney trying to make it on her own, asks her friend Stuart, a very good tax lawyer in a prestigious firm, to become co-attorney and advise her on a case. Her client has received an offer for a $40,000 settlement. As she is serving the client on a contingency basis, she will earn a percentage of the settlement without the costs of a trial if her client accepts the offer. The prospect of some immediate income is extremely attractive to Abby since she has pressing debts to pay. She is a little uncertain about the fairness of the offer, though, so she asks Stuart to go over the facts and figures and give his opinion. He does so and tells her that he thinks she has a case to support a $65,000 settlement and that she should go to court if necessary. Abby knows a court proceeding will take a long time, doesn't want to take the risk of losing, and angrily accuses Stuart of trying to undermine her. Stuart sticks with his honest assessment and adds his belief that a good lawyer doesn't sell a client short in order to pay the bills. He offers to loan Abby the money she needs to see her through. She tells him to stick his money, and his moralizing, and fires him on the spot to relieve him of his professional obligation as co-attorney to inform the client of his opinion on the case.

As her friend, Stuart had told her the truth, because it was in her best interests.

The following day, the client comes to Stuart to ask what has happened, why he is no longer on the case. Stuart does not give a straight answer, though he does not lie, because he wants the client to stay with Abby and work things out. He reiterates that Abby is a good attorney, that they don't have any serious differences but have disagreed on some figures. The client asks if Stuart thinks the settlement should be higher. Stuart says he should talk to Abby about that, and brushes off further questions.

As Abby's friend, he did not tell her client the whole truth, again because he thought it was in her best interests, and because he was under no formal obligation to say more than he did say.

As it happened, Abby lost the client and received no fee. She later came to Stuart's office to make a full and humble apology for her anger at him for telling her what she now recognized as the truth and as the right thing for him to have said. She was ashamed of herself, grateful to him, and they were closer as friends after the reconciliation. Their relationship was deepened and even more solidly based on trust, intimacy, mutual vulnerability, and caring. You see, my friend would say, that's the role of truth telling in friendship. It's that simple. Friends tell the truth to each other.

Right. But let me tell you what happened next. Before Abby left his office, Stuart told her that he had given her name to another prospective client, a very big copyright case. Stuart was afraid Abby was still hurt by his criticism, was losing confidence in herself, and he was still worried about her financial well-being. He felt he had to do something. This news visibly brightened Abby's mood, and she left in a hurry to start reading up on the technical details of copyright, with visions of a rosier future just ahead; more importantly, she had proof that Stuart still believed in her. His timing was perfect. When she left, Stuart made a phone call. He was relieved to find the prospective client in so he could now really give him Abby's name and recommend her.

In telling Abby that he had already recommended her, he actually had lied to her, and he lied for the very same reason he had for telling her the truth earlier: he thought it was in her best interests. He deceived her into thinking what he wanted her to think by saying something that was not true at the time he said it. Then he did what he could to make it true after the fact. What shall we call this if not deception? Retroactive truth telling? Leveraged truth telling? Lag time truth telling? However we qualify it, it's deception. And in this case, it's an act of friendship, too.

Stuart has given us, by saying something that was not true at the time, but later fortunately becomes true, an example of a deception created for the sake of friendship, intended to serve his friend's best interests. In fact, Abby has greater reason to trust Stuart now than she did before he lied to her. Why is that? It's because he has proved himself imaginative in figuring out ways to help her without causing harm; with her best interest at heart, he was able to rise above the principle of truth telling and do something that really made her life better. She can trust him to look after her, and that's a far greater and profounder gift of friendship than mere truth telling.

Trust in the Truth and Trust in the Person

The function of trust, I think, is to provide some confident expectation in a relationship. My friend would agree with me on that, I trust. Still, we differ, and our difference lies in a further distinction to be made in the definition of the word "trust." The *Shorter Oxford English Dictionary* helps point out this distinction when it explains that trust means "confidence in or reliance on some quality or attribute of a person or thing, *or* the truth of a statement." The key is that little word "or." Trust in friendship does not *exclusively* mean trust in the truth of your friend's statements. It also means reliance on some quality or attribute of your friend, a quality such as discretion, which is having tact with regard to the truth, or wisdom, which is having the good sense to know that not everything that *could* be said *should* be said, or resourcefulness, which is the capacity to make happen what should happen but won't happen unless somebody does something to nudge it along. Of course there is a role for truth telling in all of this, but as Stuart showed in his shrewd way of taking care of Abby, there is a role for deception, too. Trusting a person to look after your best interests is different from trusting a person never to deceive you. There are *some* things the jester should not tell his king.

HYPOCRISY CAN BE A VIRTUE

In French aristocratic life before the revolution of 1789, hypocrisy was a virtue. After the war, Robespierre and his fellow leaders declared it the greatest crime. "Purity of the heart and a passionate hatred of hypocrisy emerged as the primary virtues of those who would fight against all manner of social injustice."[10] The idea that public life and politics should in many ways be separated from private thoughts and personal morality was accepted as a necessary condition of citizenry before Robespierre's view prevailed. His view denied on moral grounds that there should be any distinction between public and private life.

> As a consequence, public ordeals of self-inspection and public protestations of honesty and purity of soul became necessary for all public actors. What thus appears in public is the naked self, indeed the moral self, who invites communal approval. But this is only ostensibly so because the suspicion of hypocrisy, of play-acting can never be entirely eliminated. Since one does not and cannot trust completely the veracity and the authenticity of one's own motives, those of others are less likely to inspire confidence and trust.[11]

This is an attack on the very idea of politics as the arena of public debate which thrives on compromise. It is a suggestion that a morality of absolute goodness, based upon the supreme value of unmasked truthfulness, replace any idea of a separate public realm. As it played out after the revolution, this morality perverted not only politics but morality itself.

Let's assume we don't want to live with the frankness of the stable as the norm for establishing our relations with each other. Does that mean necessarily that we must all become hypocrites? And must our hypocrisy be as suspect today as it was among the prerevolutionary French aristocracy? I think hypocrisy is here to stay, for a good reason, but in defending this point it is not necessary to defend the French or any other aristocracy. As an example, let's look at a column Jeff Greenfield wrote shortly after Al Campanis, a Los Angeles Dodgers executive with forty years experience in organized baseball, lost his job because he spoke frankly in a televised interview with Ted Koppel that marked the fortieth anniversary of major league baseball's integration—Jackie Robinson's debut with the Dodgers. Here is what Greenfield thinks happened:

> Asked why there are no black field managers or general managers in the game, Campanis said it wasn't because of prejudice but because "I truly believe that they may not have some of the necessities to be, let's say, a field manager or perhaps a general manager."
>
> As a "Nightline" correspondent, I have worked with anchor Ted Koppel for four years. I do not believe I have ever seen him so utterly stunned by an answer to a simple question. He invited Campanis to take another crack at the question. It got worse.
>
> "I don't say all of them, but how many quarterbacks do you have? How many pitchers do you have that are black? So it just might be—why are black men, or black people, not good swimmers? Because they don't have the buoyancy."
>
> By all accounts, Al Campanis is a decent and humane man who encouraged the development of black and Hispanic players, scouts and front-office personnel. Why, then, did the Dodgers fire him because of one appearance?
>
> Campanis was fired for lack of hypocrisy; that is, for expressing openly the opinions held by a good percentage of those who hire and fire in the world of sports—or for that matter, in finance, politics and journalism.
>
> Any public figure—candidate, baseball executive or journalist—who lacks the hypocrisy necessary to keep bigotry private is too dumb to be allowed out in public.[12]

Greenfield is surely right in recognizing the important difference between what we *think* about other people and what we *say* about what we think. Bigotry is learned by listening to bigots. If we can't change the bigot's views, we can at least use convention to muzzle

him in public in order to minimize his effectiveness, whether deliberate or inadvertent, as a teacher of bigotry to the young. In this
regard, the convention of hypocrisy can easily be considered a virtue, a minor virtue perhaps, but nevertheless a contribution to the
greater welfare of our society.

We should try to do whatever we can do to eliminate the
perniciousness of prejudice. Of course we would prefer to convert
the bigots, but that is not a practicable alternative in many cases.
Next best is to lessen their chances of spreading their odious beliefs
by inhibiting their expression. If that means, by unspoken agreement, that we expect some hypocrisy in the public forum, then so
be it.

Social progress can be marked by what some people do not
allow themselves to say in public.

EMOTIONAL LABOR

In her book *The Managed Heart*, Arlie Russell Hochschild
has written discerningly about what she calls "emotional labor" in
certain occupations, and in social life more generally. For example,
her study of flight attendants showed that "the *emotional style of
offering the service is part of the service itself*, in a way that loving or
hating wallpaper is not a part of producing wallpaper." In processing wallpaper, the product is wallpaper; however, in processing
people, "the product is a state of mind." Emotional labor

> requires one to induce or suppress feeling in order to
> sustain the outward countenance that produces the
> proper state of mind in others—in this case, the
> sense of being cared for in a convivial and safe place.
> This kind of labor calls for a coordination of mind
> and feeling, and it sometimes draws on a source
> of self that we honor as deep and integral to our
> individuality.[13]

This "coordination of mind and feeling," plus the next step of co-
ordinating the product of mind and feeling with actions calculated
to produce in somebody "the proper state of mind" for the situation, is a pretty good start at describing institutionalized, or so-
cialized, deception. For the emotional laborer there is a danger of

self-alienation, but the benefits of emotional labor can be considerable, too.

> Any functioning society makes effective use of its members' emotional labor. We do not think twice about the use of feeling in the theater, or in psychotherapy, or in forms of group life that we admire. It is when we come to speak of the exploitation of the bottom by the top in any society that we become morally concerned. In any system, exploitation depends on the actual distribution of many kinds of profits—money, authority, status, honor, well-being. It is not emotional labor itself, but the underlying system of recompense that raises the question of what the cost of it is.[14]

"Managed human feeling" has an artificial sound to it that puts many people off, in the way my friend was put off by the idea that deception could play an important, even a necessary role in friendship. We have a high regard for "natural feeling," and sometimes we seem to revere spontaneity or authenticity as if they were our most treasured virtues. The cultivation of these virtues in fact has been a focus of humanistic psychotherapy since the late 1960s. But most of us also realize the value of self-willed inhibition, and do not behave as though the exhibition of "spontaneous feeling" were the order of the day. As we have learned from Freud's rich psychological images, life is a constant navigation between the Scylla of free expression and the Charybdis of inhibition. Steering a course too close to either would be disastrous. The spectacle of actions and passions unregulated by thought (in others at least, if not in ourselves) is unnerving. Deep down we know very well that unmanaged human feeling is a general disadvantage in getting what we want, that it is a serious threat to order, to confident expectation, to trust, all of which we need in our friendships as well as our other relationships.[15] On the other hand, overmanaged feeling can lead to debilitating neurosis.

Arofa

Both the private and the public side of social life call for the management of feeling. The Hopi culture has a word for this:

"arofa," which means "feelings-as-contribution-to-the-group." In Hochschild's words, "muted anger, conjured gratitude, and suppressed envy are offerings back and forth from parent to child, wife to husband, friend to friend, and lover to lover."[16] Offerings of the edited truth back and forth—that's not a bad way to describe what we easily and frequently do contribute, day to day, in friendship, family life, teaching, flight attending, and all the other occupations that call for at least some emotional labor. (See, for an example, Patricia Neal's handling of Gary Cooper's gift of a polka-dot dress, described in chapter 4.)

THE ALTRUISTIC PERSONALITY

In their study of rescuers of Jews in Nazi Europe, Samuel and Pearl Oliner discovered some traits that are common to what they call "the altruistic personality." Key among these is the value of caring as compared with the value of equity, or justice. They explain the difference this way:

> Whereas equity is directed toward the welfare of society as a whole, based on abstract principles of fairness, care is concerned with the welfare of people without necessary regard for fairness. Whereas equity is based on reciprocity, care endorses a willingness to give more than is received. Whereas equity emphasizes fair procedures, care insists on benevolence and kindness. Equity asks that we do our duty in accordance with reason, but care insists that we act out of concern. While equity may be administered blindly—the image of Justice, blindfolded, holding her scales, is apt—care can only be given by a human face. While equity asks that we act out of a sense of self-interest as well as the interests of others, care focuses on the interests of others. Equity is based on honesty, truthfulness, and respect; care, however, can require fraud and deceitfulness. In this sense, care goes beyond what can reasonably and fairly be expected of humans in society, beginning to approach the unreasonable and the unfair.[17]

The Oliners' extensive interview data reveal that as children, a significantly higher percentage of rescuers, as compared with nonrescuers and bystanders, had learned ethical values such as the need to be helpful, concerned, generous, and expansive, while both rescuers and nonrescuers spoke frequently of their parents' concern with equity. It is interesting to note that the rescuers highlighted their parents' teaching about honesty above all other values, considering that

> while having to establish and cement trust with their colleagues in rescue, rescuers' lives were simultaneously dominated by deception; it was the absolute and enduring requirement for saving Jews. Deception was more than lying; it included trickery, subterfuge, and secrecy, striving to avoid notice and creating confusion. It began in hiding the victims from the occupier; eventually it extended to family, friends, and neighbors.[18]

For example, the Oliners tell how a Polish woman who was hiding a Jew in her apartment "hit on a masterful strategy that won her some disapproval but worked" to get rid of a suitor who would visit often unexpectedly. Her "boyfriend" stopped visiting altogether when he noticed that a photograph of a handsome Nazi officer who was stationed nearby had been hung over her bed.

An equally ingenious Dutchwoman deceived her neighbors about the impending birth of a Jewish baby in her home by "progressively padding herself with layers of clothing, letting others believe she was pregnant. None were surprised when a new baby appeared in the house."[19]

Sometimes deception of family members that was followed much later by disclosure resulted in new and deep bonds of respect. A German woman deceived her daughter and husband about the true identity of the Jewish man she was hiding in their home:

> I had told them only that his place was bombed out and that he had no place to live. I didn't tell them that he was Jewish and also a well-known Jew, a man of considerable reputation in the world of commerce. But the time came when I had to tell my husband. "I wonder how he'll react to that?" I thought. I bought some wine, and after we had drunk a little I told

him the truth. He swallowed hard, looked up at me and said, "Well, Paulachen, we've managed to get through so far with him, we'll get him the rest of the way through." Well, after that I knew what kind of husband I had. Life doesn't always give us such situations and opportunities. What a gem![20]

The moral complexity of deception is revealed in the rescuers' understanding that even though lying and secrecy was "wrong," it was nevertheless absolutely the right thing to do in the circumstances. In the words of a Dutchwoman, "I could lie really well then, but I did not lie to kill, I lied to save." One mother who was trying to help her children develop a moral point of view in the context of all this confusion explained that "one of the greatest problems in that period of our lives was on the one hand teaching them to lie in these circumstances, and on the other hand reprimanding them when they lied for other purposes, and understanding the differences between the lies."[21]

Many of these rescuers shared with André Trocmé the resolute need to avoid lying "technically." The Oliners report one witty ploy: "Faced with a nosy and untrustworthy neighbor, a woman recalled saying to her: 'I wouldn't have a single Jewish person in the house'—she had two of them."[22]

The morality of deception for these heroic, caring, righteous people must be understood in the big picture, the particularities of the time:

> The power that had taken over their lives was awesome and could indeed control much of their behavior—but not all of it. Deception was a fundamental tool for undermining that power, it was a way for the self to assert its own will. Used in the service of saving lives, rescuers had no doubt or hesitancy regarding its appropriateness. Defying the Nazi rules of destruction in whatever way possible was itself a moral victory.[23]

Integrity

Integrity, like altruism, is a complex idea that is connected both with conventional standards of morality such as honesty, truth telling, and fairness, and with personal ideals that may very well come into conflict with conventional morality. The merchant who always gives a fair measure and is careful to make the proper change for goods guaranteed to be what they appear to be has integrity in the conventional sense. The independent artist who refuses to "bow" to convention represents the other side of the coin. Consider the "unconventional" integrity of Stephen Dedalus' declaration of his independence from all conventional authority:

> Look here, Cranly, he said. You have asked me what I would do and what I would not do. I will tell you what I will do and what I will not do. I will not serve that in which I no longer believe, whether it call itself my home, my fatherland, or my church: and I will try to express myself in some mode of life or art as freely as I can and as wholly as I can, using for my defence the only arms I allow myself to use—silence, exile, and cunning.[24]

Indeed. Silence, exile, and cunning. Here is a prescription for the use of guile, wiliness, and duplicity, all in the service of personal ideals that can best be described as principles of integrity and honesty—the promise to tell the truth to oneself if not to others.

WHAT IS FRIENDSHIP FOR?

One purpose of friendship is to gain for oneself, and to provide for the other, a deeper self-understanding. But there also are times when the function of a friend is to provide a home for the soul, a place of rest, perhaps a good excuse for putting off the demands of truth-driven self-improvement to another day. Graham Greene, who got to the heart of so many matters, gets to the heart of this one, too:

> The truth, he thought, has never been of any real value to any human being—it is a symbol for mathematicians and philosophers to pursue. In human relations kindness and lies are worth a thousand truths.[25]

8 RAISING CHILDREN: THE RIGHT TRUTH AT THE RIGHT TIME

Whatever satisfies the soul is truth.

Walt Whitman

Apart from the known and the unknown, what else is there?

Harold Pinter

The most famous truth telling tale in America is about George Washington as a six-year-old, confessing, hatchet in hand, that he had hacked to bits his father's beautiful young English cherry tree. Here's the scene as it was described in *The Life of George Washington* by Parson Mason Locke Weems (1806):

> "*George,*" said his father, "do you know who killed that beautiful little cherry tree yonder in the garden?" This was a *tough question;* and George staggered under it for a moment; but quickly recovered himself: and looking at his father, with the sweet face of youth brightened with the inexpressible charm of all-conquering truth, he bravely cried out, "I can't tell a lie, Pa; you know I can't tell a lie. I did cut it with my hatchet,"—"Run to my arms, you dearest boy," cried his father in transports, "run to my arms; glad am I, George, that you killed my tree; for you have paid me for it a thousandfold. Such an act of heroism in my son is more worth than a thousand trees, though blossomed with silver, and their fruits of purest gold."

And so little George is safely conducted for a lifetime in greatest happiness along the paths of honest virtue.

The splendid and revealing irony is that the story is not true, it never happened to young George. Not only is it a fabrication, it is also plagiarized—by a parson! The Reverend Mr. Weems saw fit to lift the tale from a story by Dr. James Beattie, "The Minstrel," published in London seven years earlier.[1] So, for over a hundred years American school children have been taught always to tell the truth by being told a lie in a story plagiarized by a man of God. Of course this is not the only lie we use to teach children not to lie; it is just the best known one.

> The Teachers said, "Tell the truth, no matter what."
> "I won't lie," I lied.
> The Teachers were satisfied and said, "That's good. That's very, very good."

The point of the story remains a good one: children should not be afraid to tell their parents the truth when they have done something wrong (especially if they are caught holding the hatchet). In such cases, honesty may well lead to greater love, not less, from one's parents. But how different things would be—or would they?—if we made Parson Weems the subject of the lesson, along with George. To do that we would have to begin the lesson with the assumption that truth telling is not always a simple matter, that sometimes people are less than honest in doing what they think is right, and that deception is not always bad. This story, stolen and false though it is, has become part of our culture and is certainly a valuable fixture in parents' and teachers' attempts at moral education. But the fact that Parson Weems resorted to deception in order to make his point about honesty in such a memorable way should not be overlooked. That fact is part of the story, too. If parents and teachers decide to conceal the Parson's own deception, or postpone talking about it until the children are older, then they will also have to admit to their own complicity in this ongoing ruse, this careful selection of the right truth about truth telling. I think the reality is that both honesty and deception aid us in the manufacture of important messages; together, in some kind of balance between excess and deficiency, they help us determine many fascinating ways of getting along with each other, and getting on with business.

DID YOU TELL ME THE RIGHT TRUTH, DADDY?

One fall afternoon, when he was three, my son Noah climbed onto my lap in a big chair we often shared. We did a lot of talking there, both the serious kind and the whimsical, so I wasn't surprised when he asked, "What does 'French' mean, Daddy?"

Nevertheless, his question took me up short. I had no immediate idea how to answer. To give myself time to think I complimented him (I do this all the time with my students when they ask questions I can't answer): "That's a very good question, Son. You ask such delightful questions." Where to begin? He looked almost solemn; his little face was fixed in a pose of complete attention, showing an unselfconscious readiness to absorb what I had to say in his intense, three-year-old effort to understand everything.

What exactly did he want to know? He wasn't able to explain. Was his interest in the language, the people, Julia Child's TV program about French cooking, had he heard about French kissing, taking French leave, French cuffs, French dressing, French fried potatoes . . . what could it be? Uncertain in my purpose, I began to talk about French people and culture, trying to teach him what a culture is and how different nations have different languages, customs, and so forth—on and on, hoping to touch on some point of particular interest to him. It became clear as I struggled along in this conversation that there could be many right, good, truthful answers to his question, and that my task was to find the one to suit the situation, even though neither one of us could be perfectly sure which one it was.

I could see in his expression a mild but definite transformation from intense interest to patient indulgence. I had clearly missed the mark. This was not what he wanted to know about "French." Disappointed, he turned and looked quizzically into my eyes and said: "Did you tell me the right truth, Daddy?"

Telling the truth takes two people: one to speak it and one

to hear it. If the speaker and the listener are not on the same page, are not clearly coordinated as to purpose, getting the truth expressed rightly can be a problem.

Most of us are familiar and comfortable with the phrases "the *real* truth," "the unvarnished truth," "the truth, the whole truth, and nothing but the truth." These phrases suggest that in truth telling there is no choice: there is the truth, and if you know it, you have only one thing to say. People may be mistaken about their understanding of it, but the truth is the truth. One truth. The truth.

But consider this:

> *Teacher:* Have you finished reading the book I assigned last week?
> *Student:* No, I'm not finished quite yet. It's difficult to . . . umm . . . comprehend. You can't read this book quickly.

What the student does not say is: "I read about two pages of each chapter, then threw it across the room because it was so boring. It's pointless . . . and too difficult."

Both answers are true. The first is focused on the literal point of the question—whether the student has finished reading the book. The second, unspoken answer addresses a question that wasn't explicitly asked but is in some ways more important, and much more risky—what the student thinks about the assignment and the teacher. In this example, the student is able to select one truth that emphasizes a single point of fact, while hiding another truth about a range of personal feelings. He makes the selection of which truth to tell for the purpose of conveying an impression of seriousness, which he hopes will incline the teacher to give him more time for the assignment and in effect give him a second chance at learning something the teacher believes worthwhile. Assuming the student takes advantage of the second chance, it is possible, even likely, that this particular use of the "right" truth in order to mislead the teacher will produce a happy educational result.

Some teachers are aware of this ploy but pretend to be un-

aware of it. They reply instead with a little added pressure by selecting their own truth of higher expectation. They will say to the
student: "I'm pleased that you seem to be taking such care in reading the book; the class and I will benefit from your . . . umm . . .
comprehension. Let's focus next time on your report." What the
teacher does not say is something like this: "I don't believe you are
as serious as you want me to think you are. I also doubt your ability
to gain much from this book. However, you must try as hard as
you can anyway; it is not my job to discourage you, and who
knows—stranger things have happened—you might surprise us,
and yourself, by discovering that you can do the work."

That would not be the right thing to say to a student who
was struggling, whose own interests were unclear, whose talents
were yet undeveloped and undiscovered. Teachers try to focus their
efforts on prompting success, not predicting failure. Prompting
success often requires the careful selection of the right truth, so as
to be encouraging, and the hiding of another, so as not to be over-
bearing. This is truth telling; it is not lying, but it is at least partially
deceptive.

There is choice in truth telling; we do have a range of truths
to tell. Many questions do have more than one truthful answer. It
may sound strange to say so, but I think the virtue of truth telling
is determined by just this kind of selectivity. We ought to try for
the right truth in the right amount in order to produce the best
effects for the people involved. In other words, it is probably better
to tell the right truth rather than the whole truth or no truth at all.

What may sound even stranger, come to think of it, is that
we can say the same about deception—its virtue also consists in the
right amount between excess and deficiency. There is a certain
amount of deception needed in selecting the right truth—if by deception we mean showing or emphasizing some things while hiding others, in an artful display intended to create a well-managed
impression or idea in somebody's mind.

THE ETIQUETTE OF LYING

Mark Twain once said in his *Notebooks* that "good breeding
consists in concealing how much we think of ourselves, and how

little we think of other persons." Gloria Skurzynski explored a variation of this broad truth in her charming book for children, *Honest Andrew,*[2] in which little Andrew Otter gets caught lying (he threw away his supper but denied it because he didn't want to hurt his mother's feelings). His father gives him a stern talk about honesty, starting with the traditional motto: An Otter Ought to Be Honest. After listening to a few George Washington–type examples provided by his father, Andrew promises always to tell the truth.

The next day Andrew keeps his promise. On a walk with his mother, he meets a beaver who asks him how he is. Andrew takes the question seriously and answers in detail, at great length. His mother scolds him for talking so much and boring the beaver. Then comes Aunt Prissy Porcupine who declares, "Why, you're quite a big otter, Andrew." Andrew loudly denies this and is criticized for being sassy. His next encounter is with Mrs. Woodchuck and her baby, of whom his mother asks Andrew, "Isn't she darling?" Andrew takes a look and replies, "Darling? She's ugly. Her face is all wrinkled. She looks like she slid facedown on a mud slide." Naturally, his mother is embarrassed and enraged. That evening, when his father angrily asks why he had been so rude, boring, insulting, and hurtful, Andrew answers that he was trying to make his papa proud of him by being honest and truthful. "But you musn't hurt people's feelings," his papa warns. Andrew is choking back his tears when he says, "Last night I was trying not to hurt mama's feelings when I really hated crayfish. You got mad at me then because I didn't tell the truth." Papa Otter droops; he is confused himself and doesn't know what to say. "Papa," Andrew says, "is this what I should do? Should I always tell the truth, but be as nice and polite about it as I can?" Papa is relieved and exclaims "Yes! That's it! That's *exactly* what you should do."

Mama Otter serves salamander stew for supper. Andrew sags in his chair. "Mama," he says, "you are the sweetest, nicest mama in the whole world. Your eyes are big and bright. Your fur is warm and soft. You wear pretty earrings, and I HATE SALAMANDER STEW!"

The whole Otter family has a hard time with the truism that

good manners are inconceivable without the lie. We all have good manners, more or less; that means we're all good at the etiquette of lying, and of deceiving by selecting the right truth to tell and the right truth to hide. In fact, we often pride ourselves on our mastery of the art of selecting and weighing exactly what truth we say to whom.

My First Japanese Hamburger

As a teenager I spent a summer in Japan living with a family in which the mother was very shy and had almost no English. Since I had almost no Japanese, we felt our way along together in mutual sympathy and had great fun trying to teach each other about our respective languages, customs, special pleasures and so forth. One day she pointed questioningly to the contents of a letter I had just received. In reply to my description of the exotic Japanese diet I was struggling to enjoy, a friend had sent a full color ad for a "Big Mac." Mama-san wanted to know what it was, so I explained "hamburger and fries" and added that it was one of the things my friends and I liked to eat. She seemed satisfied and said no more about it.

Two days later the family and I were gathered at the table for lunch and mama-san was beaming with nervous pleasure. She had made a treat for me.

There on the plate was her translation of "hamburger and fries." Between two thick slabs of stale white bread was a slathering of mashed potatoes mixed with a few tiny lumps of ground beef that had been boiled. It was a huge, dry, sticky, mashed potato sandwich prepared especially for me. I knew she had gone to great efforts even to find these ingredients. Her eldest son made some rude remark about giving it to the dogs, but she kept her eyes on me.

She'll never know how abashed I was, nor will she know the difficulty I had in getting that awful stuff down my throat. I hid all that because I loved her for what she had tried to do. In fact, at that moment, I loved her enough to look her in the eye and lie outright. In the best Japanese I could muster, I exclaimed that her "hamburger and fries" was delicious, that I was enjoying my special meal

very much, and I asked whether it would be possible to have sec-
onds. (The dogs were undoubtedly more sincere in expressing their
pleasure with the leftovers, but they weren't more convincing.)

My Japanese mother had the right to be deceived just as surely as
she had the right to the truth. There are times when the truth can
destroy self-image, self-respect, and the intimacy generated by loving gestures. In these circumstances, when there is a way to avoid
the literal truth it should be taken. I think extolling the right to
truth and denying the complementary right to be deceived is to
misunderstand one of the important elements of moral decency,
which is to tell the truth selectively and deceive with discretion so
that others can find reason for self-respect and be spared suffering
whenever possible.

   Andrew Otter's solution was always to tell the truth, but
nicely and politely. His somewhat fumbled attempt to do that at
the end of the story is funny, and it works to get him out of a
bind. If only it were that easy for grown-ups, too! But it isn't. His
perspective is that of a child, his world is the fabrication of a
storyteller.

   As he gets older, Andrew will learn that it may take some
humility to deceive, even to lie, and lie well, when it is necessary
to avoid injuring a person, shattering peace, violating privacy, or
ruining self-confidence. People who steadfastly refuse to deceive or
to lie out of pridefulness in their own virtue as truth tellers will
suffer as surely as will the rest of us sinners, but they'll suffer for
sins of vanity.

THE BEST THINGS IN LIFE DON'T MAKE SENSE

   In 1897, as Christmas approached, eight-year-old Virginia
O'Hanlon thought she was old enough for her father to give her a
straight answer to an important question; but he didn't, so she
wrote a letter to the editor of the *New York Sun:* "Please tell me the
truth, is there a Santa Claus?" Editor Francis Church replied with
his now famous, seasonally celebrated lie. He said, "Yes, Virginia,
there is a Santa Claus." Was it wicked of Mr. Church (a newspaper

man!) to lie to Virginia like that? What should you say when some skeptical yet gullible little child asks, "If Santa comes down the chimney, how come he never gets dirty?"

Some parents, and even some child psychologists, undoubtedly think the best policy is to take a hard line in favor of truth telling. They might argue that the truth about Santa helps kids develop a sense of reality, so they can learn early to see the world for what it is. Or, if it's morally good to tell the truth to people, and if children are people, then it's morally good to tell the truth to children. Or, if you deceive your kids and they find out later that you did, which they surely will in this case, they won't trust you and they might learn not to trust other people because of you. Some might even call on the authority of Socrates, who thought all poets and storytellers ought to be banished, or at least forbidden to associate with children, because what they said was untrue. He knew of course that children love to listen to fanciful tales, and that they cannot easily know whether what they are listening to is true or not, which means their heads become filled with falsities that they later on have to unlearn if they are ever to know the truth. Socrates saw no point at all in learning anything that was not true. He had no kind words for poetic artists of the imagination.

The hard-line view has four parts to it: it is good for children to see the world realistically; it is morally right to tell the truth to all people, including children; truth telling teaches children to trust their parents; and learning what isn't true when you are young makes it inefficient and difficult to learn what is true later in life. As for this last claim, I don't know of any evidence that demonstrates a harmful effect of stories, myths, and romantic exaggerations on later learning. In fact, there is some reason to believe the story-telling model ought to be used more extensively in the early phases of education because it best suits the way young children's minds perceive the world, and therefore is best suited to stimulate thinking skills, imagination, and positive attitudes about learning in general.[3] As for the claim that truth telling teaches children to trust their parents, I can only repeat (see chapter 7) that there are other bases of trust that are equally important, especially to children, who need to feel taken care of and who need help in developing a strong positive sense of themselves, even at the cost of strict veracity.

THE SHARP EDGES OF REALITY

I wonder why it is so morally important to the hard-liners that children be exposed to the truth rather than at times protected from it, and see the world realistically instead of imaginatively? It seems to me that the moral character of a choice to deceive a child should be assessed according to the child's capacity for judgment. If a child hasn't yet the capacity for independent reasoning and certain rational judgments, then the so-called right to relevant information, which is often presumed among adults, doesn't clearly or automatically apply. Really, is it a good idea for kids to play with the sharp edges of reality as we older ones know it? When we snuggle in bed with our sons and daughters at night, just before sleep, and they ask innocent questions about some loathsome thing they overheard on the evening news or on the playground, should we speak of human nature candidly, let them in on the ever-presence of violence, the cruel enigma of disease, the ravages of madness and greed—the horror, the horror? If a child happens to be sick, should we discuss the limitations of medical knowledge, or should we say, "Take this stuff and you'll feel better"? What does a child need before sleep, reality or comfort? Sometimes a good myth, some barely plausible magic, something tantalizing though contrary to the day's reality, is just the right thing to sleep on.

Childhood is a time of myths and fantasy. Adults can employ fictions of many kinds for the children's benefit. Parents ought to keep the fantasies going as long as the kids are enthralled. There is no great difference between saying "Take this medicine and you'll feel better" and "Listen to this story and you'll feel better." The point is to help the kids feel better about being in this iffy world, withstanding rather than withdrawing, wobbling along aided by our love for them. Children troubled with unrealistic fears need unrealistic hope; realistic stories can be deeply disappointing.[4] There is such a thing as too much information. And there is the wrong kind of information. Childhood can be unnecessarily, harmfully foreshortened by too much of the wrong kind of information. That is a big truth which needs protection from the righteous attack of a lot of literal little truths.

This is not to say that all stories and fantasies are totally unrelated to the truth. Stories contain truths, just not literal ones. A good story is a step or two ahead of, above, or beneath the truth. It is the air around the truth that gives the truth a place to be. "Is there a Santa?" the child asks. "I don't know because I've never seen him; but he is supposed to be very, very clever—more clever than I am, anyway. So I'm not surprised I've never seen him. Maybe that's the way it has to be if he is to make so many people happy in such a short time—everybody wants to see him and talk to him, but that would slow him down too much. So he has to slip in and out when nobody is looking, to avoid conversation." Did I lie? No. Did I tell the truth? Not exactly. I did tell a story about the truth, though. I aimed the child's attention at a vision of someone who takes care of children and always will do so as long as there's a world. Did I deceive? Well, if I didn't tell the truth, and I didn't lie outright, but I did tell a story that was meant to misrepresent reality as I take it to be for the purpose of keeping a fantasy alive in the child's mind, then yes, I guess I did deceive. I did not ask the child to face reality, or tell the literal truth about Santa, because I was thinking about that child's unvoiced hope of being taken care of always, and I was trying to teach the feeling that some of the things we can't see and can't fully understand are not scary and are lovely to think about. Sometimes deceiving children about Santa's mysterious powers, to keep fantasy alive, is more valuable than truthfully explaining that Santa doesn't get dirty from sliding down those chimneys because the whole idea of Santa is phony from the start.

What better way to tuck a child into bed than with the endlessly surprising and exciting possibilities of "What if . . ."?

THE DEVELOPMENT OF DECEPTION IN CHILDREN

It comes as no surprise to many parents when psychologists tell us that children learn early and well, even before they can talk, to manage all kinds of information so as to get what they want.

Having learned to bring mom by crying when they are hungry, they learn to bring mom by crying when they aren't hungry; they try to blame the dog for spilling the milk they spilled themselves; they hide the broken toy, and if caught they say, "I didn't do it, but if I did I'm sorry"; they mask their feelings while telling a lie by smiling and appearing relaxed—all of this and lots more without the benefit of instruction.

Of course, children have to polish their skills; they're not all experts at the beginning. Here is an example of an early attempt at deception that failed.

"Daddy, can I have a fruit roll-up?" My four-year-old son had asked for a sweet treat at that time of the late afternoon known to all children and parents as "before supper," a sort of no-man's-land for growling tummies. The usual reply is "Not before supper," but this time I said, "Sure." (His mother was out and I was busy writing, so I wanted to avoid a prolonged discussion.) A few minutes later I went to his room and saw him, treat in hand, fresh and unwrapped, unnibbled. "Only one before supper," I said. He froze. His eyes, in alert intensity, darted from side to side. He said nothing. He looked like an animal whose fight-or-flight boundary had been unexpectedly penetrated. "Okay?" I asked, "Only one?" He nodded, slowly and only once, but said nothing, clutching his treat. By now I suspected that he had just opened the *second* fruit roll-up, having devoured the first in a ravenous rush. Here, in his sticky fingers, was the topper, and Daddy had just tried to extract a promise that he wouldn't eat it. I know he loves me and wants very much to do everything I ask. But this was a . . . sticky situation. Instinctively, he guarded his options. He nodded but did not speak, to introduce a little ambiguity in his response, probably. I asked, "Is that the second one, Son?" He stared into my brain— was it a real question or did I already know? He couldn't move. "Just tell me the truth, and I'll let you have that one." Now that sounded like the solution he was looking for, so he said, "Yes, it is the second. Will you really let me have it?" "Yes," I answered, "and remember it's okay to tell me the truth."

At four years old, he was able to anticipate consequences, and was motivated to manage information to avoid what he anticipated, but he was perhaps a few months away from being able to pull off the scheme. I say a few months because the same child at age five offered me a carefully printed page entitled "The Recipe for Deception" with ingredients listed in descending order of quantity:

The Recipe for Deception
Changing the subject
Imagination
Mischief
Truth
Lying

I was astonished then, as I am still, at the sophistication of this young child's understanding of deception. Where on earth did it come from?

Research on Children's Deception

The formal study of deception in children began in 1928 with Hugh Hartshorne and Mark May's landmark book *Studies in Deceit*.[5] The authors were interested in measuring three types of deception: cheating, stealing, and lying. Their study is psychological, statistical, and descriptive: their results are presented as a fabric of interesting and suggestive correlations, not causal explanations.

The authors begin their report with this preliminary statement: "One of the most interesting episodes of the history of character is the transition from this natural state of universal deception to a social order whose very foundation is its negation . . . the practice of deception is far older than language."[6] They see deception (from the bottom up) as a background for the emergence of nondeceptive, honest behavior; they see it as more natural than the necessarily contrived (top-down) social order that places a premium on the stabilizing effects of truth telling. In this sense, deception is more "natural" than truth telling, or to use their term, "honesty." Like deception, they explain,

> honesty appears to be a congeries of specialized acts which are closely tied up with particular features of the situation in which deception is a possibility, and is apparently not greatly dependent on any general ideal or trait of honesty. Motives for cheating, lying

and stealing are highly complex, and are specialized just as are the acts of deception. The most common extraneous motive [among the school children they studied] is the desire to do well in class.[7]

Consistent with their view of honesty, the authors take a general position on moral behavior that they call the doctrine of specificity. According to this doctrine, no one is honest or dishonest by nature. Rather, "a trait such as honesty or dishonesty is an achievement like ability in arithmetic, depending of course on native capacities of various kinds, but *consisting* in the achieved skills and attitudes of more or less successful and uniform performance."[8] These deceptive skills and attitudes show up as attributes of the child's mode of adjustment to the conflicts in the environment, and their routine development would seem to be guaranteed, because

> as long as there is conflict between the teacher and the school authorities generally on the one side, and the pupils on the other, there will be deception. . . . If there is anything in school procedure which puts a premium on subterfuge, it would be folly to imagine that any teaching of honesty, whether in school or out, would greatly alter the actual practice of the children.[9]

Children learn naturally to use deception in adjusting to conflict in their environment, even before going to school. Hartshorne and May's overall conclusion is that everybody deceives, that all children will cheat, lie, and steal in the "right" circumstances and there is not much of anything we can do about it. They do suggest an approach, though, that emphasizes modifying behavior by structuring the environment rather than by direct instruction: don't teach honesty as a trait, but reconstruct school practices to provide regular opportunities for teachers and students to act honestly. The authors believe that children must experience honesty as a "natural and rewarding behavior" in situations where they are "ethically at home" in order to develop the self-mastery necessary to control deceit in other areas of life.

While Hartshorne and May were pioneers in measuring children's deceptive behavior, Jean Piaget was the first to study children's conceptions of lying together with their understanding of intentionality.[10] Piaget's interviews with children showed that their understanding of lying progressed from viewing it as using naughty words, to making untrue statements (errors, mistakes), and finally to making intentionally false statements. More generally, Piaget showed that "the child's ability to engage in or cope with lying rests upon his or her communicative competence, perspective-taking skill, and appreciation of intentionality."[11] These are basic aspects of the ability to deceive and, as George Herbert Mead has illustrated through his notion of the "generalized other," they are also basic aspects of human social intelligence in general.[12]

Having learned to share a common perspective through language, children at around the age of six years experience a budding awareness that not everybody's perspective is the same. Other people see things differently, and it is possible to learn how to see as they do; it is possible to take another person's perspective. This monumental cognitive breakthrough makes moral empathy possible, but at the same time it makes a new kind of deception possible—deception not about things, but about states of mind, about intention. In this first phase of empathetic awareness, however, the child is apt to think his own inner state is private, even though he can know the other's. Thus, while carrying out a cunning plan the child does not even try to disguise his motives, which are "childishly" obvious to the observer. Within a short time, the child will realize that with regard to perspective-taking, others can do to him what he can do to them, and will become able to perceive self and other in a reciprocal relationship at the same time. Given this new understanding, successful deception calls for concealment of his own state of mind as well as concealment of his planned action.

Jules Henry thought that "in the interest of mental health, it would be important to know how, spontaneously, so many children, knowing the world to be fake, learn how to deal with it without going mad, while others never learn—either that it is fake or how to deal with it."[13] He went on to generalize that "sanity is nothing more than the capacity to deal with falseness, in a false world; and it can take three forms—Albee's, which is to believe sham to be the truth; to see through sham while using it; or to see through sham but fight it."[14] (The theme of Albee's play *Tiny Alice* is that if you don't learn to accept sham, you'll be shot.)

Several recent studies offer convergent data "showing that the essential cognitive skills for tactical deception emerge within the period of four to six years,"[15] even though much younger children can produce deceptive behavior. There may be a biological explanation for why most children "spontaneously" see through sham and use it. Age four-to-six is the time when most children go to school, where they begin to interact much more with peers and the wider social community; it is at least hypothetically possible that these cognitive skills may serve an adaptive function. Furthermore, skills at deception certainly do appear much earlier in children's behavior, without explicit training, which suggests that there may be a genetic basis for deception. In young children, "the tendency to tell lies is a natural tendency, so spontaneous and universal that we can take it as an essential part of the egocentric thought."[16] Deception, it would appear, comes naturally to children, while truth telling is a matter of education. This should not be surprising once we see that deception is a mechanism much favored by evolution in most, if not all, species. Deceptive behavior is believed by some scientists to have a genetic basis in promoting individual as well as group adaptation. It is probably necessary to the survival of any gene pool in the long term, and to the preservation of self right now.[17]

While the sociobiologists continue to study the genetic question, social psychologists have extended the early works of Piaget. Marie Vasek summarizes her review of psychological research on the emergence of deception in children in these words:

> To lie successfully, one must have knowledge of another's knowledge and beliefs, recognize the information required to sway the beliefs of the listener, and communicate such that this information, rather than information which suggests one's intent to deceive, is passed on. Perspective-taking skills and understanding of intentionality are developed enough in children over five years of age to allow them to manipulate their opponents in complex games . . .

and to understand convoluted deceptions in narra-
tives. . . . Children of the same age can also modify
their speech to suit the informational needs of their
listeners. Thus, at the beginning of the school years
children have all the skills theoretically necessary to
lie effectively. All they need, perhaps, is some practice with deception and the inclination to deceive.[18]

Children are inclined to deceive for many reasons.[19] They do it to
be playful; deceiving can be exciting and fun, it can provoke laughter and gain attention. They do it to be defensive; deceiving helps
to escape blame or punishment, or to create a false impression that
makes a person appear to be better than he or she really is. Of
course some children deceive out of aggression; they want to harm
another and escape responsibility. Competition can be a strong
motive, too; children learn in our culture that achievement often
requires besting other children, and sometime the desire to do this
is so strong that cheating, or unfairly influencing others in an official position, seems the right strategy. But we should not forget
that children sometimes will deceive in order to protect the feelings
of other people also, to protect them from shame. Older children
will deceive others, especially their parents, to preserve privacy.
Secrets play an important, and often a very disturbing, role during
adolescence.[20]

    At school, children will learn much about the subtleties of
deception, such as what forms and degrees are acceptable in which
circumstances, through the games they play and through other co-
operative activities. Vasek has noted that selfishly motivated deception in nonplay contexts is most likely to be punished by parents
and school authorities, but "whether this punishment will influence
the child to avoid telling lies or to become a more adept liar is not
known." (Of course, the successful deception is not detected, and
therefore not punished; so we can never know what a child's actual
rate of success at deceiving us really is.) Furthermore, "the positive
regard which people show for deceptions intended to benefit others
may allow children to recognize that the intent of a deception, and
therefore typically its effects, are often what are judged, and not the
fact of deception alone."[21]

The moral complexity of deception in children is brought out nicely by Vasek, whose thinking has been influenced by Mead:

> The skills which make deception possible seem also responsible for developing the more positive social skills such as empathy and compassion. Thus, perspective-taking may act as a natural check on a person's more antisocial deceptive practices when, because he is able to take another's perspective, he becomes aware that the other has goals and desires just as the self does. Greater communicative competence allows the child to use his or her knowledge that another is without some knowledge not only to deceive but also to aid that person in understanding. The same process which allows the child to develop the ability to deceive also allows her to develop, toward her own actions, the attitude of the social group to which she belongs. . . . The skills required in deception are also used in being compassionate and in coordinating our actions with those of others, and without them human society might not exist.[22]

I will return to this observation and explore its moral importance in the concluding chapter.

Deceiving in School

More than twenty years ago, in the opening chapter of *Life in Classrooms,* Philip Jackson introduced the concept of the "hidden curriculum." In discussing the student's task of adjusting to evaluation in school, he identified three related "jobs": learn to behave in such a way as to enhance the likelihood of praise and reduce the likelihood of punishment; publicize positive evaluations and conceal negative ones; and learn how to satisfy two audiences at the same time by being a good student and a good guy. Jackson showed us that "learning how to make it in school involves, in part, learning how to falsify our behavior."[23] The hidden curriculum exists in other cultures, too. Take this example of a Japanese schoolboy:

> Without going about it in a deliberate way, I made a practice of pulling the wool over the eyes of adults.

These included not just my tight-collared teachers but also my mother and father. I didn't have any trouble reading their unsubtle eyes and facial expressions in order to estimate how best to make them happy or to extract praise from them, sometimes playing the innocent role, sometimes that of the bright child. I perceived by a sort of instinct exactly what adults wanted to see in me: a blend of naïveté and wisdom. Overplaying naïveté wouldn't do nor, on the other hand, would seeming too wise. However, if one doled out these commodities to adults in just the right measure, they would inevitably respond with praise. The me who is writing now, today, doesn't look upon the me of that time, the bright little boy, as having been especially crafty. I'd like you to think a bit about your own childhood. All bright children have more or less the same kind of slyness about them. And then it sometimes happens that they foster in themselves the congenial illusion that they are good children precisely because of this capacity.[24]

Later in the story, the young student explains another aspect of his real education about schooling. When he wrote a composition, he always put in a couple of "purple patches," because that's the sort of thing his teachers were delighted by. In one essay he wrote:

"As a present for the sick Master Kimura, I picked out a box of butterfly specimens, which I had gone to great efforts to collect, and started for his house. As I was walking through the onion fields, I was suddenly struck by misgivings about what I had decided to do. Any number of times, I was on the point of stopping and going back home; but finally I came to Master Kimura's house. Then after I had seen the expression of joy on his face, I felt great peace of heart."[25]

Predictably, his teacher was impressed, especially by what he pointed out as the boy's conscientiousness in writing exactly what he felt: "'When he was walking through the onion fields, he felt sorry about giving the butterflies, and that's just the way he wrote it down. All of you sometimes put lies into your compositions. But

Master Toda here has frankly written exactly how he felt. That's being conscientious.'"[26] Of course Master Toda was conscientious, but not at all in the way his teacher believed. The boy's father was rich and would have bought him any number of collections just like the one he gave away; he had felt no regret at all. His purpose in writing the essay was to impress his teacher, and he was clear-headed about how to do it: "My conscience wasn't at all troubled about having lied or having deceived the teacher and my class-mates. That was the way I had always acted whether at school or at home. And by so doing, I had become known as a good boy and a first-class student."[27]

There has been very little written about the actual role of deceiving and truth telling in the classroom that is helpful to our understanding of their dynamics and moral character. Perhaps this deficiency can be explained by Martin Hoffman's judgment that "the primary problem [with research on moral education] is not one of measurement, but rather of conceptualization. Mistaken conclusions and simplistic characterizations of moral behavior and what produces it are not so much a matter of observation error as of the failure to construct an adequate scientific understanding of exactly what is being observed."[28] Throughout the educational lit-erature on classroom interactions, if it is mentioned at all, deception is treated obliquely and negatively either as a vulgar strategy for survival[29] or as a mockery of the principle of respect for persons.[30] For example, the educator and educationist John Holt has bravely called attention to some realities about dishonesty among teachers, aspects of the job that are not mentioned in teacher education courses:

> It didn't take me long to find out that if I gave my students surprise tests, covering the whole material of the course to date, almost everyone flunked. This made me look bad, and posed problems for the school. I learned that the only way to get a respect-able percentage of decent or even passing grades was to announce tests well in advance, tell in some detail what material they would cover, and hold plenty of advance practice in the kind of questions that would be asked, which is called review. I later learned that

teachers do this everywhere. We know that what we
are doing is not really honest, but we dare not be the
first to stop. . . .[31]

In addition to this cover-up about the nature of "knowledge" mea-
sured by testing, Holt identifies several other ways teachers misrepresent reality about themselves:

> We think it our right and duty, not to tell the truth,
> but to say whatever will best serve our cause—in
> this case, the cause of making children grow up into
> the kind of people we want them to be, thinking
> whatever we want them to think. . . . Worse yet,
> we are not honest about ourselves, our own fears,
> limitations, weaknesses, prejudices, motives. We pre-
> sent our selves to children as if we were gods, all-
> knowing, all-powerful, always rational, always just,
> always right. This is worse than any lie we could tell
> about ourselves. . . . As we are not honest with them,
> so we won't let children be honest with us. To begin
> with, we require them to take part in the fiction that
> school is a wonderful place. . . .[32]

While he sees these deceptions clearly, Holt categorically condemns
them all as harmful. He sees schools as contrivances for preparing
the young to succeed in the larger contrivance of society. He sees
also that deception is part of the logic of society and has become
part of the logic of schools. What Holt does not mention, and what
we too often forget in thinking about what goes on in schools, is
that deception is part of the logic of caring, too. It is not all clear
what we must do to care for, to love a child, a student, a person.
When a student needs help or advice, teachers don't always know
what to say that will make the best pedagogical result more probable. We have scant knowledge of pedagogy. This is our lot, partly
because education is not only or mostly a social science that is intent
on identifying and solving problems by the numbers. Education is
also a humanistic enterprise, somewhat more like literature, intent
on dealing with the contrariety of experiences, beliefs, values, and
visions of the good life. Education must contend with the indefi-

nite, the unprovable—with human choice, remorse, mystery, the craving to be thought well of, and so on and on. The methods we might use as educators are not easily established through the observations of social science; rather, they are likely to be discovered in our communicative competence, perspective-taking skills, and in our appreciative understanding of other people's intentionality. That is, in those very skills required for deception as well as for compassion and coordination with others.

9 TRUTH, VERDICTS, AND JUSTICE

I like to know what the truth is so I can decide whether to believe it or not.

Queen Elizabeth I

I've been economical with the truth, yes, I admit that. But I haven't lied.

Sir Robert Armstrong

Fitzhugh had been certain that if he could find the damaged helmet he could persuade the court that his client did indeed suffer brain damage as a result of the accident. He might even name the helmet manufacturer as co-defendant in the suit. Since the collision, the young man had suffered dizziness, headache, and some memory loss. For example, he couldn't remember where he had been going, or how fast he had been traveling through the intersection when he collided with the sports car that slowed to make a left turn. He was also in jeopardy of losing his job because he couldn't concentrate for long periods of time. The doctor's testimony confirmed the fact that there had been a head injury, but the full extent and the exact cause were undetermined. The doctor alluded to "the damaged helmet" in his statement even though no evidence about the helmet had been introduced. His allusion went unnoticed by the defense counsel and the judge.

As the trial progressed, a junior associate in Fitzhugh's firm returned to the scene of the accident and found the helmet. It was in perfect condition except for a scrape. There was obviously no damage that could in any way indicate a source or cause of head injury. Fitzhugh was very disappointed; he put the helmet in his office and said nothing about it to anyone.

When it came time for the judge to sum up the case, she mentioned "the damaged helmet" as a factor. Defense counsel objected angrily this time that there had been no evidence about the helmet. Fitzhugh stood up to say that he agreed with the objection; that there had been no evidence about the helmet. As he did so, he had two things in mind: he thought he was being exceedingly considerate of his adversary, offering support for his objection when none was called for, an act that would certainly influence others' perception of his principles of fair play; he also knew that the judge would have it in the back of her mind that the helmet was in fact damaged, even though there was no formal evidence to establish the truth of her belief. The doctor's mistaken allusion had been enough to plant the idea which had taken root in her conception of the case.

At no time did Fitzhugh consider presenting the undamaged helmet itself as evidence to clear up the matter of its role in the accident and injury. As far as he was concerned, there being "no evidence about the helmet" was good for his client, under the circumstances, and it was his job—and his ethical obligation, as he saw it—to do what was good for his client. He won a generous settlement for the young man, a third of which he took for his fee, and he still has the helmet in his office.

In this case, Fitzhugh deceived the court through silence about a germane material fact, and by offering one truth ("I agree there is no evidence about the helmet") to hide the more important truth only he knew (the helmet is tucked away in my office, undamaged). He managed to handle the truth in a composition of display and concealment while avoiding lies. There is a legal sanction for perjury, but none for omission through silence, and certainly none for emphasizing the wrong truth in an effort to deflect attention from the right truth. But to be fair we have to ask, what is the right truth in this context? The attorney, after all, is not a scientist whose professional obligation is to discover and report the (scientific) truth without distortion, to make all the facts of his investigation public for the scientific community to scrutinize in a joint effort to improve our understanding of the laws of nature.

The scientist's client is human understanding, the laboratory is his court, and the jury is comprised of other scientific experts. Attorneys work in a different world. Their clients are individuals; their court is a theater of sorts, where persuasion and story telling play a crucial role in handling information, where not all is done that could be done in the pursuit of truth, and where juries consist of ordinary people rather than experts.

THE RIGHT STORY — BUT NOT ALL OF IT

There is a difference between deliberately telling a story you believe to be false and not telling all of the right story. The first is lying, the second is deception through selective omission. A friend of mine found selective omission an indispensable aid in coping with the early stage of an important family relationship: "When I introduced Cheryl to my father, I didn't mention the fact that she had been divorced twice. He's eighty and he believes divorce is wrong, period. But he didn't ask, so I didn't tell him. Because he's been open to her from the start, he and Cheryl have had a chance to get to know each other, and they like each other. If he finds out now it will be very difficult for him to dismiss her as 'a divorcee' because he has become close to her and has experienced her as the wonderful woman she is. Maybe I'll never tell him the truth. There is still a chance he wouldn't speak to her again."

The statement "You didn't tell the truth" covers both telling a lie—the wrong story (perjury)—and not telling all of the right story—selective silence. Fitzhugh didn't tell the whole truth, but neither did he lie. Attorneys hope their clients will not be asked certain questions precisely because they would have to answer "truthfully" and might thereby provide relevant, but damaging, information for the judge or jury to consider in determining "the truth." If the opposing attorney doesn't ask the question, the information remains hidden in silence. Just in case the question will be asked, the client is very likely to have been coached by his attorney to give a reply that is designed to conceal at least part—the most important part—of the answer. (Robert MacFarlane is reported to have offered this advice to Oliver North: "Don't lie. Put your own interpretation on the truth.") Fitzhugh knew that the opposing attorney had the right to ask his client whether he was able "to dispose of" (produce as evidence) the helmet, and for this reason he kept his client ignorant of the fact that the helmet had been found. If asked this question, his client could truthfully answer, "No."

There is a similar problem with asking expert witnesses to testify: some of them will damage a case by telling too much truth. The expert witness who is also expert at being a witness knows how to tell the right story—but not necessarily all of it.

Is this attitude to truth telling always wrong? Is it ever wrong? Do we have an obligation to tell the truth to our adversaries as we do to our partners in voluntary agreements?

TRUTH TELLING, LIES, AND AGREEMENTS

In his bold and fresh book *Ethics: Inventing Right and Wrong,* J. L. Mackie makes the point that because people normally and properly live

> as members of various circles, larger and smaller, with different kinds and degrees of cooperation, competition, and conflict in these circles, the appropriateness of telling the truth becomes disputable. Truth telling naturally goes along with cooperation; it is not obviously reasonable to tell the truth to a competitor or to an enemy.[1]

Mackie elaborates this observation by suggesting that when someone "intrudes" with a question, the person questioned may well resent the question, the questioner, or both. When it is not possible to tell the intruder "to mind his own business, a lie may be an appropriate defence of privacy." Of course, as we have seen, the lie is only one kind of deception that might be used in the defence of privacy. In defending his position on the appropriateness of lying, Mackie makes the important distinction between simply telling the truth and keeping an agreement (to tell the truth):

> There is no question of keeping an agreement unless one has first made it, and making an agreement is voluntary and in general deliberate, whereas one often gets quite involuntarily into a position where one has to decide whether or not to tell the truth. Saying nothing may well be no real option: to give no an-

swer to a question may well be, by implication, to give one answer rather than another, and a round, confident, lie may be the only practicable alternative to an undesirable revelation of the truth.[2]

Keeping agreements, keeping promises, being reliable and trustworthy are aspects of mutually beneficial cooperation, which we need to help bring stability to a world in which limited sympathies and limited resources generate so much conflict. All that competition and conflict, which springs up from need and is exacerbated by selfish motives, untethered by cooperation, would make for a very unfriendly and inhospitable world. In a broad sense, stabilizing interactions with cooperation is what morality is for. Telling the truth goes with cooperation, and within voluntary agreements that are meant to generate cooperation we should generally try to tell the truth. Our obligation to tell the truth outside such agreements is not so clear.

ETHICS AND TACTICS

A man named Whiteside stabbed another man to death in Cedar Rapids, Iowa, and was charged with murder. He knew his only hope was in arguing self-defense, and so he wanted to testify that he had seen something "metallic" in the victim's hand just before he killed him, to justify his claim that he thought the man had a gun. Whiteside had previously told his attorneys that he had not seen a gun, and no gun was found at the scene. In other words, he was planning to lie and his attorneys knew it. What should they do? They were duty bound to be zealous advocates for their client and to keep his confidence. They were also duty bound not to use false evidence knowingly to deceive the court.

Attorneys live in several societies: a small one with their clients which is private and bounded by an ethic of confidentiality; a larger one with their fellow attorneys and judges which includes an ethic enjoining the "knowing" use of perjury; and the largest one with the rest of us which, as we have seen, includes many contradictory ethical positions on truth telling.

Whiteside's principal attorney warned him that if he said he saw a gun that would be perjury, and if he went ahead with it, he, the attorney, would withdraw from the case and expose the perjury to the judge and jury. Whiteside did not testify about the gun and was convicted of second-degree murder. He appealed, and his new attorneys argued that his previous counsel's threat had violated his constitutional rights. That appeal was rejected by the Iowa Supreme Court, which commended the "high ethical manner" of the previous counsel. Later, a panel of the United States Court of Appeals overturned the conviction saying that Whiteside had been denied a fair trial. "Despite counsel's legitimate ethical concerns, counsel's actions were inconsistent with the obligations of confidentiality and zealous advocacy," the panel said. Finally, the Supreme Court ruled in 1986 that a defendant's right to assistance of counsel is not violated by an attorney who refuses to cooperate in presenting perjured testimony.[3]

Should attorney–client confidentiality yield to the duty not to use, or let clients use, false evidence knowingly to deceive the court? The American Bar Association says it should, but the American College of Trial Lawyers and other groups disagree. They say the criminal defense lawyer is the client's—especially the indigent client's—most important champion against the powers of the state or the United States Government, and in that context the attorney–client relationship should be absolutely protected. In taking this position, one lawyer and professor of law, Monroe Freedman, became the focus of tremendous controversy and the object of disbarment proceedings (which failed) when he posed these three questions to his colleagues in a law review article:

1. Is it proper to cross-examine for the purpose of discrediting the reliability or credibility of an adverse witness whom you know to be telling the truth?
2. Is it proper to put a witness on the stand when you know he will commit perjury?
3. Is it proper to give your client legal advice when you have reason to believe that the knowledge you give him will tempt him to commit perjury?[24]

Freedman's answer to all three questions was "Yes." Since then, he has even argued that "if a criminal defendant insisted on lying to conceal his guilt, the lawyer has an ethical obligation to put him on the stand, pretend to believe him and use the perjured testimony to argue for acquittal."[5] The reasoning behind such a view is that the lawyer's promise of confidentiality is necessary to build trust in the client; without such trust the lawyer may never get the client to say all in private; and the lawyer needs to know all in order to give the best, most informed advice. Once given, the promise must be kept, even if the client then insists on lying.

Many attorneys disagree with Freedman's view of moral obligation and want no part of lying in court, or helping a client to lie. They argue that the lawyer's obligation to the client is secondary to his obligation "to procedures and to institutions; he must fulfill that obligation no matter the cost. No lawyer may allow a lie to corrupt the adversary system."[6] They deplore the fact that lying and deception have come to be so common, and are so commonly perceived by the public as almost inherent in all aspects of their professional practice (counseling, negotiating, and especially advocating).[7] But they still want to be effective in their work and maintain a competitive advantage for their clients. One way around this conflict, for those looking for a way around it, is to insist on an exactly literal interpretation of "knowingly" in the rule stating that attorneys may not knowingly make use of false evidence. After all, how often does an attorney "know" anything for certain? Isn't there a little ambiguity in everything? In the true, false, meaningful, and meaningless words of Sri Syadasti:

> All affirmations are true in some sense, false in some
> sense, meaningless in some sense, true and false in
> some sense, true and meaningless in some sense, and
> true and false and meaningless in some sense.[8]

Isn't it possible—even easy—to remain selectively ignorant about certain matters that the attorney suspects might be true, or false? Attorneys who take this view don't often ask their clients to tell them everything about what really happened, because they don't want to hear the whole truth if the truth is damaging to the case. They want to hear whatever truth will help, and that's all. This view also allows for trying to discredit an opposing witness who is very likely telling the truth, by probing for some area of ambiguity in the testimony to show that the witness cannot be certain of all the facts, either. This tactic works very well with honest, intelligent witnesses:

Dr. Ashby has been called as an expert witness in the murder trial of Dr. Adams.

> As he steps down, nobody can be wholly pleased; nor can anybody be really vexed with Dr. Ashby, his honesty was too patent. His was no hedging; here was a man clear-minded enough, conscientious enough, come to think of it: brave enough, to refrain from tidying up the ambiguities of fact.[9]

"Ambiguities of fact" is a condition of life we must endure; skilled trial lawyers know how to exploit this condition for the purpose of creating doubt, and sometimes for the purpose of deceiving the jury about what they themselves believe to be true.

> *Zealous lawyer:* I know she's telling the absolute truth, *and* I have it within my power to make her *appear* unreliable. I can destroy her with the truth by asking for more and more clarification on smaller and smaller points until the ambiguity is exposed, until she says she is not sure, she can't be positive. My goal is to deceive the jury. That's allowed by our system.
> *Honorable judge:* Even when lawyers are trying to deceive the jury, if they stay within the rules, I will allow it. The system has worked for a long time.
> *Zealous lawyer:* The only true evidence I want is that which is helpful to my case. Therefore, I will encourage the jury to disbelieve true evidence that is harmful to my case.
> *Honorable judge:* The adversarial system is not set up to produce the truth. It produces verdicts. Sometimes justice.

Truth in the adversarial system is not an absolute value. We have built-in Constitutional constraints on our rights and abilities to find the truth: the Fifth Amendment privilege against self-incrimination, for example, and the Fourth Amendment prohibition of unreasonable searches and seizures, as well as double-jeopardy provisions. No attorney, even those who think Professor Freedman is dead wrong, would deny someone accused of a crime the right to plead not guilty (even when in fact he is guilty) in order to have a chance at a fair trial. If discovering and exposing the truth were the sole point of the process, there would be no attorney–client privilege at all. But there is such a privilege, and it is held to be a very strong value in the system.

However, attorney–client confidentiality is not an absolute value, either. Let's say a client is guilty and is a liar willing both to deny truthful complaints against him and to perjure himself. The conventional view in American law says that impeaching a truthful witness is allowable, even appropriate, while introducing perjury is not. It is also the consensus that lawyers ought to make full use of the evidence available regardless of their beliefs about the truth of the witness's testimony and the falsity of the client's denial. The reason given for this is that it's not the lawyer's role to determine the verdict—that's for judge and jury to do. The lawyer's role is to create "reasonable doubt" in the minds of the jurors so they will not believe that the case against the defendant has been proved. (Some wag on a television program once said, "Lawyers don't lie; they tell the truth judiciously to guarantee confusion.") The state is obliged to prove its case, and this means that the defending attorney has a right to try to discredit truthful witnesses.

The rules now forbid an attorney to make "knowing" use of perjury. What does that mean? Well, if we get technical about what anybody can really know with certitude, we have to admit that we can find some ambiguity in almost every question as well as every statement of "fact." It is possible, also, to remain selectively ignorant in the course of preparing a case. Barbara Babcock, professor of law at Stanford Law School and former assistant attorney general of the United States in charge of the civil division, puts the point starkly:

> What I'm really trying to avoid is the point at which
> you say to a client, "I'm your lawyer and you can
> trust me; anything you say to me is completely con-

fidential. Now tell me everything about what really happened." Suppose he says, "Well, I had nothing else to do that night, it [a rape] seemed like an easy thing to do so I did it." *I don't want to hear that.*[10] [My emphasis.]

So, if an attorney suspects a client of being guilty and/or of lying, it is possible to try to remain uncertain about it for the sake of being able to say, "I don't *know* that my client is guilty, or is lying." This is obviously a pretense that is valued in the legal profession because its official codes of ethics allow it as a compromise position on the question of protecting client confidentiality versus being an active accomplice to perjury.

DECEPTION IN POLICE WORK

An undercover officer's observations are reliable and have well-established credibility within the criminal justice system. To be in a position to make these observations, undercover operators must assume an identity other than their own for the purpose of gaining the confidence of individuals whom they suspect of criminal connections or illegal activities. Once established, this confidence, or trust, makes it possible for the officer to infiltrate a world otherwise inaccessible to the police, make first-hand observations, and provide information essential to successful prosecution. This trust, and the officer's success, would not be possible without very highly developed skills of deception.

There are limits that govern the use of deception in undercover work, the most important being prohibitions against entrapment. The law will not tolerate a law enforcement officer generating the original intent to commit a crime in the mind of an otherwise innocent person who, acting alone, would not have thought to do what the officer, or a decoy, entices him to do. In principle, the law permits deception of criminals, and it encourages providing the occasion for criminals to do their crimes in order to catch them at their trade, but it discourages the seduction of law-abiding citizens into criminal activity for the sake of making an arrest.

Techniques of Interrogation

Interrogation is formal and systematic questioning. Normally, the person under interrogation, if guilty, will resist the efforts of police to get the desired information. Indeed, experienced criminals know that no one has a *legal* obligation to provide factual information to the police while under interrogation. Since effective interrogation is vital to police work, several techniques have been developed to achieve success with reluctant suspects, witnesses, informants, and even victims. All of these techniques involve deception.[11]

Bluffing. When a suspect offers an alibi that places him in some other location when the crime was committed, pretend to accept it as the truth. Go on with other questions for a while, then ask a detailed question about an incident at the alibi location that the suspect could not have failed to see. If the suspect's alibi is that he was at the symphony, for example, ask whether the conductor had recovered sufficiently from the flu to take the podium. Then watch carefully as the answer comes.

Good guy, bad guy. We've all seen this one on TV. Two investigators come in together: the first plays the role of the hardened, unsympathetic, even vindictive person; the second is sympathetic and mild. The first takes over the interrogation, becomes belligerent and threatening, appears to be losing control. The other officer remains calm and supportive of the suspect to the point of actually criticizing her partner, who then leaves the room, muttering all sorts of threats on the way out. The goal now is for the sympathetic officer to convince the suspect that it would be wise to cooperate with her, because she might be able to get a better deal and prevent the first investigator from making things worse than they already are.

Fear. When the suspect is a novice criminal, or an accessory to a serious crime, it is often effective to make him think that he is legally subject to greater penalties than is in fact the case. The guideline is to amplify fear if the suspect appears to be fearful already.

Blatant neglect. Some subjects who are deeply insecure crave attention. It is possible to exploit this attribute by openly focusing on what others have to say, with the subject able to see but not to hear what you are doing. The point is to convey the impression that you are getting a lot of incriminating information while denying the subject an opportunity to refute any of it. Sometimes this sort of pressure works to convert a silent subject into a talkative one, because being ignored is actually harder to bear than being found out.

False identification. If a suspect has victimized someone, it is sometimes possible by prearrangement to invite more "victims" to view a lineup and identify the suspect as the one who got them, too. The idea is to fool the suspect into admitting the one crime in order to convince the investigators that she is innocent of the others of which she has been accused.

Interrogators must always be mindful that suspects' statements are made out of self-interest and therefore are likely to be false or at least distorted. Many subjects have an interest in protecting some financial stake, and often there is another person affected by the crime whom the suspect wishes to protect. Even when a suspect is cooperative and gives a confession, it should be kept in mind that interrogation is much more likely to bring about a partial confession than a full and complete one. A suspect will use cooperation and confession deceptively to counter the efforts of interrogation to uncover the whole truth. The objective of the investigator is to acquire accurate and complete information. To this end she may use legitimate deceptive techniques. The objective of the suspect is to conceal accurate and complete information. Often his best bet is to offer accurate but incomplete information in hopes that the interrogation will be concluded before the truth is told.

THE CODE

There is one more aspect of deception in police work that should be mentioned. It is called the code of secrecy among the police themselves. The code is simple: Officers do not testify against officers, period. Secrecy is a bond between the sharers and a shield against the outside. Police work requires absolute confidence in partners to provide backup assistance when needed, in situations that are dangerous and often life-threatening. Hence the necessity of the bond. Police work also sometimes requires actions that are themselves illegal, actions which if widely known would erode public confidence in law enforcement and hinder police effectiveness. Hence the necessity of the shield. There are two unfortunate consequences of this code. The first, totally unanticipated consequence is that police have become intensely suspicious of each other, never knowing who knows what about whom, who might tell what, and who might be investigating them.

The second consequence is that because the existence of the code itself has been exposed, it is no longer as effective as it once was in shielding the police from public suspicion of wrongdoing. Perhaps that is a good thing, perhaps not. Does this suspicion work out in the long term to the benefit of criminals more than to the benefit of law-abiding citizens? I don't know any way to be sure of an answer. In any case, the ability to keep secrets remains so important among police that successful careers depend on it, and they are willing to break the law to support it.[12]

A NOTE ON THE ANCIENT ARTS OF WAR

In his *Philoctetes* (lines 79–122), Sophocles dramatizes two incompatible conceptions of honorable conduct by focusing on the difficulty one noble man has in accepting another noble man's proposal to use deception as a means in dealing with foes. He shows in this discussion how the very question of deceit is deeply disturbing to the younger and less experienced warrior, who would rather risk his life and "fail with honor" than "succeed by fraud":

> *Odysseus:* I know, my son, thy honest nature shrinks
> From glozing words and practice of deceit;
> But (for 'tis sweet to snatch a victory)
> Be bold to-day and honest afterwards.
> For one brief hour of lying follow me;
> All time to come shall prove thy probity.
> *Neoptolemus:* Son of Laertes, what upon my ear
> Grates in the telling, I should hate to do.
> Such is my nature; any taint of guile

I loathe, and such, they tell me, was my sire.
But I am ready, not by fraud, but force
To bring the man; for, crippled in one foot,
Against our numbers he can prove no match.
Natheless, since I was sent to aid thee, prince,
I fear to seem a laggard; yet prefer
To fail with honor than succeed by fraud.
Odysseus: Son of a gallant sire, I too in youth
Was slow of tongue and forward with my hand;
But I have learnt by trial of mankind
Mightier than deeds of puissance is the tongue.
Neoptolemus: It comes to this that thou would'st have
me lie.
Odysseus: Entangle Philoctetes by deceit.
Neoptolemus: Why not persuade him rather than
deceive?
Odysseus: Persuasion's vain, and force of no avail.
Neoptolemus: What arms hath he of such miraculous
might?
Odysseus: Unerring arrows, tipp'd with instant
death.
Neoptolemus: Might not a bold man come to grips
with him?
Odysseus: No, as I told thee, guile alone avails.
Neoptolemus: Thou deem'st it, then, no shame to tell
a lie?
Odysseus: Not if success depends upon a lie.
Neoptolemus: With what face shall one dare to speak
such words?
Odysseus: If thou would'st profit thou must have no
qualms.
Neoptolemus: What gain to me, should he be brought
to Troy?
Odysseus: Without these arms Troy-town cannot be
sacked.
Neoptolemus: Ye told me I should take it. Was that
false?
Odysseus: Not thou apart from these nor these from
thee.
Neoptolemus: The quarry's worth the chase, if this be
so.

Odysseus: Know that success a double meed shall win.

Neoptolemus: Make plain this twofold prize and I'll essay.

Odysseus: Thou wilt be hailed as wise no less than brave.

Neoptolemus: I'll do it—here's my hand—and risk the shame.

Odysseus: Good. My instructions—thou rememberest them?

Neoptolemus: I have consented; trust me for the rest.[13]

Odysseus succeeds in his effort to convince Neoptolemus that in dealing with enemies, deception is sometimes required when persuasion and force will not avail, and like persuasion and force, it is justified by the purpose which it serves. He even goes on to say that if Neoptolemus uses deception well in protecting Troy from attack by "unerring arrows, tipp'd with instant death," he will win the double honor of being "hailed as wise no less than brave." The younger man was willing to settle for being hailed as brave, even brave but dead, rather than "risk the shame" he felt he would deserve if he tried to "entangle Philoctetes by deceit." It would seem that Neoptolemus was willing to risk the loss of battle, the fall of Troy, and even his own death, all for the sake of a sense of personal integrity that for him was defined in terms of truth telling: "Such is my nature; any taint of guile I loathe."

Perhaps this difference in perspective on the role of deception can be described as a contrast between the pull of culture (honor, face-saving, honesty) and the pull of nature (survival, self-protection, strategy). I don't mean to put too much emphasis on this metaphor, but there does seem to me to be a tension of this kind in our lives. Education is in many ways a fine thing, but it does tend to weaken instinct. We are taught that "honor" requires us to despise the use of deceitful strategies and tactics in waging our personal battles against the sources of our fears and anxieties, against the "slings and arrows of outrageous fortune." The result is that our instinct for survival, which tells us that guile, misdirection, camouflage, faking of all sorts are very successful strategies in a pinch, is implicated as "uncivilized" (which it is) and "immoral" (which I question) and is therefore to be suppressed.

All Warfare Is Based on Deception

Sun Tzu wrote a handbook called *The Art of War* more than two thousand years ago, in which he said: "All warfare is based on deception. Hence, when able to attack, we must seem unable; when using our forces, we must seem inactive; when we are near, we must make the enemy believe we are far away; when far away, we must make him believe we are near."[14]

In discussing tactics, Sun Tzu emphasized the avoidance of battle: "True excellence is to plan secretly, to move surreptitiously, to foil the enemy's intentions and balk his schemes, so that at last the day may be won without shedding a drop of blood."[15]

He knew the value of showing what he wished the enemy to believe, especially when it was not true: "If we do not wish to fight, we can prevent the enemy from engaging us. . . . All we need do is to throw something odd and unaccountable in his way." And he tells this story:

> Tu Mu relates a stratagem of Chu-ko Liang, who in 149 B.C., when occupying Yang-p'ing and about to be attacked by Ssu-ma I, suddenly struck his colors, stopped the beating of the drums, and flung open the city gates, showing only a few men engaged in sweeping and sprinkling the ground. This unexpected proceeding had the intended effect; for Ssu-ma I, suspecting an ambush, actually drew off his army and retreated.[16]

Sun Tzu was wise and right and radical in his thinking when he said, "Success in warfare is gained by carefully accommodating ourselves to the enemy's purpose." Likewise, success in social life is gained by carefully accommodating ourselves to each other's purpose. Such accommodation is in our culture most often associated with the "feminine way" of doing things and is not highly regarded by modern Neoptolemuses, who would rather fight than accommodate. Sun Tzu and Odysseus knew better. So, in his own way, does Fitzhugh.

PART *three*

DECEPTION AND
MORAL DECENCY

10 INVENTING RIGHT AND WRONG

That's the worst of acting on principle . . . one begins thinking of one's attitude instead of the use of what one is doing.

Harley Granville Barker

It is neither possible for a man to know the truth fully nor to avoid the error of pretending that he does.

Reinhold Niebuhr

Throughout this book I have tried to challenge our current conceptions of truth telling and deceiving, by exploring their logical as well as moral complexity and by providing examples of ways in which deception might actually work to improve the moral character of our relationships with others. Now it is time to fit these pieces together into an intelligible moral point of view, so we can see why deception and moral decency are not necessarily, and not always, at odds with each other.

ETHICAL THINKING

It is at the very heart of being human to recognize the importance of ethical ideas. These are the ideas we have about how relations between people can be, might be, ought to be. They are beliefs about how life ought to be lived; they are the interests and ideals that help us in shaping purposes of life that give meaning to the variety of ways human beings can interact with each other, with other species, and with the environment. Ethical thought consists in the orderly examination of these ideas, beliefs, interests, and ideals, as well as in raising new questions about them in the context of our own present circumstances.

In ethical thinking, we cannot confine our attention to the great impersonal forces which sway or magnetize or, as some think, determine the way our lives will go. Nor can we look only at the familiar laws of rationality in sorting out the truth of what we want to understand, for much of moral life goes on beyond the limits of what is strictly rational. Modern neuroscience is showing us how the conventional wisdom that we make "rational" decisions mainly through clear, logical deduction is not anywhere close to the whole picture. Our brains react to questions in very complicated, sophisticated ways that are more powerful than mere deduction. We must instead look at human conduct in light of *all* we know and understand, even if imperfectly, and we should examine what we do with every resource our intellects and sentiments can provide. If we hope to comprehend this world we live in— alternating as it does between peace and violence, bliss and wretchedness, stunning beauty and repulsive ugliness, trust and treachery, imaginative creativity and mindless conformity, control and catastrophe—and with this comprehension try to live better lives, then ethics is the vital field of thought where we must necessarily begin.

The moral universe is the same for everyone in that it is based on concern for human dignity, decency, voluntary relations that are not oppressive, and some kind of spiritual fulfillment. These norms, which make up moral lives, are construed differently at different ages, in different places, and the particulars vary depending on the kind of brain we have (we are all similar, but we're not identical), the evolution of local histories and customs, and the models generated for their expression. But the basis of concern is the same.

Within this common moral universe values can clash. Nations, and cultures within nations, are incompatible because they hold conflicting values—not because they hold no values. Individuals, too, can find it difficult or impossible to reconcile different values. Are human beings able to see clearly that some actions are intrinsically right or wrong? Yes and no. You may believe in telling the truth always and in every case, because to you it is self-evident that there is an element of wrongness in not telling the truth, which means you have an obligation in principle not to lie or deceive. I may not believe that truth telling is always right, or that lying and deceiving are always wrong, because sometimes the truth can be too costly or painful, too destructive, or too much to expect of human sensitivity, and other virtues must override the virtue of truth telling. Our differences can be discussed, our ends in life compared, but reconciliation may not come as a result. Values can even clash within the mind of one person. Is this the time to tell the truth, or is it better for both of us that I avoid doing so in this case and risk damaging your trust? Should I tell the truth or should I instead say something close to it?

THE HEDGEHOG AND THE FOX

The problem we are talking about here is really a problem of two deeply divergent attitudes, or personalities, which characterize different human beings. In his essay "The Hedgehog and the Fox," Isaiah Berlin took a line from the Greek poet Archilochus—"The fox knows many things, but the hedgehog knows one big thing"—and used it figuratively to identify these attitudes. The kinds of personality which belong to the hedgehogs

> relate everything to a single central vision, one system less or more coherent or articulate, in terms of which they understand, think and feel—a single, universal, organizing principle in terms of which alone all that they are and say has significance.[1]

Foxes, on the other hand,

> pursue many ends, often unrelated and even contradictory, connected, if at all, only in some de facto way, for some psychological or physiological cause, related by no moral or aesthetic principle. . . . Their thought is scattered or diffused, moving on many levels, seizing upon the essence of a vast variety of experiences and objects for what they are in themselves, without, consciously or unconsciously, seeking to fit them into, or exclude them from, any one unchanging, all-embracing, sometimes self-contradictory and incomplete, at times fanatical, unitary inner vision.[2]

Berlin goes on to illustrate his categories with famous names. He counts among the hedgehogs Plato, Lucretius, Dante, Pascal, Hegel, Dostoevsky, Nietzsche, Ibsen, and Proust. The foxes include Herodotus, Aristotle, Montaigne, Erasmus, Molière, Goethe, Pushkin, Balzac, and Joyce. (I suppose Mrs. Ramsay, Huck Finn, and the likes of John Lennon would be foxes, while Mr. Ramsay, Pastor Trocmé, and perhaps Shirley McLaine would feel more at home with the hedgehogs.)

The fox's idea of rationality is that people can think and act in ways they themselves can understand and alter, that individuals are not merely victims of structural causes, and that justifications and explanations of human conduct must include terms of personal, subjective motives and reasons, however idiosyncratic they may seem. In this view, our ignorance of how things happen in the social world is not due to our incapability to fathom first causes; it is due rather to our inability to take in and remember and consider enough details of all the partial, contributing small causes that influence what people do.

The hedgehog's view of rationality is that people should strive for economy of means in thought by coming up with a single conception that applies to an enormous number of cases. Ideas that are extensive, inclusive, and universal are best. The notion of the perfect whole guides efforts to discover (not invent) laws that govern nature, spirit, morality—truth in every realm of the whole. In this view our ignorance of how things happen, and of what should happen in the social world, is due to spiritual and intellectual confusion, abandonment of the search for the rules which govern the universe.

These characterizations are oversimple, but they make a point. We must recognize and accept the fact that there exist conflicting moral visions of the world, not only between individuals and groups who are as deeply divided as the hedgehogs and the foxes, but also within one consciousness. Human beings live in a world of competing genuine values, and this pluralism of values is as much a part of each individual consciousness as it is of society.

This collision of values is the moral core of what it is to be human. Such conflict of values between peoples, or within one's own moral universe, should not always lead to a forced choice of *the* right one, *the* wrong one, the *only* true or false one. Truth telling is a value that is likely to exist in conflict with many others—kindness, compassion, self-regard, privacy, survival, and so on. Simply to be aware of the conflict is enough to keep conscience alive, and conscience will play a key role in helping both hedgehogs and foxes resolve moral conflict in a morally acceptable way.

To put it bluntly, it is the nature of moral values that they are in conflict—because it is our nature to see things differently from one another. Human perception is not a passive process; our brains use images to compose pictures of the world, images of ourselves, of right and wrong, good and bad. Nietzsche provides a helpful model for this insight: "As a genius of construction man raises himself far above the bee in the following way: Whereas the bee builds with wax that he gathers from nature, man builds with the far more delicate conceptual material which he first has to manufacture from himself."[3] As there is no "moral wax" to gather from nature, the ideal of ultimate value-harmony, no matter how fondly or gravely imagined in the abstract, is simply and forever impossible on this earth, where we all think and feel and need and generate our lives in our own ways. For example, you may still prefer to believe there is one true value-harmony—and that our clashes indicate at least one of us must be wrong. I may believe, in accord with my argument above, such harmony is only a wish that cannot be fulfilled and that clashes in value, while they may sometimes involve mistakes, indicate a deep truth about personhood. There is surely a difficult tension generated in a society that values freedom and equality at the same time, or in an individual feeling bound to the loyalty of friends and to the impartiality of justice simultaneously, but there is no clear wrong or mistake involved in the fact that these tensions exist.

MAKING ADJUSTMENTS

If collisions of value are unavoidable, if only some but not all conflicting values can live easily together, if human lives can be fashioned and lived imaginatively only in a pattern of mutually exclusive choices, then what can we do? The answer is: make adjustments as best we can, to avoid extremes of suffering and soften the blows.

Practicing morality, like maintaining a house, or dancing, is a matter of attending to particulars and making adjustments. We may well believe in the principle of truth telling, for example, but that principle must be adjusted, as must all moral principles, to improve our chances of having what we need to live decently, enjoying what we do, and preventing things from going too far wrong. Children in their games, especially girls, come naturally to this need for constant adjustment. When there is a dispute, when some unfortunate flubs a chance, or when the day's lucky child is about to run away with all the prizes, they either adapt the rules to keep everybody playing or they discontinue the game in order to preserve the relationships of the players.[4]

Context is important, too. It is not easy to abstract a particular act or practice from its place in a complete set of concerns, values, ideals, relationships, standards of taste, educational experiences, and visions of self and of the future if we have any hope of fully understanding that act or practice. We cannot fairly judge a particular lie merely through comparisons with abstractions from other lives, or by calling up philosophical theories about value and truth.

A history of conventions, attachments to particular people and institutions, commitment, a sense of character or integrity—all of these go into a moral point of view, along with whatever guidance reason, rules, principles can provide. In the end, if anything binds us to moral conduct of a certain kind it cannot be only principles or rules. More likely it will be a sense not wholly understood, an intuition that this is the right thing to do, all things considered. We may not do the best thing we can imagine doing, but it will be the best we can manage in the circumstances. In his play *Man and Superman,* G. B. Shaw brought out this sense of morality:

> *Octavius:* I assure you all, on my word, I never
> meant to be selfish. It's so hard to know what to do
> when one wishes earnestly to do right.
> *Tanner:* My dear Tavy, your pious English habit of
> regarding the world as a moral gymnasium built ex-
> pressly to strengthen your character in, occasionally
> leads you to think about your own confounded prin-

ciples when you should be thinking about other
people's necessities. The need of the present hour is
a happy mother and a healthy baby. Bend your en-
ergies on that; and you will see your way clearly
enough.[5]

Moral associations are built on shared confidence in one another.
What is it that gives us confidence in another person? More often
than not it's personality, or something like character. A good and
loving personality, a character you can count on, judgment that is
informed by various principles but is not dominated by any one of
them—these are the sources of our confidence in others. I don't
mean to mock anyone who tries to be a "person of principle," for
I believe we all try to be that, more or less. I do mean to point out,
however, that adherence to the idea of adjusting the principle of
truth telling to fit the circumstances is a sound moral position just
as surely as is adherence to the ideal of honesty itself.

Granville Barker's play *The Voysey Inheritance* is about a conflict of this sort between father and son. Mr. Voysey, a lawyer, long
ago misused some of his clients' trust funds (he secretly borrowed
from them for an investment that didn't work out well). He has for
some years been juggling accounts to make sure that his clients get
the annuity they expect each month while trying to restore the lost
capital. As he is nearing death, he reveals the nature of the losses to
his son, who is to inherit the firm, and asks him to help repair the
harm without going to the authorities first.

> *Mr. Voysey.* My dear Edward, you've lived a quiet
> humdrum life up to now, with your books and your
> philosophy and your agnosticism and your ethics of
> this and your ethics of that . . . and you've never
> before been brought face to face with any really vital
> question. Now don't make a fool of yourself just
> through inexperience. Try and give your mind freely
> and unprejudicedly to the consideration of this very
> serious matter. And it's for your own sake and not
> for mine, Edward, that I do beg you to—to—to be
> a man and try and take a practical common sense
> view of the position you find yourself in. It's not a
> pleasant position, I know, but it's unavoidable.[6]

Edward is shocked at his father's behavior and his suggestion that the son carry on, trying his best to restore the lost money without the clients knowing anything about it. Going to the authorities would bring about bankruptcy and scandal, deplete the family estate entirely, and leave his clients much worse off than they would be if Edward could succeed in building up the capital in secret, as indeed his father has been trying to do for years. Edward reluctantly considers the path of covering his father's tracks, and seeks the advice of Alice, whom he greatly respects and wishes to marry.

> *Edward:* Shall I do this?
> *Alice:* [Turning away] Why must you ask me?
> *Edward:* You mocked at my principles, didn't you?
> You've taken them from me. The least you can do is
> give me advice in exchange.
> *Alice:* [After a moment] No . . . decide for yourself.
> He jumps up and begins to pace about, doubtful,
> distressed.
> *Edward:* Good Lord . . . it means lying and
> shuffling!
> *Alice:* [A little trembling] In a good cause.
> *Edward:* Ah . . . but lying and shuffling takes the
> fine edge off one's soul.
> *Alice:* [Laughing at the quaintness of her own little
> epigram] Edward, are you one of God's dandies?
> . . .
> *Edward:* Alice, if my father's story were true . . . he
> must have begun like this. Trying to do the right
> thing in the wrong way . . . then doing the wrong
> thing . . . then bringing himself to what he was . . .
> and so me to this. [He flings away from her] No,
> Alice, I won't do it. I daren't take that first step
> down. It's worse risk than any failure. Think . . . I
> might succeed.[7]

Well, despite his upright conviction about the goodness of telling the whole truth to everybody as soon as he finds it out, Edward does decide to try to cover his father's tracks for the sake of his own family and for the sake of the clients, who have a real chance of recovery. He realizes that this chance depends upon his willingness to adopt a policy of speaking only as truthfully as he thinks suitable. He therefore hesitantly adjusts his principle of truth telling to fit the circumstances.

In this case, who really knows what the son should do? Should Edward have the freedom to choose a solution that he believes will work out in the long run for the benefit of all, even though it involves "lying and shuffling"? Should he instead keep things "simple" by telling the whole story to the authorities, and thereby forfeit the family estate (including its good name) along with any chance of recovering the funds his father lost? What are his relative obligations to his father and the rest of his family, his clients, his own future career, and his commitment to the principle of truth telling? In this case, is it better to tell the whole truth or to be as truthful as he thinks suitable?

What any one of us really needs in the way of truth telling is not at all clear. We all take pride in our differences from others in matters of talent, appearance, or particular relationships. We don't think of ourselves first as human beings in general; rather, we think of ourselves as special sons and daughters who can do certain things well, or as mothers and fathers who have certain visions of the future for our children, as friends who occupy a unique place in someone else's life. We are interconnected, but not universal; we are local, not ubiquitous; we are historical, not timeless. It is in our differences, and our particular web of relations, not in our general humanity, that we find recognizable identity. And it is here in our identities as particular social persons in structured but flexible relationships with others that we find out what the morality of truth telling means to us.

PRINCIPLES AND MORAL INTUITION

A good way to learn conceptions of what is right and what is not right is to be presented with examples and mull over alternative interpretations and decisions. If we pay attention to the particulars of concrete situations, we may learn to see that not all moral claims have equal force at any one time. The claims of principles can be traded off against the claims of other kinds of values in light of circumstances.[8] (All moral principles are themselves values, but not all moral values are principles: "Always tell the truth" is a moral principle; "I love you and I won't risk hurting you by telling you

this truth" is a personal value.) The frequently recommended alternative way of learning moral conceptions is to start with moral
theories which provide the principles and procedures for resolving
moral problems in general. But, as Edmund Pincoffs argues, often
"the structures known as ethical theories are more threats to moral
sanity and balance than instruments for their attainment. They have
these malign characteristics principally because they are, by nature,
reductive. They restrict and warp moral reflection by their insistence that moral considerations are related in some hierarchical order . . . there is no such order."⁹

William Gass uses a striking example to show the concrete,
intuitive nature of moral knowledge and the limited usefulness of
moral principles in "The Case of the Obliging Stranger":

> Imagine I approach a stranger on the street and say to
> him, "If you please, sir, I desire to perform an ex-
> periment with your aid." The stranger is obliging,
> and I lead him away. In a dark place conveniently by,
> I strike his head with the broad of an axe and cart him
> home. I place him, buttered and trussed, in an ample
> electric oven. The thermostat reads 450° F. There-
> upon I go off to play poker with friends and forget
> all about the obliging stranger in the stove. When I
> return, I realize I have overbaked my specimen, and
> the experiment, alas, is ruined.
>
> Something has been done wrong. Or something
> wrong has been done.
>
> Any ethic that does not roundly condemn my ac-
> tion is vicious.¹⁰

Gass's point is that this case is a clear case of immorality. It is evi-
dently, obviously, intrinsically wrong to bake a stranger this way.
No moralist's principle will help in the least to explain why this act
should be condemned. The moral certainty we feel in this case we
feel directly; we do not derive it from grander or generalizable cer-
tainties in the shape of principles. Furthermore, when cases are not
so clear, when there may be a conflict of obligations, we decide
what to do not by appeal to principle, but by stating what puzzles
us, and by gathering more information until enough clarity is
achieved. Gass gives this example:

"She left her husband with a broken hand and took the children."

"She did!"

"He broke his hand on her head."

"Dear me; but even so!"

"He beat her every Thursday after tea and she finally couldn't stand it any longer."

"Ah, of course, but the poor children?"

"He beat them, too."

"My, my, and was there no other way?"

"The court would grant her no injunction."

"Why not?"

"Judge Bridlegoose is a fool."

"Ah, of course, she did right, no doubt about it."[11]

The judgment unfolds as details are put in place. No general principles are required to clear up the picture. "People have been wrongly persuaded that principles decide cases and that a principle which fails in one case fails in all. So principles are usually vehicles for especially powerful feelings and frequently get in the way of good sense."[12] This is a contextualist morality in which the main theme is finding compatibility among feelings and beliefs, particulars and principles, responsiveness and impartiality, clarity and simplicity. It is a morality that has room for natural impulse and intuition, as well as rationality.

Always to choose principles, or worse, The One Right Principle, over individual values and needs in resolving specific moral situations may sometimes be the road to martyrdom and sainthood, but it is also the road to inhumanity, which ironically is paved with illusions of perfection. The prophet who believes he has the truth and therefore knows what all people need is likely to put down resistance by taking up arms, is likely to find a way to justify the sacrifice of hundreds of thousands of individuals for the sake of humankind. A far better general rule would be to balance the competing claims of values and principles in light of concrete particulars, aiming to avoid the intolerable and achieve the beneficent. Thomas Jefferson expressed a similar thought in a letter to his nephew, Peter Carr, when he wrote: "State a moral case to a ploughman and a professor. The former will decide it as well, and often better than the latter, because he has not been led astray by artificial rules." [13] Jefferson's ploughman represents a middle ground between impulse and "artificial rules" that is found in a person of good sense, acting for a purpose, who can form a judgment using some measure of inventiveness and ingenuity while taking in the pertinent facts and details of the case.

CLARITY AND SIMPLICITY

This distinction between moral principles and personal values is made to illustrate two broad orientations toward formulating moral judgments. They are not meant to be mutually exclusive in any strict sense; rather, they represent stronger and weaker tendencies in people. The moral-principle orientation favors such categories as the universal and the absolute, or in William James's terms, *simplicity*. The personal-value orientation favors such categories as particular life story or singular situation or, again in James's terms, *clarity*. James believed that "the passion for parsimony, for economy of means in thought, is the philosophic passion par excellence." [14] A philosophic thinker gets satisfaction from this passionate state when he or she comes up with a single conception that applies to an enormous number of cases. For these philosophers, as for the hedgehogs, ideas that are extensive, inclusive, universal, and elegant in their simplicity are preeminent. Alongside this passion, however, lives another. It is "the passion for distinguishing; it is the impulse to be acquainted with the parts rather than to comprehend the whole. Loyalty to clearness and integrity of perception, dislike of blurred outlines, of vague identifications, are its characteristics." [15] For this group of philosophic thinkers, as for the foxes, it is seeing individuals with perfect clarity, in all their literal, particular, factual fullness that is the best—no matter how fragmented the world may then seem.

There will always be human beings whose most powerful emotional and practical tendencies run toward the hedgehog's ideal of simplicity, and there will be others who are drawn toward the fox's aim of clarity in recognizing all the complex aspects and relations of a living, discrete individual case, no matter how seemingly incoherent and fragmented. Most of us will feel both tendencies, and for most of us no philosophy of moral value is going to seem reasonable unless it satisfies our needs for both clarity and simplicity in some kind of balanced manner. Thomas Nagel's list of five fundamental types of value that people consider in making moral judgments represents such a balanced view. His list, summarized:

1. Specific obligations to individuals or institutions, such as family members, students, or the organization where one works;
2. General rights that everyone has, such as freedom from assault or coercion;
3. Utility, or the effects of what one does on everyone's welfare, not just on those with whom one has special and direct relationship;
4. The intrinsic value of certain achievements that Nagel calls perfectionist ends or values, such as scientific discoveries or certain works of art;
5. And finally, commitment to one's own projects or undertakings that, once begun, take on remarkable importance (such as writing a book about the moral complexity of deception!).[16]

The divisions among these values run deep. There is no unifying value that bridges these divisions. We are left with the burden of having to make judgments anyway, even when we don't know for sure what to do. When there are good reasons for doing two or three different things, we still have to choose somehow. It is important to say that we should not fail to decide and to act merely because we are not able to provide a completely satisfactory, impartial statement of principles in justification of what we want to do. Impartial principles play a part in making moral judgments, but not the only part. I love and care for my child not because doing so is universally recognized as a father's duty, or because it will benefit the general welfare; I love him and care for him because he is *my* child. I will have different motives for taking care of your child, if the need should arise.

This view of ethics is not exciting or dramatic, for it evokes no romantic ideal; it sounds more humble than heroic; it stresses the necessary more than the noble. All it asks, really, is that we take into account all the relevant factors of concrete situations (including our own complex inner worlds) when making moral choices. In the words of Mies van der Rohe, "God is in the details." Of course Mies was speaking of good architecture, but I think his observation carries weight in the realm of moral conduct as well. If a principle leads to a decision that does not feel right, don't automatically mistrust your feeling. Rather, entertain the possibility that there is something inappropriate about the principle in the circumstances. People and their situations are made up of particulars: gender, age, family, occupation, health, motive, memory, attachments, etc. The details are everything—almost. I am not suggesting that we should allow ourselves to be pushed and pulled, willy-nilly, by impulsive emotion. Rather, like Jefferson's ploughman, we should aim for the middle ground between impulse and abstract rules, for, as Shakespeare said so memorably:

> . . . bless'd are those
> Whose blood and judgment are so well co-mingled
> That they are not a pipe for fortune's finger
> To sound what stop she please.[17]

Some may fear that by yielding on principles we open the gates to a chaos of runaway relativism. I don't share such a fear, though, because I can see that even as values clash, there is also a great deal of agreement within the moral universe about right and wrong, good and bad, which the majority of humankind assumes. Human dignity, decency, voluntary relations that are not oppressive, and some kind of spiritual fulfillment together preclude any justification of slavery, torture, or baking strangers in the oven—and there is today no compromise on this.

ALTRUISTIC RESPONSIVENESS

In his reflections on the relevance of social science to moral philosophy, Lawrence Blum lays out a conception of morality that centers on responsiveness, in contrast to the Kantian emphasis on rationality. With "responsiveness" he refers to "an action expressive of an altruistic motive toward others."[18] Responsiveness does not mean merely reacting to another person, or merely the intent to help someone (which could result from unaltruistic motives), nor is it limited to the relief of stress or pain. Rather,

> responsiveness involves both cognitive and affective dimensions. It involves a cognitive grasp of another's condition . . . and at the same time the altruistic aspect of responsiveness involves our emotional natures, in that responsiveness is not a purely rational willing of another person's good. . . . The cognitive and affective dimensions of responsiveness are not rightly understood as merely two separate 'components'—a cognition and a feeling-state—added together; rather they inform one another.[19]

As an example of responsiveness in young children, Blum describes a time when his own son and daughter—three-and-a-half-year-old Ben and his six-month-old sister Sarah—were playing together on the floor. Ben noticed a pin and took it to his mother, explaining that it might hurt Sarah. Blum's interpretation of this action is that Ben felt a natural sense of connection with his sister, and his sense of her was fundamental in his sense of himself. The fundamental likeness between the two allowed Ben to empathize easily with his sister, in spite of their differences.

Blum stresses the point that

> the moral significance of responsiveness does not lie in the child's appreciation of moral *standards*. There is no necessary implication that a child who is responsive to another necessarily thinks of helping the other as conformity to a standard of right and wrong, or good or bad, nor that she sees herself as behaving in conformity with a standard of behavior which defines what it is to be a good person. All that is necessary is that the child understand the other child's state, believe that the other child will be made better off by her action, and have some altruistic sentiment or motivation toward the other child.[20]

What matters more than standards is the particulars of the personal situation. The response is contextual rather than categorical. Carol Gilligan has a view of responsiveness and standards very similar to

Blum's, which she illustrates by her interviews with young women who are willing to "make exceptions all the time" and summarizes with the words of George Eliot: "Since 'the mysterious complexity of our life' cannot be 'laced up in formulas,' moral judgment cannot be bound by 'general rules' but must instead be informed 'by a life vivid and intense enough to have created a wide fellow-feeling with all that is human.'"[21]

Gilligan calls this the ethic of caring; Blum calls it the ethic of altruistic responsiveness. For both it is important to remember that moral decisions are seldom made once and for all; we must make moral decisions over and over again. We decide which (or whether any) principles, formulas, or general rules are relevant in each instance, and the particulars of each instance matter greatly to us in making such decisions. As Gilligan's subjects reveal, moral decisions often can be agonizingly difficult. However, for many children and adults, the ethic of caring brings about moral action naturally, spontaneously, without any agony of analysis. For example, Philip Hallie found in his interviews with the people of Le Chambon, whom Pastor Trocmé led in their extraordinary achievement of saving an estimated five thousand refugees during the Nazi occupation of France, that they scoffed at his praise for their morality.

> In almost every interview I had with a Chambonnais or a Chambonnaise there came a moment when he or she pulled back from me but looked firmly into my eyes and said, "How can you call us 'good'? We were doing what had to be done. Who else could help them? And what has all this to do with goodness? Things had to be done, that's all, and we happened to be there to do them. You must understand that it was the most natural thing in the world to help these people."[22]

These French "ploughmen" prove that in order to do good it is not necessary to employ a moral standard, or even to see oneself as doing good. Nor is it necessary to be honest. These people used cunning, secrecy, and lying (although their pastor could not bring himself personally to lie) to do good. Still, they worried about the long-term effects of their dishonesty on the children who lied jointly with the adults. Magda Trocmé, the pastor's wife, anguished aloud over the children who had to lie, then "unlearn lying" after the war.

> But usually when she says this, she suddenly straightens up her body, with typical abruptness and vigor, and adds, "Ah! Never mind! Jews were running all over the place after a while, and we had to help them quickly. We had no time to engage in deep debates. We had to help them—or let them die, perhaps—and in order to help them, unfortunately we had to lie."[23]

Nevertheless, she worried, as do the hard-liners discussed in chapter 8, that children would be harmed by lying and being lied to. But what did the children think about the problem of unlearning lying? It turned out not to be such a problem, after all. The Trocmés' daughter Nelly pointed out that

> the children, as far as [she] could see, never had the problem of unlearning lying. She remembers the children, among them herself, seeing the situation with the clear eyes of youth. She remembers their seeing that people were being helped in a desperate situation by these lies. And the children were convinced that what was happening in the homes of Le Chambon was right, simply right.[24]

Their responsiveness involved both a cognitive grasp of the refugees' condition and a feeling-state, which informed each other and produced an attitude that cannot be adequately described as rationally willing to act in accord with, or for the sake of, any impartial standard. As Blum argues, "there are some morally valuable actions which cannot be accounted for in wholly impartialist terms," even if it can be shown "that the same action *could* be performed from a purely impartialist set of considerations."[25]

In explaining his theory of "cooperative utilitarianism," a similar yet distinctly different moral point of view, Donald Regan offers an arresting analogy of how impartial rules can actually hamper people who are trying to act morally. His analogy helps portray the meaning of responsiveness Blum finds so important:

A chorus can make a fairly decent sound, and even sing moderately expressively, if the individual singers are adequate, if each individual knows his part, and if each hews to his part to the best of his ability, more or less ignoring everyone else. [However] if the chorus is really to work as a chorus, it is necessary for each individual to listen to all the others, to tune to them, to breathe with them, to swell and diminish with them, and so on. The unity that is required for really successful choral work cannot be guaranteed even by everyone's paying attention to a conductor, although that helps. Everybody just has to listen to everybody else and feel himself part of a community. "Rules", in the form of individual parts, are not enough, and preoccupation with the rules interferes both with the achievement of the joint goal and with the individual satisfaction from taking part.[26]

In my somewhat Darwinian view, variety is all: cooperation is a high achievement, and essence is illusion. With regard to our moral obligations, I think we have evolved into a loose confederation of choosers who need to listen to each other's voices, and to cooperate with one another. The price for being free to choose has been the loss of a sort of mythic certainty about essence, the ideal of a universal, impartial moral standard. Perhaps the foxes have a better chance of long-term survival in this moral world of constant changes and adjustments because of their flexible adaptiveness and their willingness to live with uncertainty. Hedgehogs thrive in an environment that suits and supports them, but when that environment changes, if they can't adapt to new conditions, they may find themselves left out in the cold.

VISION AND CHOICE IN MORALITY

The idea that deception could be complex in a morally interesting way does not even occur to the many who believe there is a universal morality that has been settled either through revelation or through the rational specification and definition of principles to govern behavior. Of that attitude I share Thomas Nagel's opinion: "The idea that the basic principles of morality are known, and that the problems all come in their interpretation and application, is one of the most fantastic conceits to which our conceited species has been drawn."[27]

We do not fully understand the principles of morality and we do not fully understand ourselves. We don't even have the methods we would need for such understanding. We don't even know what it is exactly that we are trying to understand. It has something to do with living well, or living a good life, or at least living peacefully and respectfully with others; at a minimum it has to do with avoiding pain and not causing too much harm.

In deciding moral questions and in rising to moral action, people often proceed, rightly, on "moral insight, as communicable vision or as a quality of being."[28] Such vision is not reducible to definition and does not always allow for disinterested reflection about facts. Our basic goals and the directions of our striving are set out first of all by who we are, or who we think we are. The most trustworthy sign that something good has been done, that the right policy has been chosen, is the happiness, or sense of well-being, or welfare that comes about as a result. If the action produces happiness at not too great a cost, then it is good. This alternative line of thinking that calls attention to the importance of vision has plenty of room for ideas such as the moral complexity of deception because it is not restricted by the belief that morality is basically a procedure for generating, or a set of already generated, universal rules. Persons may reflect deeply on their lives and see "a certain meaning, and a certain kind of movement." They may regard themselves as "set apart from others, by a superiority which brings special responsibilities, or by a curse, or some other unique destiny." These people will make judgments of importance to their own lives and the lives of others.

If you are attracted to this view of moral judgment, which includes a role for personal vision and choice, then you will have to be prepared to answer the question: "Would you wish anyone else in a similar situation to act the same way?" One answer is, of course: "Yes; in fact that's the best test to use in determining the moral worth of an action." But you could also answer: "No, because nobody else is set apart in exactly the same way as I am. No one could be in my position without being me." Moral judgment and moral action come out of moral attitudes, and attitudes have personal histories. The universal rules model simply doesn't fit, nor does it describe this perspective. We can say that somebody's attitudes are not desirable, and that we do not agree with them, but it is quite another thing to say that we all *ought* to have (assuming that we *could* have) the same attitudes universally.[29]

Iris Murdoch puts the contrast in perspective succinctly:

> There are people whose fundamental moral belief is that we all live in the same empirical and rationally comprehensible world and that morality is the adoption of universal and openly defensible rules of conduct. There are other people whose fundamental belief is that we live in a world whose mystery transcends us and that morality is the exploration of that mystery in so far as it concerns each individual.[30]

The passion for clarity is characteristic of the second belief, which requires paying attention to endless detail in pursuing an unclouded apprehension of unique, individual cases. This passion runs in the opposite direction from the first belief, which is bent on discovering the deep unity beneath surface differences.

We are talking about the hedgehog and the fox again in this contrast between the search for universal rules that apply to human nature and the exploration of individuals in all their mysterious but earthly detail. The hedgehog wants to establish universal moral rules and defend them by proving that we ought to follow them. The fox believes that there is no knowledge which could serve as such proof, and sees all attempts to attain it as doomed to failure.

Suppose we come to doubt whether we ought to tell the truth—that is, doubt the nature of our conviction to tell the truth. What is the remedy? In my view, we are unlikely to find it in general thinking, or thinking about general principles that support truth telling. Sometimes knowing the truth is a good, either in itself or as a means to something else, and when it is we have a good reason to tell the truth. Sometimes, however, knowing the truth is a curse, and our duty is to conceal it. Sometimes the truth is merely a nuisance and we have no clear duty to do one thing or another with it. The test of whether we ought to tell the truth is in getting face to face with somebody in a situation that calls for a choice, and directly appreciating the obligations which arise.[31] Truth telling may be one of these obligations. There will be others.

In thinking about all this I am haunted by the opening scene in Shakespeare's enigmatic play *King Lear*. In that scene, Lear asks his three daughters to tell him how much they love him. His intention is to divide his kingdom among them on the strength of their love. Cordelia, his favorite, who loves her father profoundly, refuses to say she loves him more than her husband. She is sincere but unyielding. When Lear rebukes her—"So young, and so untender?"—she replies, "So young, my lord, and true." A. C. Bradley interprets her reply as a perversion of her truth:

> Yes, "heavenly true." But truth is not the only good in the world, nor is the obligation to tell the truth the only obligation. The matter here was to keep it inviolate, but also to preserve a father. And even if truth *were* the only obligation, to tell much less than the truth is not to tell it. And Cordelia's speech not only tells much less than the truth about her love, it actually perverts the truth when it implies that to give love to a husband is to take from a father. There surely never was a more unhappy speech.[32]

Cordelia knew the significance for her own future of her father's question, and she couldn't have been ignorant of the king's needs as an aging, fearful man badly needing reassurance from his most beloved daughter. Yet somehow, for some reason of her own, she got stuck on a rather strict interpretation of the principle of truth telling. What unimaginable suffering, what awesome tragedy are to come of that judgment! Yes, she could say of herself that she was "so young, my lord, and true." But at what price? Even if Lear was acting with incredible impropriety in the opening scene, and even if Cordelia would have been wrong to compete with her sisters in hyperbole, it still would not have been wrong for her to humor her father and find a way to offer him the reassurance he needed at no expense to herself except that of momentarily giving up literal truth telling.

Returning to an earlier example, we can ask whether Edward Voysey should cover his father's tracks even if it means "lying and shuffling." If his purpose is to bring about something good, or to bring about the thing which causes the good result, then maybe he is justified in adjusting his principle of truth telling. Moral principles stated in terms of specific acts (Always tell the truth) do not account for this sense of obligation, which is to find some way to bring about a good result in a particular situation.

I am suggesting that if we have any general moral obligation, it is to consider all the circumstances and to base action on the opinion we reach with respect to the likelihood of bringing about something good. However, as C. S. Lewis plaintively pointed out, there are limits on our capacities to "consider the circumstances":

> Five senses; an incurably abstract intellect, a haphazardly selective memory, a set of preconceptions and assumptions so numerous that I can never examine more than a minority of them—never become even conscious of them all. How much of total reality can such an apparatus let through?[33]

In addition, we have only so much time and skill, so sometimes we must decide what to do in a hurry, as Magda Trocmé said, by overriding the demands of a more thorough and deliberate investigation. All these are severe limitations on our ability to make a judgment, "all things considered." Nevertheless, our moral decisions and actions are dependent upon the facts of the situation *such as we are able to know them* and upon our thoughts about the information we have. We may be ill-informed, or partially informed, about the facts, and we may interpret mistakenly what facts we have, to boot. Therefore, we may never know with certainty what our obligation is, or at least we may *not always* be able to know what it is.

About the best way I can summarize this sense of moral obligation is by saying that we really ought to try to bring about a good result when we think we can. There is an important difference between asking, "How can I help this person?" and the question, "What is the right thing to do?" In the responsiveness, or caring, view of morality, there are many ways to envision a moral life, and many ways to help a particular person in a particular situation. The emphasis is on action guided by concrete intuitive knowledge. We do not have to employ any universal, impartial moral principles to know the right thing to do before we act. The "ought" statement above is about the person—not about the specific act that the person performs. The emphasis is on "trying to bring about a good result" rather than on conforming to a principle in determining what is the right thing to do.

DRAWING THE LINE SOMEWHERE

To live in high spirits but not recklessly, to be lighthearted without swaggering or rampaging, to show trust and truthfulness but not unconditionally and not naively, and to face uncertainty with imagination instead of fatalism—this is the art of living. This art, like morality, consists in drawing the line somewhere. One of the most interesting lines to be drawn is the one between innocence (happiness that comes at the cost of being gullible, or less than fully awake) and ingeniousness (satisfaction achieved by astute manipulation of effects). There are some who are proud to be known as innocent, but I think the majority of us—if forced to choose— would prefer to be thought ingenious. This is because most of us fear being known as inept and credulous more than we fear being known as shrewd, wily, or crafty. Which of these rival characteristics is more likely to win a promotion for you at your place of work? Which of these types is going to be the more successful negotiator in the marketplace? Which one will make the more respected teacher? Who makes better company? Better art? Better love?

Perhaps one route toward moral progress lies in the exploration of various ways of drawing this line between innocence and ingeniousness, between guileless, unworldly openness and canny, clever cunning. Between truth telling and deception.

KEEPING COMPANY

Ethics is a subject about which we cannot be certain. What comes of that conclusion? One quick, easy, and mistaken reply is (to paraphrase Ludwig Wittgenstein) "Of that about which you are not certain, do not speak." The major virtue of this advice is the immensely prolonged silence it would afford us in which to enjoy our private thoughts. If only certainty gives the right to speak, I for one would have little to say. A more productive response to the lack of certainty in ethics is to realize that uncertainty may be a sign of importance. The most important things about being human—such as love, spirit, mindfulness, goodness—have expansive and elusive meanings that far transcend attempts to reduce them to the rigorous specifications of logical certainty, or proof of any kind. Nevertheless, we have every right—not to mention a strong desire—to go on thinking and talking about them, nudging each other with new ideas and arguing about the choices we could make, taking seriously what matters in the best way we can. If we can't have certainty, it's not so bad as long as we have company.

CONCLUSION

They lie, we lie, all lie, but love no less . . .
George Gordon, Lord Byron

I have tried to give a picture of the role of deception in our lives, and thereby alter our map of knowledge about moral decency. By knowledge I don't mean a set of irrefutable truths but a coherent interpretation of experience. Deception is not merely to be tolerated as an occasionally prudent aberration in a world of truth telling: it is rather an essential component of our ability to organize and shape the world, to resolve problems of coordination among individuals who differ, to cope with uncertainty and pain, to be civil and to achieve privacy as needed, to survive as a species and to flourish as persons. Deception is ancient, it is universal, it is to be expected in any communications that can be intentionally managed by an organism capable of having beliefs about another's state of mind. This is because, as the hunter and the hunted know well, success and survival sometimes require "seeing without being seen."

I have tried to show that our culture, and other cultures, give us ambivalent philosophical and religious teachings about the morality of truth telling and deceiving. In learning that some deceits are intolerable we also learn that certain others are not only tolerated, even rewarded, but indeed are required. Perhaps this ambivalence enables us to glimpse a large, vague truth about morality: if our sentiments draw us toward whatever is useful and agreeable and not harmful to ourselves or others, then morally we are on the right track.[1]

For those who think making a case for greater appreciation of deception's role in morality is somehow wrong or injurious I can only say that our humanity is not diminished by our efforts to master the secrets of social intelligence. In seeking such mastery, I think we will do better if our attitude to deception and truth telling is fired by an imagination that lets us break through the surface of rationality, penetrate the customary, and delve into the mysterious reality beneath, where wonder, amazement, festivity, and play may give birth to less innocent, more ingenious images of who we are. Simplicity is good, but richness is better when it comes to descriptions of humankind.

Deception is very much with us, but that should be no cause for despair. On the contrary, there are many reasons why we ought to be thankful for the inventive craft, and for all those agreeable and useful things it enables us to do.

> And, after all, what is a lie? 'Tis but
>   The truth in masquerade; and I defy
> Historians, heroes, lawyers, priests, to put
>   A fact without some leaven of a lie.
> The very shadow of true Truth would shut
>   Up annals, revelations, poesy,
> And prophecy—except it should be dated
> Some years before the incidents related.[2]

NOTES

CHAPTER 1

1. For a broad selection of articles on these general themes, see Robert W. Mitchell and Nicholas S. Thompson, eds., *Deception: Perspectives on Human and Nonhuman Deceit* (Albany: State University of New York Press, 1986).

2. This and the following quotations are from "The Doctor as Dramatist," *Newsweek*, February 1, 1988.

3. This is a modified version of a story told by Professor Robert Sternberg, who said it was true.

4. *The New York Times Education Supplement*, Winter 1988, p. 46.

5. Sissela Bok, *Lying: Moral Choice in Public and Private Life* (New York: Pantheon, 1978).

6. Bok, p. xviii.

7. Bok, p. xix.

8. Bok, p. 13.

9. Bok, p. xviii.

10. Bok, p. 22.

11. Bok, p. 26.

12. Bok, pp. 26–27.

13. Immanuel Kant, "On a Supposed Right to Lie from Altruistic Motives," in his *Critique of Practical Reason and Other Writings in Moral Philosophy*, ed. and trans. Lewis White Beck (Chicago: University of Chicago Press, 1950), pp. 346–47.

14. Bok, p. 45.

15. Bok, p. 31.

16. Bok, p. 76. These principles are taken from G. J. Warnock, *The Object of Morality* (London: Methuen, 1971), p. 79.

17. Bok, p. 86.

18. Bok, p. 88.

19. Bok, p. 89.

20. Bok, chap. 7, passim.

21. Bok, p. 91.

22. Bok, pp. 105–6.

23. Bok, p. 181.

24. Bok, p. 104.

25. Bok, pp. 105–6. The quotation comes from Augustine, "Against Lying," in his *Treatises on Various Subjects,* ed. R. J. Deferrari (New York: Catholic University Press, 1952), p. 172.

26. George Steiner, *After Babel: Aspects of Language and Translation* (New York: Oxford University Press, 1975), p. 214.

CHAPTER 2

1. This and the following quotation come from Ronald W. Clark, *Einstein: The Life and Times* (New York: World Publishing Company, 1971), p. 192.

2. Clark, p. 622.

3. Aristotle, *Metaphysics,* 1011 b26 ff.

4. Erving Goffman, *The Presentation of Self in Everyday Life* (Garden City, N.Y.: Doubleday Anchor Books, 1959); and *Relations in Public* (New York: Harper and Row, 1971).

5. This is one of Euclid's famous geometric axioms that is certainly and self-evidently true, but only if one assumes, as did Euclid, that the earth is flat. His geometry works perfectly well over small areas such as this page, but it would lead to catastrophe in ocean navigation. The ocean is not a flat surface; it is part of the surface of a sphere, where the shortest distance between two points is not a straight line but an arc (a curve known as a geodesic). Furthermore, two straight lines intersect no more than once, whereas two geodesics always intersect in exactly two points, and they always enclose a space, to boot.

6. Lewis Carroll, *The Annotated Alice* (New York: Bramhall House, 1960), p. 251.

CHAPTER 3

1. See St. Augustine, "Lying," in his *Treatises on Various Subjects,* ed. R. J. Deferrari (New York: Catholic University Press, 1952), pp. 54–56.

2. Immanuel Kant, "On a Supposed Right to Lie from Altruistic Motives," in his *Critique of Practical Reason and Other Writings in Moral Philosophy,* ed. and trans. Lewis White Beck (Chicago: University of Chicago Press, 1950), p. 349.

3. Karl E. Scheibe, "In Defense of Lying: On the Moral Neutrality of Misrepresentation," *Berkshire Review* 15 (1980), p. 16.

4. In his *The Man Who Corrupted Hadleyburg and Other Stories and Essays* (New York: Harper and Brothers, 1902).

5. "Of Liars," in *The Complete Works of Montaigne,* trans. Donald M. Frame (Stanford: Stanford University Press, 1957), p. 24.

6. Mark Twain, *Adventures of Huckleberry Finn,* 2d ed. (New York: W. W. Norton, 1977), pp. 73–75.

7. Montaigne, p. 24.

8. St. Augustine, "Lying," pp. 68–70, 105–7.

9. Homer, *The Iliad,* trans. Robert Fitzgerald (Garden City, N.Y.: Doubleday, 1974), p. 213 (book 9, lines 282–84).

10. Philip Hallie, *Lest Innocent Blood Be Shed* (New York: Harper and Row, 1979), pp. 226–30.

11. This is the central question Tom Stoppard asks in his play *Every Good Boy Deserves Favor* (New York: Grove Press, 1978). He doesn't answer it either.

12. Virginia Woolf, *To the Lighthouse* (New York: Harcourt, Brace and World, 1927), pp. 50–51.

13. I first came across this analogy in Scheibe, "In Defense of Lying."

14. *The Poems of Emily Dickinson,* ed. Thomas H. Johnson (Cambridge: Harvard University Press, 1955), vol. 2, p. 729.

CHAPTER 4

1. Agnes Hankiss, "Games Con Men Play: The Semiosis of Deceptive Interaction," *Journal of Communication* 30 (1980), pp. 108–9.

2. Charles W. Wolfram, *Modern Legal Ethics,* Practitioner's Edition (St. Paul, Minn.: West Publishing Co., 1986), pp. 720–21.

3. This categorization owes much to Barton Whaley, "Toward a General Theory of Deception," *Journal of Strategic Studies* 5 (1982), pp. 178–92.

4. Eric Hoffer, *The Passionate State of Mind* (New York: Harper and Row, 1955), p. 117.

5. Leo Tolstoy, *War and Peace,* part 3, chap. 7.

6. Balthasar Gracian, *The Art of Worldly Wisdom* (New York: Frederick Unger, 1967), p. 34.

7. Francis Russell, "The Return of T. S. Eliot," *Harvard Magazine,* Sept.–Oct. 1988, p. 54.

8. See Roger Fisher and William Ury, *Getting to Yes: Negotiating Agreement Without Giving In* (New York: Penguin Books, 1983).

9. Robert Gittings, *The Nature of Biography* (Seattle: University of Washington Press, 1978), pp. 69–71.

10. Maya Angelou, *I Know Why the Caged Bird Sings* (New York: Random House, 1969), p. 189.

11. This general framework is adapted from Roderick M. Chisholm and Thomas D. Feehan, "The Intent to Deceive," *Journal of Philosophy* 74, no. 3 (March 1977), pp. 143–59.

12. Robert Trivers, *Social Evolution* (Menlo Park, Cal.: Benjamin/Cummings, 1985), p. 420.

13. Patricia Neal (with Richard de Neut), *As I Am: An Autobiography* (New York: Simon and Schuster, 1988), p. 104.

14. For a discussion of these issues see Anne Kelleher, *Sex Within Reason* (London: Jonathan Cape, 1987), chap. 4, "Adultery."

CHAPTER 5

1. Donald P. Spence, *Narrative Truth and Historical Truth: Meaning and Interpretation in Psychoanalysis* (New York: W. W. Norton, 1982), pp. 61, 31.

2. Robert Boyers, "Observations on Lying and Liars," *Salmagundi* 29 (Spring 1975), p. 48.

3. See Richard Wollheim, *The Thread of Life* (Cambridge: Harvard University Press, 1984), chap. 2.

4. For some interesting work that focuses on the "leakage" see Paul Ekman, *Telling Lies: Clues to Deceit in the Marketplace, Politics, and Marriage* (New York: W. W. Norton, 1985); and Daniel Druckman and Robert A. Bjork, eds., *In the Mind's Eye: Enhancing Human Performance* (Washington, D.C.: National Academy Press, 1991), chap. 9, "Hiding and Detecting Deception."

5. Leon Festinger, *A Theory of Cognitive Dissonance* (Stanford: Stanford University Press, 1957).

6. Elliott Aronson, "Self-Justification," in *Readings about the Social Animal,* 3d ed., ed. Elliott Aronson (San Francisco: W. H. Freeman, 1981), p. 98.

7. Leon Festinger and J. Merrill Carlsmith, "Cognitive Consequences of Forced Compliance," *Journal of Abnormal and Social Psychology* 58 (1959), pp. 203–10.

8. Aronson, p. 115.

9. T. S. Champlin, "Double Deception," *Mind* 85 (1976), p. 102. Champlin's discussion is a reply to D. W. Hamlin, "Self-Deception," *Proceedings of the Aristotelian Society,* supp. vol. XLV (1971), pp. 45–60.

10. See M. R. Haight, *A Study in Self-Deception* (Atlantic Highlands, N.J.: Humanities Press, 1980), and David Kipp, "On Self-Deception," *Philosophical Quarterly* 30 (1980), pp. 305–17.

11. See Bela Szabados, "Wishful Thinking and Self-Deception," *Analysis* 33 (1973), pp. 201–5.

12. Herbert Fingarette, *Self-Deception* (London: Routledge and Kegan Paul, 1969).

13. M. Beldoch, "On Liars and Lying," *Salmagundi* 29 (Spring 1975), p. 143.

14. Fingarette, p. 42.

15. For insightful discussion on this see Michael Polanyi, *Personal Knowledge* (Chicago: University of Chicago Press, 1958), and *The Tacit Dimension* (Garden City, N.Y.: Doubleday, 1966).

16. Fingarette, p. 140.

17. Friedrich Nietzsche, *Beyond Good and Evil* (Harmondsworth: Penguin, 1973), p. 72.

18. See Jon Elster, ed. *The Multiple Self* (Cambridge: Cambridge University Press, 1986), and Brian P. McLaughlin and Amelie Oksenberg Rorty, eds., *Perspectives on Self-Deception* (Berkeley and Los Angeles: University of California Press, 1988) for a range of excellent essays on the concept of self and self-deception.

19. Benzion Chanowitz and Ellen J. Langer, "Self-Protection and Self-Inception," in *Self-Deception and Self-Understanding*, ed. Mike W. Martin (Lawrence, Kan.: University Press of Kansas, 1985), p. 125.

20. Matthew Arnold, "The Buried Life," in *Arnold: Poetical Works*, ed. C. B. Tinker and H. F. Lowry (London: Oxford University Press, 1950), pp. 245–47.

21. Jorge Luis Borges, "Everything and Nothing," in his *Labyrinths* (New York: New Directions), p. 249.

22. Roy Mottahdeh, *The Mantle of the Prophet: Religion and Politics in Iran* (New York: Simon and Schuster, 1985), pp. 182–82.

23. Mottahdeh, p. 182.

24. Shahla Haeri, *Law of Desire: Temporary Marriage in Shi'i Iran* (Syracuse: Syracuse University Press, 1989), pp. 51–52.

25. Haeri, p. 2.

26. David Pears, "Freud, Sartre, and Self-Deception," in *Freud*, ed. Richard Wollheim (Garden City, N.Y.: Anchor Books, 1974), p. 112.

27. *King Richard II*, act 5, sc. 5.

28. The term was introduced by Robert K. Merton in *Social Theory and Social Structure* (New York: Free Press, 1957), pp. 421–36.

29. See Robert Rosenthal and Lenore Jacobson, *Pygmalion in the Classroom* (New York: Holt, Rinehart & Winston, 1968); Ray C. Rist, "Student Social Class and Teacher Expectations: The Self-Fulfilling Prophecy in Ghetto Education," *Harvard Educational Review* 40:3 (August 1970), pp. 411–51; and Jere E. Brophy, "Research on the Self-Fulfilling Prophecy and Teacher Expectations," *Journal of Educational Psychology* 75:5 (1983), pp. 631–61.

30. See Bernard Williams, "Deciding to Believe," in his *Problems of the Self* (Cambridge: Cambridge University Press, 1973), pp. 136–51.

31. Charles Sanders Peirce, "The Fixation of Belief," *Popular Science Monthly* 12 (1877), pp. 1–15; reprinted in Barbara Mac Kinnon, ed., *American Philosophy* (Albany: State University of New York Press, 1985), pp. 174–83.

32. Peirce, p. 175.

33. Peirce, p. 175.

34. Peirce, p. 176.

35. Peirce, p. 177.

36. Lionel Tiger, *Optimism: The Biology of Hope* (New York: Simon and Schuster, 1979), p. 15.

37. William James, *The Varieties of Religious Experience* (New York: New American Library, 1958), p. 397.

38. Tiger, p. 18.

39. Tiger, p. 24.

40. Shelley E. Taylor, *Positive Illusions: Creative Self-Deception and the Healthy Mind* (New York: Basic Books, 1989), p. 108.

41. Taylor, p. 115.

42. Taylor, p. 116.

43. Arthur K. Shapiro, "Factors Contributing to the Placebo Effect: Their Implications for Psychotherapy," *American Journal of Psychotherapy* 18 (1964), p. 35; quoted in Taylor, p. 117.

44. Taylor, p. 120.

45. Claude Levi-Strauss, *The Savage Mind* (Chicago: University of Chicago Press, 1968), p. 28.

CHAPTER 6

1. George Steiner, *After Babel: Aspects of Language and Translation* (New York: Oxford University Press, 1975), p. 49.

2. Steiner, p. 51.

3. Steiner, p. 54.

4. Michel de Montaigne, "Of Liars," in *The Complete Works of Montaigne,* trans. Donald M. Frame (Stanford: Stanford University Press, 1957), p. 24.

5. Lewis Thomas, *Late Night Thoughts on Listening to Mahler's Ninth Symphony* (New York: Viking, 1983). The following quotations are from the same source.

6. H. H. Munro (Saki), *The Complete Works of Saki* (Garden City, N.Y.: Doubleday and Co., 1976), pp. 108–14.

7. Oliver Sacks, "The President's Speech," in his *The Man Who Mistook His Wife for a Hat* (New York: Summit Books, 1985), pp. 76–80. The following quotations are from the same source.

8. My thanks to the anonymous reader for the University of Chicago Press who pointed out that Wellington *did* use deception at Waterloo. By posting the main body of his forces on reverse slopes he deceived Napoleon as to the strength of those forces.

9. Mario Pei, *The Voices of Man: The Meaning and Function of Language* (London: George Allen and Unwin, 1964), pp. 10–12.

10. Pei, p. 26.

11. Hannah Arendt, *Eichmann in Jerusalem: A Report on the Banality of Evil* (New York: Viking, 1965), pp. 85–86.

12. Pei, p. 32.

13. The same can be said of languages like German which have all three genders.

14. Pei, pp. 109, 110.

15. For a discussion of ambiguity in social thought see Donald N. Levine, *The Flight from Ambiguity* (Chicago: University of Chicago Press, 1985).

16. This example comes from Peter S. Hawkins, "The Truth of Metaphor: The Fine Art of Lying," *Massachusetts Studies in English* 8, no. 4 (1982), pp. 1–14.

17. Max Black, "Metaphor," in his *Models and Metaphors* (Ithaca: Cornell University Press, 1962), pp. 25–47.

18. Edward H. Levi, *An Introduction to Legal Reasoning* (Chicago: University of Chicago Press, 1948), p. 6.

19. For views similar to mine see Richard A. Posner, *The Economics of Justice* (Cambridge: Harvard University Press, 1981), esp. pp. 231–48, 268–76.

20. Posner, p. 231.

21. Posner, p. 271. The Privacy Act referred to is U.S.C. §552(a) (1976).

22. See Erving Goffman, *The Presentation of Self in Everyday Life* (Garden City, N.Y.: Doubleday Anchor Books, 1959).

23. Ivy Compton-Burnett, *A Father and His Fate* (Oxford: Oxford University Press, 1984).

24. J. B. Priestly, *Dangerous Corner* (London: Samuel French, 1932).

25. For a discussion that brings these themes together with self-deception see Jerome Neu, "Life-Lies and Pipe Dreams: Self-Deception in Ibsen's 'The Wild Duck' and O'Neill's 'The Iceman Cometh'," *Philosophical Forum* 19:4 (Summer 1988).

CHAPTER 7

1. "Philip Roth on Bernard Malamud," *The New York Times Book Review,* April 20, 1986, p. 41.

2. *The Journal of Eugène Delacroix,* trans. Walter Pach (New York: Viking, 1972), pp. 188–89.

3. Niklas Luhmann, quoted in Annette Baier, "Trust and Antitrust," *Ethics* 96:2 (1986), p. 244.

4. Baier, p. 244.

5. Baier, p. 245.

6. Baier, p. 259.

7. Kathryn Pauly Morgan, "Let's Play Dominoes Again: The Moral Impossibility of Universalizing Deception as a Moral Maxim," in *Philosophy of Education 1987,* ed. Donald Arnstine and Barbara Arnstine (Normal, Ill.: The Philosophy of Education Society, 1987), pp. 27–38.

8. Sissela Bok, *Lying: Moral Choice in Public and Private Life* (New York: Pantheon, 1978), p. 31.

9. Bok, pp. 26–27.

10. Hannah Arendt as quoted in Shiraz Dossa, "Arendt on Billy Budd and Robespierre," *Philosophy and Social Criticism* 9, nos. 3 & 4 (1982), p. 313.

11. Dossa, p. 313.

12. Jeff Greenfield, "Hypocrisy's Virtue," *The San Francisco Examiner,* April 12, 1987.

13. Arlie Russell Hochschild, *The Managed Heart* (Berkeley and Los Angeles: University of California Press, 1983), p. 7.

14. Hochschild, p. 12.

15. F. G. Bailey, *The Tactical Uses of Passion: An Essay on Power, Reason, and Reality* (Ithaca: Cornell University Press, 1983).

16. Hochschild, p. 18.

17. Samuel Oliner and Pearl Oliner, *The Altruistic Personality* (New York: Free Press, 1988), pp. 163–64.

18. Oliner and Oliner, p. 105.

19. Oliner and Oliner, p. 107.

20. Oliner and Oliner, pp. 109–10.

21. Oliner and Oliner, p. 112.

22. Ibid.

23. Ibid.

24. James Joyce, *A Portrait of the Artist as a Young Man* (New York: Viking, 1956), p. 247.

25. Graham Greene, *The Heart of the Matter* (New York: Viking, 1948), p. 59.

CHAPTER 8

1. Curtis D. MacDougal, *Hoaxes* (New York: Dover, 1958), pp. 106–7.

2. Gloria Skurzynski, *Honest Andrew* (New York: Harcourt Brace Jovanovich, 1980).

3. See David Nyberg and Kieran Egan, *The Erosion of Education* (New York: Teachers College Press, 1981), chap. 5; and Kieran Egan, *Teaching as Story Telling* (Chicago: University of Chicago Press, 1986).

4. See Bruno Bettelheim, *The Uses of Enchantment: The Meaning and Importance of Fairy Tales* (New York: Vintage Books, 1977); and Roger Sale, *Fairy Tales and After: From Snow White to E. B. White* (Cambridge: Harvard University Press, 1978).

5. Hugh Hartshorne and Mark A. May, *Studies in Deceit* (New York: Macmillan, 1928), published as the first volume in their *Studies in the Nature of Character,* sponsored by the Character Education Inquiry project at Teachers College, Columbia University, in cooperation with the Institute of Social and Religious Research.

6. Hartshorne and May, p. 19.

7. Hartshorne and May, p. 15.

8. Hartshorne and May, p. 379.

9. Hartshorne and May, p. 400.

10. Jean Piaget, *The Moral Judgment of the Child* (New York: Free Press, 1965 [1932]).

11. Peter J. LaFrenière, "The Ontogeny of Tactical Deception in Hu-

mans," in *Machiavellian Intelligence: Social Expertise and the Evolution of Intellect in Monkeys, Apes, and Humans,* ed. Richard W. Byrne and Andrew Whiten (Oxford: Clarendon Press, 1988), pp. 238–52. See also Marie E. Vasek, "Lying as a Skill: The Development of Deception in Children," in *Deception: Perspectives on Human and Nonhuman Deceit,* ed. Robert W. Mitchell and Nicholas S. Thompson (Albany: State University of New York Press, 1986), pp. 271–92.

12. George Herbert Mead, *Mind, Self and Society* (Chicago: University of Chicago Press, 1974 [1934]).

13. Jules Henry, *On Sham, Vulnerability and Other Forms of Self-Destruction* (New York: Random House, 1973), p. 126.

14. Henry, p. 126.

15. La Frenière, pp. 243–44.

16. Piaget, p. 139.

17. See, for example, Robert Trivers, *Social Evolution* (Menlo Park, Cal.: Benjamin/Cummings, 1985), chap. 16, "Deceit and Self-Deception"; Richard W. Byrne and Andrew Whiten, eds., *Machiavellian Intelligence: Social Expertise and the Evolution of Intellect in Monkeys, Apes, and Humans* (Oxford: Clarendon Press, 1988); Robert W. Mitchell and Nicholas S. Thompson, eds., *Deception: Perspectives on Human and Nonhuman Deceit* (Albany: State University of New York Press, 1986); Joan S. Lockard and Delroy L. Paulhus, eds., *Self-Deception: An Adaptive Mechanism?* (Englewood Cliffs, N.J.: Prentice Hall, 1988); and Richard D. Alexander, *The Biology of Moral Systems* (New York: Aldine de Gruyter, 1987).

18. Vasek, p. 287. See also an earlier review by Roger V. Burton, "Honesty and Dishonesty," in *Moral Development and Behavior,* ed. Thomas Lickona (New York: Holt, Rinehart and Winston, 1976), pp. 173–97.

19. I have adapted this taxonomy from La Frenière, p. 251, and Svenn Lindskold and Pamela S. Walters, "Categories for Acceptability of Lies," *The Journal of Social Psychology* 120 (1983), pp. 129–36.

20. For seventeen life studies of adolescents' secrets, and the subterranean life of their families, see Thomas Cottle, *Children's Secrets* (Garden City, N.Y.: Doubleday Anchor, 1980).

21. Vasek, pp. 288–89.

22. Vasek, pp. 289, 291.

23. Philip W. Jackson, *Life in Classrooms* (New York: Holt, Rinehart and Winston, 1968), pp. 26–27.

24. Shusaku Endo, *The Sea and Poison* (London: Peter Owen, 1972), p. 102.

25. Endo, p. 106.

26. Endo, p. 107.

27. Endo, p. 107.

28. U.S. Department of Education, Office of Educational Research and Improvement, *Moral Education and Character* (U.S. Government Printing Office, 1988), p. 19.

29. See, for example, Linda McNeil, *Contradictions of Control* (New York and London: Routledge, 1986), especially chap. 7, "Defensive Teaching and Classroom Control."

30. See Daniel Pekarsky, "Education and Manipulation," in *Philosophy of Education 1977*, ed. W. S. Steinberg (Urbana, Ill.: The Philosophy of Education Society, 1977), pp. 354–62.

31. John Holt, *How Children Fail*, rev. ed. (New York: Dell Publishing Company, 1982), p. 254.

32. Holt, p. 282.

CHAPTER 9

1. J. L. Mackie, *Ethics: Inventing Right and Wrong* (New York: Penguin Books, 1977), p. 182.

2. Mackie, p. 183.

3. Nix v. Whiteside, 475 U.S. 157, 106 S. CT. 988, 1986.

4. Monroe H. Freedman, "Professional Responsibility of the Criminal Defense Lawyer: The Three Hardest Questions," *Michigan Law Review* 64 (1966), p. 1469.

5. Quoted in Stuart Taylor, Jr., "Legal Community and Top Court Debate Lawyer's Duty When Clients Lie," *The New York Times*, Sunday, May 5, 1985, p. 40.

6. Robert L. Lawry, "Lying, Confidentiality, and the Adversary System of Justice," *Utah Law Review* (1977), pp. 653, 693.

7. See Richard K. Burke, "Truth in Lawyering: An Essay on Lying and Deceit in the Practice of Law," *Arkansas Law Review* 38:1 (1984), pp. 1–23.

8. Quoted in Jon Winokur, ed., *Zen to Go* (New York: New American Library, 1989), pp. 105–6.

9. Sybille Bedford, *The Trial of Doctor Adams* (New York: Time Inc. Book Division, 1962), p. 194.

10. "A Case of Competing Loyalties," *The Stanford Magazine*, Fall 1983, p. 43.

11. The following section draws upon Joseph DeLadurantey and Daniel Sullivan, *Criminal Investigation Standards* (New York: Harper and Row, 1980), p. 83ff.

12. William Westley, "Secrecy and the Police," in *The Ambivalent Force: Perspectives on the Police*, ed. Arthur Niederhoffer and Abraham S. Blumberg (Waltham, Mass.: Ginn and Co., 1970), pp. 129–32.

13. Sophocles, *Philoctetes*, in *An Introduction to Philosophy through Literature*, ed. R. C. Baldwin and J. A. S. McPeek (New York: Ronald Press, 1950), pp. 96–97.

14. Sun Tzu, *The Art of War* (New York: Delacorte, 1983), p. 11.

15. Sun Tzu, p. 20.

16. Sun Tzu, p. 27.

CHAPTER 10

1. Isaiah Berlin, "The Hedgehog and the Fox," in his *Russian Thinkers* (New York: Viking, 1978), p. 22.

2. Berlin, p. 22.

3. Friedrich Nietzsche, "On Truth and Lies in a Nonmoral Sense," in *Philosophy and Truth: Selections from Nietzsche's Notebooks of the Early 1870's,* ed. Daniel Breazeale (Atlantic Highlands, N.J.: Humanities Press, 1979), p. 85.

4. Carol Gilligan, *In a Different Voice* (Cambridge: Harvard University Press, 1982), pp. 9–11.

5. G. B. Shaw, *Man and Superman,* in G. B. Shaw, *Collected Plays,* vol. 3 (New York: Dodd, Mead and Co., 1963), act 1.

6. Harley Granville Barker, *The Voysey Inheritance,* in *Three Plays by Granville Barker* (London: Sidgwick and Jackson, 1909), act 1.

7. Barker, act 3.

8. For a discussion defending the universality of moral principles, see Marcus Singer, "Moral Rules and Principles," in *Essays in Moral Philosophy,* ed. I. A. Melden (Seattle: University of Washington Press, 1958), pp. 160–97.

9. Edmund L. Pincoffs, *Quandaries and Virtues* (Lawrence, Kan.: University Press of Kansas, 1986), p. 2.

10. William H. Gass, "The Case of the Obliging Stranger," *Philosophical Review* 66:2 (1957), pp. 193–204.

11. Gass, p. 202.

12. Gass, p. 203.

13. Quoted in Richard Hofstadter, *Anti-intellectualism in American Life* (New York: Alfred A. Knopf, 1963), p. 155.

14. William James, "The Sentiment of Rationality," in *The Writings of William James,* ed. John J. McDermott (New York: Random House, 1967), p. 318.

15. James, p. 319.

16. Thomas Nagel, *Mortal Questions* (New York: Cambridge University Press, 1979), pp. 129–30.

17. *Hamlet,* act 3, sc. 2.

18. Lawrence Blum, "Particularity and Responsiveness," in *The Emergence of Morality in Young Children,* ed. J. Kagan and S. Lamb (Chicago: University of Chicago Press, 1987), pp. 306–37.

19. Blum, pp. 311–12.

20. Blum, p. 319.

21. Gilligan, p. 130. Gilligan's references are to George Eliot's novel *The Mill on the Floss* (1860).

22. Philip Hallie, *Lest Innocent Blood Be Shed* (New York: Harper and Row, 1979), p. 20.

23. Hallie, pp. 126–27.

24. Hallie, p. 127.

25. Blum, p. 323.

26. Donald Regan, *Utilitarianism and Co-operation* (Oxford: Clarendon Press, 1980), p. 209.

27. Thomas Nagel, *The View from Nowhere* (New York: Oxford University Press, 1986), p. 187.

28. This and the following quotations are taken from Iris Murdoch, "Vision and Choice in Morality," *Proceedings of the Aristotelian Society,* suppl. 30 (1956), pp. 32–58.

29. For an enlightening discussion of this and related issues, see E. A. Gellner, "Ethics and Logic," *Proceedings of the Aristotelian Society* 55 (1954–55), pp. 157–78; reprinted in Joseph Margolis, ed., *Contemporary Ethical Theory* (New York: Random House, 1966), pp. 227–48.

30. Murdoch, p. 47.

31. See H. A. Prichard, "Does Moral Philosophy Rest on a Mistake?" in his *Moral Obligation* (Oxford: Clarendon Press, 1949), pp. 1–17.

32. A. C. Bradley, *Shakespearean Tragedy* (London: Macmillan, 1904), pp. 320–21.

33. Quoted in Jon Winokur, ed., *Zen to Go* (New York: New American Library, 1989), p. 49.

CONCLUSION

1. For a full articulation of this perspective see David Hume, *An Enquiry Concerning the Principles of Morals* (Oxford: Clarendon Press, 1975).

2. George Gordon, Lord Byron, *Don Juan: A Satiric Epic of Modern Life* (New York: Heritage Press, 1943), canto 11, stanza 37.

SELECTED BIBLIOGRAPHY

Alexander, Richard D. *The Biology of Moral Systems*. New York: Aldine de Gruyter, 1987.

Aronson, Elliot. "Self-Justification." In *Readings about the Social Animal*, ed. E. Aronson. San Francisco: W. H. Freeman, 1981.

Augustine of Hippo, St. "Lying" and "Against Lying." In *Treatises on Various Subjects*, ed. R. J. Deferrari. New York: Catholic University Press, 1952.

Baier, Annette. "Trust and Antitrust." *Ethics* 96, no. 2 (1986): 231–60.

Bailey, F. G. *The Tactical Uses of Passion: An Essay on Power, Reason, and Reality*. Ithaca: Cornell University Press, 1983.

Bailey, F. G. *Humbuggery and Manipulation: The Art of Leadership*. Ithaca: Cornell University Press, 1988.

Barber, Bernard. *The Logic and Limits of Trust*. New Brunswick, N.J.: Rutgers University Press, 1983.

Behrens, Roy R. *Art and Camouflage: Concealment and Deception in Nature, Art and War*. Cedar Falls, Iowa: The North American Review, University of Northern Iowa, 1981.

Black, Max. *Models and Metaphors: Studies in Language and Philosophy*. Ithaca: Cornell University Press, 1962.

Black, Max, ed. *The Importance of Language*. Englewood Cliffs, N.J.: Prentice-Hall, 1962.

Bok, Sissela. *Lying: Moral Choice in Public and Private Life*. New York: Pantheon, 1978.

Bok, Sissela. *Secrets: On the Ethics of Concealment and Revelation*. New York: Pantheon, 1982.

Bolinger, Dwight. *Language—The Loaded Weapon*. London and New York: Longman, 1980.

Bonhoeffer, Dietrich. *Ethics*. New York: Macmillan, 1962.

Bowyer, J. Barton. *Cheating*. New York: St. Martin's Press, 1982.

Broad, William, and Nicholas Wade. *Betrayers of the Truth: Fraud and Deceit in the Halls of Science*. New York: Simon and Schuster, 1982.

Burton, Roger V. "Honesty and Dishonesty." In *Moral Development and*

Behavior, ed. Thomas Lickona. New York: Holt, Rinehart and Winston, 1976.

Byrne, Richard W., and Andrew Whiten, eds. *Machiavellian Intelligence: Social Expertise and the Evolution of Intellect in Monkeys, Apes, and Humans.* Oxford: Clarendon Press, 1988.

Canfield, J. V., and D. F. Gustafson. "Self-Deception." *Analysis* 23 (1962): 32–36.

Carr, Albert Z. "Is Business Bluffing Ethical?" In *Ethics in Practice,* ed. Kenneth R. Andrews, 99–109. Boston: Harvard Business School Press, 1989.

Champlin, T. S. "Double Deception." *Mind* 85 (1976): 100–102.

Chisholm, Roderick, and Thomas D. Feehan. "The Intent to Deceive." *Journal of Philosophy* 74 (1977): 143–59.

Cialdini, Robert B. *Influence: How and Why People Agree to Things.* New York: William Morrow and Co., 1984.

Demos, R. "Lying to Oneself." *Journal of Philosophy* 57 (1960): 588–95.

DePaulo, B. M., and A. Jordan. "Age Changes in Deceiving and Detecting Deception." In *Development of Nonverbal Behavior in Children,* ed. R. S. Feldman. New York: Springer-Verlag, 1982.

DePaulo, B. M., M. Zuckerman, and R. Rosenthal. "Humans as Lie Detectors." *Journal of Communication* 30 (1980): 129–39.

de Waal, F. *Chimpanzee Politics: Power and Sex among Apes.* New York: Harper and Row, 1982.

Dostoevsky, Fyodor. *The Grand Inquisitor.* Ed. Jerry S. Wasserman. Columbus, Ohio: Charles E. Merrill, 1970.

Eck, Marcel. *Lies and Truth.* London: Macmillan, 1970.

Ekman, Paul. *Telling Lies: Clues to Deceit in the Marketplace, Politics, and Marriage.* New York: W. W. Norton, 1985.

Ekman, Paul. *Why Kids Lie: How Parents Can Encourage Truthfulness.* New York: Charles Scribner's Sons, 1989.

Elster, Jon. *Sour Grapes: Studies in the Subversion of Rationality.* Cambridge: Cambridge University Press, 1983.

Elster, Jon, ed. *The Multiple Self.* Cambridge: Cambridge University Press, 1986.

Feldman, R. S., and J. B. White. "Detecting Deception in Children." *Journal of Communication* 30 (1980): 121–28.

Festinger, Leon. *A Theory of Cognitive Dissonance.* Stanford: Stanford University Press, 1957.

Fingarette, Herbert. *Self-Deception.* London: Routledge and Kegan Paul, 1969.

Fisher, Roger, and Scott Brown. *Getting Together: Building a Relationship That Gets to Yes.* Boston: Houghton Mifflin, 1988.

Fisher, Roger, and William Ury. *Getting to Yes: Negotiating Agreement without Giving In.* New York: Penguin Books, 1981.

Frank, Robert H. *Passions within Reason: The Strategic Role of Emotions.* New York: W. W. Norton, 1988.

Fried, Charles. *Right and Wrong*. Cambridge: Harvard University Press, 1978.

Gardiner, P. L. "Error, Faith, and Self-Deception." *Proceedings of the Aristotelian Society* 50 (1970): 221–43.

Gass, William H. "The Case of the Obliging Stranger." *Philosophical Review* 66, no. 2 (1957): 193–204.

Gilligan, Carol. *In a Different Voice*. Cambridge: Harvard University Press, 1982.

Gilligan, Carol, J. V. Ward, and J. M. Taylor, eds. *Mapping the Moral Domain*. Cambridge: Harvard University Press, 1988.

Goffman, Erving. *The Presentation of Self in Everyday Life*. Garden City, N.Y.: Doubleday Anchor Books, 1959.

Goffman, Erving. *Relations in Public*. New York: Harper and Row, 1971.

Goleman, Daniel. *Vital Lies, Simple Truths: The Psychology of Self-Deception*. New York: Simon and Schuster, 1986.

Greenwald, A. G. "The Totalitarian Ego: Fabrication and Revision of Personal History." *American Psychologist* 35 (1980): 603–18.

Gur, R. C., and H. A. Sackeim. "Self-Deception: A Concept in Search of a Phenomenon." *Journal of Personality and Social Psychology* 37 (1979): 147–69.

Haeri, Shahla. *Law of Desire: Temporary Marriage in Shi'i Iran*. Syracuse: Syracuse University Press, 1989.

Haight, M. R. *A Study of Self-Deception*. Atlantic Highlands, N.J.: Humanities Press, 1980.

Hallie, Philip. *Lest Innocent Blood Be Shed: The Story of the Village of Le Chambon and How Goodness Happened There*. New York: Harper and Row, 1979.

Hampshire, Stuart. *Morality and Conflict*. Cambridge: Harvard University Press, 1983.

Harris, Kenneth Marc. *Hypocrisy and Self-Deception in Hawthorne's Fiction*. Charlottesville: University Press of Virginia, 1988.

Hawkins, Peter S. "The Truth of Metaphor: The Fine Art of Lying." *Massachusetts Studies in English* 8, no. 4 (1982): 1–14.

Hediger, H. *The Psychology and Behaviour of Animals in Zoos and Circuses*. New York: Dover, 1968.

Hochschild, Arlie Russell. *The Managed Heart*. Berkeley and Los Angeles: University of California Press, 1983.

Hofmeister, H. E. M. "Truth and Truthfulness." *Ethics* 82, no. 3 (1972): 262–67.

Isenberg, Arnold. "Deontology and the Ethics of Lying." *Philosophy and Phenomenological Research* 24, 1964: 465–480.

James, Henry. "The Tree of Knowledge." In *The Norton Anthology of Short Fiction*, ed. R. V. Cassill. New York: W. W. Norton, 1978.

Kant, Immanuel. "On a Supposed Right to Lie from Altruistic Motives." In *The Critique of Practical Reason and Other Writings in Moral*

Philosophy, ed. Lewis White Beck. Chicago: University of Chicago Press, 1949.

Kant, Immanuel. "Ethical Duties towards Others: Truthfulness." In *Lectures on Ethics*. New York: Harper and Row, 1963.

Kurtines, William M., and Jacob L. Gewirtz, eds. *Morality, Moral Behavior, and Moral Development*. New York: John Wiley and Sons, 1984.

Levine, Donald N. *The Flight from Ambiguity*. Chicago: University of Chicago Press, 1985.

Lickona, Thomas, ed. *Moral Development and Behavior*. New York: Holt, Rinehart and Winston, 1976.

Lockard, Joan S., and Delroy L. Paulhus, eds. *Self-Deception: An Adaptive Mechanism?* Englewood Cliffs, N.J.: Prentice-Hall, 1988.

Ludwig, Arnold M. *The Importance of Lying*. Springfield, Ill.: Charles C. Thomas, 1965.

Mackie, J. L. *Ethics: Inventing Right and Wrong*. New York: Penguin Books, 1977.

Marietta, Don E., Jr. "On Using People." *Ethics* 82, no. 3 (1972): 232–38.

Martin, Mike W. *Self-Deception and Morality*. Lawrence, Kan.: University Press of Kansas, 1986.

Martin, Mike W., ed. *Self-Deception and Self-Understanding: New Essays in Philosophy and Psychology*. Lawrence, Kan.: University Press of Kansas, 1985.

McLaughlin, Brian P., and Amelie O. Rorty, eds. *Perspectives on Self-Deception*. Berkeley and Los Angeles: University of California Press, 1988.

Mele, A. R. *Irrationality: An Essay on Acrasia, Self-Deception, and Self-Control*. Oxford: Oxford University Press, 1984.

Mitchell, Robert W., and Nicholas S. Thompson, eds. *Deception: Perspectives on Human and Nonhuman Deceit*. Albany: State University of New York Press, 1986.

Montefiore, Alan, ed. *Philosophy and Personal Relations*. London: Routledge and Kegan Paul, 1973.

Mottahdeh, Roy. *The Mantle of the Prophet: Religion and Politics in Iran*. New York: Simon and Schuster, 1985.

Muecke, D. C. *The Compass of Irony*. London: Methuen, 1969.

Murdoch, Iris. "Vision and Choice in Morality." *Proceedings of the Aristotelian Society* supp. 30 (1956): 32–58.

Murdoch, Iris. *The Sovereignty of Good*. New York: Schocken Books, 1971.

Nagel, Thomas. *The View from Nowhere*. New York: Oxford University Press, 1986.

Nathanson, Stephen. *The Ideal of Rationality*. Atlantic Highlands, N.J.: Humanities Press, 1985.

Neu, Jerome. "Life-Lies and Pipe Dreams: Self-Deception in Ibsen's 'The Wild Duck' and O'Neill's 'The Iceman Cometh'." *Philosophical Forum* 19, no. 4 (1988): 241–69.

Nietzsche, Friedrich. "On Truth and Lies in a Nonmoral Sense." In *Philosophy and Truth: Selections from Nietzsche's Notebooks of the Early 1870's,* ed. Daniel Breazeale. Atlantic Highlands, N.J.: Humanities Press, 1979.

Nowell-Smith, P. H. "Contextual Implication and Ethical Theory." *Proceedings of the Aristotelian Society* supp. XXXVI, 1962: 1–18.

Nyberg, David. "The Moral Complexity of Deception." In *Philosophy of Education 1987,* ed. Donald Arnstine and Barbara Arnstine. Normal, IL: The Philosophy of Education Society, 1987.

Oliner, Samuel, and Pearl Oliner. *The Altruistic Personality.* New York: Free Press, 1988.

Pears, David. *Motivated Irrationality.* Oxford: Oxford University Press, 1984.

Pei, Mario. *The Voices of Man: The Meaning and Function of Language.* London: George Allen and Unwin, 1964.

Piaget, Jean. *The Moral Judgment of the Child.* New York: Free Press, 1965.

Pincoffs, Edmund L. *Quandaries and Virtues: Against Reductivism in Ethics.* Lawrence, Kan.: University Press of Kansas, 1986.

Prichard, H. A. *Moral Obligation.* Oxford: Clarendon Press, 1949.

Quine, W. V. O., and J. S. Ullian. *The Web of Belief.* New York: Random House, 1978.

Regan, Donald. *Utilitarianism and Co-operation.* Oxford: Clarendon Press, 1980.

Reisman, David. "Values in Context." In *Selected Essays from Individualism Reconsidered.* Garden City, N.Y.: Doubleday Anchor Books, 1954.

Rorty, Amelie Oksenberg. "Belief and Self-Deception." *Inquiry* 15, no. 4 (1972): 387–410.

Rorty, Amelie Oksenberg. "Adaptivity and Self-Knowledge." *Inquiry* 18, no. 1 (1975): 1–22.

Roskill, Mark, and David Carrier. *Truth and Falsehood in Visual Images.* Amherst, MA: University of Massachusetts Press, 1983.

Ross, W. D. *The Right and the Good.* Oxford: Clarendon Press, 1930.

Sackeim, H. A., and R. C. Gur. "Self-Deception, Self-Confrontation, and Consciousness." In *Consciousness and Self-Regulation: Advances in Research,* ed. G. E. Schwartz and D. Shapiro, vol. 2. New York: Plenum, 1978.

Sackeim, Harold A. "Self-Deception, Self-Esteem, and Depression: The Adaptive Value of Lying to Oneself." In *Empirical Studies of Psychoanalytic Theories,* ed. Joseph Masling, vol. 1. Hillsdale, N.J.: Analytic Press, 1983.

Scheibe, Karl E. "In Defense of Lying: On the Moral Neutrality of Misrepresentation." *Berkshire Review* 15 (1980): 15–24.

Schoeman, Ferdinand D., ed. *Philosophical Dimensions of Privacy.* Cambridge: Cambridge University Press, 1984.

Shklar, Judith N. *Ordinary Vices.* Cambridge: Harvard University Press, 1984.

Siegler, F. A. "Demos on Lying to Oneself." *Journal of Philosophy* 59 (1962): 469–75.

Sloan, Tod Stratton. *Deciding: Self-Deception in Life Choices.* New York and London: Methuen, 1987.

Snyder, C. R., R. L. Higgins, and R. J. Stucky. *Excuses: Masquerades in Search of Grace.* New York: John Wiley and Sons, 1983.

Spence, Donald P. *Narrative Truth and Historical Truth.* New York: W. W. Norton, 1982.

Steffen, Lloyd H. *Self-Deception and the Common Life.* New York: Peter Lang, 1986.

Steiner, George. *After Babel: Aspects of Language and Translation.* New York: Oxford University Press, 1975.

Storr, Anthony. *Solitude: A Return to the Self.* New York: Free Press, 1988.

Sun Tzu. *The Art of War.* New York: Delacorte, 1983.

Szabados, Bela. "Wishful Thinking and Self-Deception." *Analysis* 33 (1973): 201–5.

Szabados, Bela. "Self-Deception." *Canadian Journal of Philosophy* 4, no. 1 (1974): 51–68.

Szabados, Bela. "Rorty on Belief and Self-Deception." *Inquiry* 17, no. 4 (1974): 464–73.

Taylor, Shelley E. *Positive Illusions: Creative Self-Deception and the Healthy Mind.* New York: Basic Books, 1989.

Tiger, Lionel. *Optimism: The Biology of Hope.* New York: Simon and Schuster, 1979.

Trilling, Lionel. *Sincerity and Authenticity.* Cambridge: Harvard University Press, 1972.

Trivers, Robert. *Social Evolution.* Menlo Park, Cal.: Benjamin/Cummings, 1985.

Watzlawick, Paul. *How Real Is Real?* New York: Random House, 1976.

Weiss, Ann E. *Lies, Deception, and Truth.* Boston: Houghton Mifflin, 1988.

Wilde, Oscar. "On the Decay of Lying." In *The Soul of Man under Socialism and Other Essays.* New York: Harper and Row, 1970.

Williams, Bernard. *Problems of the Self.* Cambridge: Cambridge University Press, 1973.

Williams, Bernard. *Moral Luck.* Cambridge: Cambridge University Press, 1981.

Williams, Bernard. *Ethics and the Limits of Philosophy.* Cambridge: Harvard University Press, 1985.

Wilson, John R. S. "In One Another's Power." *Ethics* 88, no. 4 (1978): 299–315.

Winch, Peter. "Nature and Convention." *Proceedings of the Aristotelian Society* 60 (1959–60): 231–52.

Wolff, Geoffrey. *The Duke of Deception: Memories of My Father.* New York: Random House, 1979.

Zagorin, Perez. *Ways of Lying: Dissimulation, Persecution, and Conformity in Early Modern Europe.* Cambridge: Harvard University Press, 1990.

INDEX

Truth: coherence theory of, 33–35; and the community of discourse, 38; constitutional constraints on finding, 183–84; correspondence theory of, 35–37; degrees of, 34; friends' expectation of, 140; human role in making, 38; illusion as source of, 133; images of, 31–32; as interplay of memory and imagination, 9–10; as an invention, 31; moral value of, 9; and the need for certainty, 30–31; as object of worship, 29; performance theory of, 38–41; political contempt for, 40; pragmatic theory of, 37–38; rights to, 10; its role in redemption, 30; self-evident, 42–43; unvarnished, 3
Truth alloys, 61
Truthfulness, 10, 20–21, 36–37
Truth telling: casual attitude toward, 19; and children, 162–63; choice in, 158; and cooperation, 179–80; and the greater good, 43–44; as communication strategy, 53; hypocrisy about, 7; and keeping an agreement, 179, 180; in *King Lear,* 215; limits on obligation, 78; moderation in, 136; morality of, 199, 203; and pridefulness, 161; principle of, 11, 145, 203; and religious tradition, 60; in science and scholarship, 2

Turnbull, Colin, 81
Twain, Mark, 52, 55, 56, 158

Undercover operations, 185

Vagueness, 48. *See also* Ambiguity
Varieties of Religious Experience (James), 105
Vasek, Marie, 169–71
Vauvenargues, 63
Veterinary deception, 12–13
Voysey Inheritance (Granville-Barker), 201

Washington, George, 154–55
Weems, Parson Mason Locke, 154–55
Welles, Orson, 65
Wellington, Duke of, 121
Whitehead, Alfred North, 29
Whitman, Walt, 154
Wiesel, Elie, 111
Wilde, Oscar, 61, 85, 87
Wishful thinking, 89–90
Witnesses: discrediting truthful, 181, 184; expert, 179
Wittgenstein, Ludwig, 217
Wolfram, Charles, 65–66
Woolf, Virginia, 59

Yeats, William Butler, 70